TLC

THE WRITER'S OPTIONS

College Sentence Combining

**DONALD A. DAIKER • ANDREW KEREK •
MAX MORENBERG**
Miami University • Oxford • Ohio

HARPER & ROW • PUBLISHERS
**NEW YORK • HAGERSTOWN • PHILADELPHIA •
SAN FRANCISCO • LONDON**

Cover photo: Michel Craig

Sponsoring Editor: Phillip Leininger
Project Editor: Eleanor Castellano
Designer: Michel Craig
Production Manager: Marion A. Palen
Compositor: Bi-Comp, Incorporated
Printer and Binder: The Murray Printing Company
Art Studio: J & R Technical Services, Inc.

THE WRITER'S OPTIONS: College Sentence Combining

Library of Congress Cataloging in Publication Data
Daiker, Donald A., 1938–
    The writer's options.

    1. English language—Rhetoric. 2. English language—
Sentences. I. Kerek, Andrew, 1936–   joint author.
II. Morenberg, Max, 1940–   joint author. III. Title.
PE1441.D3   808'.042   78-11393
ISBN 0-06-041475-8

For
**Vicky
Yvonne
Avis**

CONTENTS

PART TWO: STRATEGIES

PART THREE: BEYOND

PREFACE

The idea for *The Writer's Options* evolved from research made possible by a grant from the Exxon Education Foundation. This research suggests that sentence-combining practice is a highly successful way to improve the writing of college composition students.

During the fall of 1976 almost 300 Miami University freshmen participated in a controlled research study designed to test the effectiveness of two teaching methods in improving writing quality. Half of the students, following a traditional method, read and analyzed essays from a college reader and worked closely with a standard college rhetoric; the other half practiced sentence combining exclusively. After 15 weeks, the sentence-combining students wrote original compositions that a panel of experienced college instructors judged to be superior in overall quality to the compositions written by traditionally trained students.

The achievement of the students trained in sentence combining encouraged us to write a textbook that would emphasize—through sentence-combining exercises varying in length, format, and focus—the wide range of options open to college writers. *The Writer's Options* includes exercises that teach students to control structures like participles, appositives, absolutes, and subordinate clauses; to employ strategies of coherence and rearrangement, as well as emphasis and tone; and even to define a thesis, select supporting details, and effectively organize an essay. Actually, the sentence-combining exercises consistently move beyond the sentence to provide the larger context of a paragraph or entire essay for student writing. In the same way, there are a number of exercises which instruct the student not to combine sentences but to simplify ones that have become too long and unwieldy. After all, "not to combine" always remains one of the writer's major options. But despite their variety, the sentence-combining exercises are alike in providing students with the disciplined practice that helps to develop writing skills and to build confidence.

Because any significant element of composition and rhetoric can be taught through sentence-combining exercises, particularly if student versions of the exercises are compared during class, *The Writer's Options* can serve as the sole textbook in a writing course, or it can be used with an essay reader and/or a rhetoric. *A Guide for Teaching The Writer's Options,* available from Harper & Row, includes sample syllabi both for courses in which *The Writer's Options* is used by itself and for courses that include a reader or rhetoric.

Many people have helped put this book together. Dennis Herron, Beth Neman, Susan Russell, Janet Ziegler, and especially Russell Reising and John Streamas helped construct the exercises. Professors Paul V. Anderson, James J. Sosnoski, Patricia Sosnoski, Edward L. Tomarken, Randolph Wadsworth, and Jack E. Wallace—all of Miami University—and Kathleen Spencer of Wright State University class-tested an earlier version of the book and provided us with valuable suggestions for revision. Our own students were often helpful in telling us what needed improvement. And Betty Marak is simply the best typist we know.

For what they have taught us about the theory and practice of sentence combining, we are indebted to Kellogg W. Hunt and William Strong. Our reviewers—John Clifford, Richard L. Larson, and Elisabeth McPherson—have given us the benefits of their insights and constructive criticism. And, finally, we want to thank our editors for combining encouragement and enthusiasm with warnings, threats, and other necessary forms of intimidation.

DONALD A. DAIKER
ANDREW KEREK
MAX MORENBERG

Introduction

The Writer's Options has only one purpose—to help you become a better writer.

The book is guided by two basic assumptions. The first is that you will develop writing skills not by analyzing essays, studying grammar, or even reading books about writing, but by writing itself. The second is that your writing will improve as you learn to express yourself in different ways and then to choose the most effective option.

In order to involve you actively in the writing process and to help increase your writing options, the book is organized around a series of sentence-combining exercises. Although these exercises vary in length, format, and focus, each of them provides disciplined writing practice in constructing a sentence, paragraph, or essay. And because there are usually no right or wrong answers, the exercises encourage you to explore various possibilities by experimenting with different structures and strategies.

In doing the exercises, you will always have choices to make. For example, the first sentence-combining exercise in the book asks you to combine the following four sentences as the conclusion of a short paragraph on hockey:

> The referee blew his whistle.
> The referee called to the team captains.
> The referee dropped the puck.
> The referee began the game.

Perhaps the simplest way to combine the four sentences is this:

> The referee blew his whistle, called to the team captains, dropped the puck, and began the game.

But you have other options as well:

> The referee blew his whistle, called to the team captains, and then dropped the puck to begin the game.
> After blowing his whistle and calling to the team captains, the referee dropped the puck and began the game.
> The referee blew his whistle and, calling to the team captains, dropped the puck to begin the game.
> The game began after the referee blew his whistle, called to the team captains, and dropped the puck.

If you tried, you could probably make several more sentences from the original four. Your ability to create a number of longer, more complex sentences from four shorter ones indicates that you have already learned many important writing skills. It also shows that the English language enables you to express essentially the same information in a variety of different ways. Sentence-combining exercises build upon your writing skills to help you develop new writing options.

But sentence-combining exercises, despite their name, do not always require that you combine shorter sentences into longer ones. Long, complex sentences are often appropriate, but so are short, simple sentences. For example, you can rewrite the four sentences about hockey like this:

> After blowing his whistle, the referee called to the team captains and dropped the puck. The game began.

The sentence "The game began," shorter and less complex than any of the original four, illustrates that you always have the option of not combining. Indeed, your writing is most likely to improve if you consider all your options and if you do the exercises creatively rather than mechanically. Since there is no one correct answer for any exercise, don't worry whether your version is the right one. Instead, try to respond to the exercises as if they were a game in which you occasionally take risks and experiment with different moves. Don't be afraid to substitute words, rearrange sentences, or even add details whenever such changes make your writing clearer or more interesting. To give more excitement to your sentences about hockey, you might rewrite them this way:

> After blowing his whistle and calling to the team captains, the referee dropped the puck between two slashing sticks. The game was on.

If you do the sentence-combining exercises carefully and creatively, you can expect to become a better writer. A controlled study at Miami University in 1976 showed that Freshman English students who practiced sentence combining for a term wrote compositions that college instructors graded higher than those written by students who had not practiced sentence combining. This study strongly suggests that the writing skills you develop by working out the exercises, and by comparing your versions to those of your classmates and instructor, will transfer to your actual writing. Constructing exercise sentences with participial or appositive phrases will help you use the same structures effectively in your own compositions. Building coherent exercise paragraphs makes it more likely that your own compositions will consist of coherent paragraphs. That is, sentence-combining exercises are only a means to an end. The end is improved writing. The real test of your writing ability will come in the original compositions assigned by your instructor. They will demonstrate how fully the writing skills developed through the exercises transfer to the writing that really counts. Few things in a student's life are certain, but if you consciously use in your compositions the structures and strategies you practice in the exercises, it's a good bet that you'll become a much better writer. Your instructor will probably think so, too.

The Writer's Options is organized into two main parts, "Structures" and "Strategies," and a short third part concerned with the selection and organization of ideas. The units in "Structures" give you practice in writing specific kinds of sentences—sentences that illustrate constructions often found in effective prose. But at the same time that you're building sentences which include specific structures, you'll also be incorporating such sentences into paragraphs and entire essays. So even in "Structures" you will usually write sentences not in isolation but as part of a larger whole. With "Strategies," the second major part of the book, the focus shifts more directly to the paragraph and the essay. Here, the units provide practice in using rearrangement and repetition, in achieving coherence, and in controlling emphasis and tone.

With the exception of "Warm-Ups" and three "Summing Up" units, each unit consists of a brief introductory section followed by six exercises. The introductory section explains a structure or strategy and illustrates its use. But the essence of each unit—and of the whole book—are the exercises, which give you active practice in writing and revising. The three Sentence Combining Exercises are especially important because they ask you to combine sets of short sentences into whole paragraphs or essays, and thus provide a context for your combining practice.

The three Sentence Combining Exercises alternate with others, such as basic pattern and creative pattern exercises, which focus more specifically on a given structure or strategy. By working out the Basic Pattern Exercise before doing the first Sentence Combining Exercise, you can test your understanding of the structure or strategy in the unit. If you have difficulty with the Basic Pattern Exercise, this is a good place to stop. You might want to reread the introductory section or raise questions in class.

The Creative Pattern Exercise takes you one step further. It asks you to complete or expand sentences by adding ideas of your own in the form of the construction practiced in the unit and thus helps you develop the habit of creating such constructions on your own. In this way, Creative Pattern Exercises can help you transfer sentence-combining skills into actual writing.

Here is a sentence-combining exercise like those you'll sometimes be given as a homework assignment. The instructions are simply to construct an effective paragraph from the given sentences. The spaces between groups of sentences indicate where one of your sentences may end and another begin, but you may ignore the spaces whenever you choose.

HYPNOTISM

1. Franz Mesmer was a physician.
2. Franz Mesmer was from Germany.
3. Franz Mesmer invented hypnotism.
4. Hypnotism was invented in the eighteenth century.

5. Hypnotism remained an amusing gimmick.
6. It remained a gimmick for over a century.
7. The gimmick was for nightclub acts.
8. The gimmick was for parlor games.

9. Physicians now use hypnotism.
10. Dentists now use hypnotism.
11. Psychiatrists now use hypnotism.
12. Hypnotism is used to treat various ailments.
13. Hypnotism is used to control chronic pain.
14. Hypnotism is used as a replacement for anesthesia.

In constructing a paragraph from these sentences, you're likely to be most successful if you follow three suggestions. First, go slow. The easiest way to put sentences together is not always the best. Second, experiment with different combinations. See what happens when you rephrase or reorder parts of sentences and when you shift sentences within the paragraph. Only by experimenting will you increase your writing options, and only by increasing your options will you extend your power over language. Third—and this is most important of all—listen to what you have written. As you are writing out different combinations, sound them out as well. Because you've listened to many more sentences than you've read, your ear is often a better judge than your eye.

After you've constructed several versions of "Hypnotism" and then chosen the best of them, your instructor may ask three or four students to write their completed paragraphs on the blackboard or to submit them before class so that they can be duplicated and distributed. The paragraphs may look something like these:

1. Franz Mesmer was a physician from Germany. He invented hypnotism in the eighteenth century. Hypnotism re-

mained an amusing gimmick for over a century. It was used for nightclub acts and parlor games. Physicians, dentists, and psychiatrists now use hypnotism. It is used to treat various ailments, to manage chronic pain, and as a replacement for anesthesia.

2. Franz Mesmer, a German physician, invented hypnotism in the eighteenth century. But for over a century it remained an amusing gimmick for nightclub acts and parlor games. Physicians, dentists, and psyhiatrists now use it to treat various ailments, to manage chronic pain, and to replace anesthesia.

3. Hypnotism was invented by the German physician Franz Mesmer in the eighteenth century. Yet for over a hundred years it remained merely an amusing gimmick for nightclub entertainers and party hosts. Now physicians, dentists, and psychiatrists use it not only to replace anesthesia but to manage chronic pain and to treat various ailments.

4. Physicians, dentists, and psychiatrists now use hypnotism to replace anesthesia, to manage chronic pain, and even to treat various ailments. But it had been invented by Franz Mesmer, a German physician, in the eighteenth century. For over a century it had been used merely as an amusing gimmick for nightclub acts and parlor games.

Once the four paragraphs have been read aloud so that the differences among them can be heard as well as seen, your class can begin discussing those differences. It's likely that discussion will begin with students either praising versions #2 and #3 or voicing reservations about version #1. There is, of course, nothing "wrong" with #1: it is clear, grammatically correct, and free from common writing errors. But it sounds dull in comparison to the other versions. It is also the longest and most repetitive of the four versions. What accounts for its dullness? For one thing, every sentence in #1 is approximately the same length. For another, each sentence follows the same order, beginning with the subject, which is immediately followed by the predicate. Although the English language provides writers with many ways of varying sentence length and order, the writer of #1 has not taken advantage of them.

Now compare the beginnings of paragraphs #1 and #2:

1. Franz Mesmer was a physician from Germany. He invented hypnotism in the eighteenth century.

2. Franz Mesmer, a German physician, invented hypnotism in the eighteenth century.

One difference between the two verions is that #2 is three words shorter than #1, yet at least as clear and informative. How has the writer of version #2 managed to say in 11 words what took 14 words in version #1? First, she made the phrase "from Germany" into the single word "German." Then she combined the two sentences "Franz Mesmer was a German physician" and "Franz Mesmer invented hypnotism in the eighteenth century" into the single sentence, "Franz Mesmer, a German physician, invented hypnotism in the eighteenth century." To make this combination, she shortened the full sentence "Franz Mesmer was a German physician" to the phrase "a German physician." Through such changes, the writer of version #2 made her sentence not only more concise but also more focused. That is, her sentence makes clear to the reader that Mesmer's invention of hypnosis is a more important fact than his having been a German physician. By contrast, the sentences in version #1 make those two facts seem equally important. The options you choose will often affect the meaning you convey.

The writer of version #3 made use of still another option. He changed the order of his first sentence to make "hypnotism," instead of "Franz Mesmer," its subject and first word. By doing so, he seems to be indicating to the reader that he regards "hypnotism" as the more important term. Do you think this change is an effective one? As you discuss this question, others will arise. Do the paragraphs become more coherent when their second sentence begins with a connecting word like "but" or "yet"? Why has the writer of version #3 substituted the phrase "over a hundred years" for "over a century"? Why has he added the word "merely" before "an amusing gimmick"? Which of the paragraphs ends most successfully? How do you like the reversal of time sequence in version #4? Discussing such questions with your classmates and instructor will increase your awareness of the possibilities open to you as a writer and at the same time will help develop your sensitivity for those options which work best in specific situations.

PART ONE

STRUCTURES

1. Warm-Ups

Combine the following sentences into an effective paragraph. The spaces between groups of sentences indicate where one of your sentences may end and another begin. Unless your instructor says otherwise, feel free to ignore the spaces whenever you choose.

OPENING FACE-OFF

1. The fans leaned forward.
2. The fans were eager.
3. The players leaned forward.
4. The players were eager.

5. The referee skated to center ice.
6. He was going to drop the puck.

7. The colors of the players' uniforms were reflected.
8. The reflection was from the surface of the ice.

9. The surface was glassy.
10. The ice was newly made.

11. The colors of the Boston uniforms were black and yellow.
12. The colors of the Detroit uniforms were red and white.

13. The referee blew his whistle.
14. The referee called to the team captains.
15. The referee dropped the puck.
16. The referee began the game.

Combine the following sentences into an effective paragraph.

BLUE JEANS

1. The girl is wearing blue jeans.
2. The blue jeans are her favorite pair.

3. The blue jeans are faded.
4. They are worn thin.
5. Their cuffs are frayed.
6. The blue jeans show signs of constant wear.

7. The blue jeans are punctuated by patches.
8. There are scores of patches.
9. They are of different materials.
10. Some of them are stripes.
11. Some are paisleys.
12. Some are solid colors.

13. Studs line the seams.
14. The studs are brass.
15. They add to the wide variety of colors.
16. They add metallic luster.

17. The jeans fit just right.
18. They are like an old friend.
19. They are not just another pair of pants.

Combine the following sentences into an effective paragraph.

DELUXE PIZZA

1. The pizza sits on the table.
2. It is fresh from the oven.
3. It is in the middle of the table.

4. Its crust rises up.
5. The crust is thick.
6. The crust is golden brown.
7. It is like a wall.
8. The wall surrounds the rest of the ingredients.

9. The sauce steams.
10. The sauce bubbles.
11. Its smell drifts upwards.
12. The smell is slightly sweet.

13. Pepperoni slices lie on the pizza.
14. They are shiny.
15. They are dappled.
16. They contrast with the sauce.
17. The sauce is dull red.

18. Mushroom slices rest in the sauce.
19. The slices are now shriveled.
20. The slices are now soft.
21. Their edges are curved up.
22. The curving is slight.

23. Green olives are scattered about.
24. Black olives are scattered about.
25. They dot the surface.

26. Cheese melts over the pizza.
27. The cheese is creamy.
28. It enmeshes everything in its strands.
29. The strands are weblike.

30. They trap the tastes until someone releases them.
31. They are released with a bite.

Combine the following sentences into an effective paragraph.

ANTEATERS

1. Anteaters are mammals.
2. Anteaters are common to tropical America and Africa.
3. Anteaters have long snouts.
4. Anteaters feed on white ants.
5. White ants are also called termites.

6. The ant bear, the three-toed anteaters, and the silky ant-eater are common types of anteaters.
7. These common types have mouths.
8. The mouths are small.
9. These common anteaters have tongues.
10. The tongues are long.
11. The tongues can be extended to catch insects.

12. Anteaters have claws.
13. The claws are long.
14. The claws are hooked.
15. The hooking is for digging insect nests.

16. The claws are strong.
17. The claws are sharp.
18. The strength and sharpness are for self-defense.

19. The anteater generally sleeps during the day.
20. The anteater is a nocturnal animal.
21. The anteater's tail is curled around him.
22. The tail protects him from the elements.

Combine the following sentences into an effective paragraph.

LAGER BEER

1. A cold draft of beer sits in front of you.
2. It sits invitingly.

3. A foamy head caps the golden brew.
4. Refreshing drops stream down the side.

5. Most likely the beer is a lager.
6. Lager is the largest selling type in the United States.

7. Lager is unlike ale.
8. Lager is produced by bottom fermentation.
9. Ale is a top fermentation beer.
10. Ale is popular in England.

11. That is, the yeast ferments for about 10 days.
12. Then the yeast settles to the bottom.
13. This happens during fermentation.

14. The settling is completed.
15. The beer is stored for two months or more.
16. It is stored at temperatures near 32° Fahrenheit.
17. It is stored in huge tanks.

18. This gives the beer its light taste.
19. This gives the beer its clear color.
20. And this gives the beer its most distinguishing characteristic.
21. Its most distinguishing characteristic is high carbonation.

22. After storage, the beer is canned.
23. Or it is bottled.
24. Or it is kegged.

25. It eventually reaches you.
26. It is delicious.
27. It is ready to be drunk.

Combine the following sentences into an effective paragraph.

CABLE CAR

1. The cable car approaches.
2. It is empty.
3. It clangs its bell.
4. It sways as though slightly drunk.

5. The brakes grind.
6. The grinding is harsh.
7. The grinding is metallic.
8. The grinding drowns out the babbling.
9. The people are babbling.
10. The people are waiting in line.

11. Most of them are tourists.
12. They are adorned with sunglasses.
13. They are adorned with cameras.
14. They press to secure a good view.
15. The pressing is excited.

16. One man refuses to move.
17. He has a good vantage point.
18. His stomach is swollen.
19. The swelling is from too many lager beers.
20. He angers the other passengers.
21. He forces them to squeeze past.

22. The tourists are all crammed inside.
23. The cable car lurches away from the station.
24. The lurching is awkward.
25. It heads down to Fisherman's Wharf.

26. At Fisherman's Wharf it will pick up another batch of passengers.
27. The passengers will be impatient.
28. It will struggle back up the hill.

2. Relative Clauses

Combining short, simple sentences allows you to write without needless repetition. Writing about the technological development of prehistoric peoples, for instance, you might begin a paragraph with these two statements:

> The Cro Magnons developed a spear-throwing device. The spear-throwing device improved the range of their weapons by 30 yards.

Since the phrase "spear-throwing device" occurs in both sentences, you can combine the two by replacing the repeated phrase with **which:**

> The Cro Magnons developed a spear-throwing device **which improved the range of their weapons by 30 yards.**

Because the two ideas are now linked within a single sentence, they seem more closely related than before. By combining the sentences with **which,** you have shown more directly that the spear-throwing device improved the range of the Cro Magnons' weapons.

Words like **which, who, whom, that,** and **whose** are called RELATIVES, and the new structure created from the second sentence is a RELATIVE CLAUSE. Which relative is used depends on the type of noun it replaces. **Which** replaces nouns that refer to things and animals. **Who** replaces nouns that refer to people, such as **peasant farmers** in the following:

> The peasant farmers still work in the ancient ways of their ancestors.
> The peasant farmers till the Nile Delta.

↓

> The peasant farmers **who till the Nile Delta** still work in the ancient ways of their ancestors.

In the following sentence, the relative clause begins with **whom:**

> The women **whom Gloria Steinem addressed** support the Equal Rights Amendment.

The relative **whom** is optional; without **whom,** the sentence will sound less formal:

> The women **Gloria Steinem addressed** support the Equal Rights Amendment.

You also have the option of using **that** instead of **whom:**

> The women **that Gloria Steinem addressed** support the Equal Rights Amendment.

In fact, **that** is the most versatile of the relatives, since it can replace nouns that refer to either people or things:

> The Cro Magnons developed a spear-throwing device **that improved the range of their weapons by 30 yards.**

The peasant farmers **that till the Nile Delta** still work in the ancient ways of their ancestors.

Whose replaces possessive nouns—nouns that take an apostrophe, like **child's** in the next example:

The policeman picked up the child.
The child's arm was broken.

↓

The policeman picked up the child **whose arm was broken.**

Note that commas change the meaning of relative clauses:

The governors **who took bribes from construction companies** misused the public trust.

The governors, **who took bribes from construction companies,** misused the public trust.

The first sentence, without commas, implies that only *some* of the governors took bribes from construction companies and thereby misused the public trust. The second sentence, with commas, states that all of the governors took bribes from construction companies and that all of them misused the public trust.

Here are two more sentences, one with commas and one without. Decide how they differ in meaning:

History books **which ignore the accomplishments of blacks and other minorities** should not be used in the schools.

History books, **which ignore the accomplishments of blacks and other minorities,** should not be used in the schools.

The second sentence states that all history books ignore the accomplishments of blacks and other minorities and should therefore not be used in the schools. The first says that only some history books ignore the accomplishments of blacks and other minorities and that only they should not be used in the schools. It implies that there are other history books.

When the noun that you are replacing is a proper noun, the name of someone or something, then you must use commas around it:

> Paul McCartney has been more successful than the other ex-Beatles.
> Paul McCartney is the founder of Wings.

↓

> Paul McCartney, **who is the founder of Wings,** has been more successful than the other ex-Beatles.

As in the previous examples, relative clauses modify nouns by adding details to them. And details make your writing vivid and forceful. Compare the sentence

> Until 1942, blacks were limited to stereotyped film roles.

with the next one that adds new information in a relative clause:

> Until 1942, blacks were limited to stereotyped film roles **that portrayed them as mammies or shuffling incompetents.**

Sometimes an added detail creates an interesting effect:

> A gust of wind suddenly broke the eerie silence.
> The gust of wind began as a faint sigh.

↓

> A gust of wind, **which began as a faint sigh,** suddenly broke the eerie silence.

Not only is the new construction more concise, but the relative clause interrupts the sentence just as the gust of wind breaks the silence.

Relative clauses can also strengthen paragraph structure:

> The Norway rat is regarded by experts as the most destructive mammal on earth and the most adaptive to changing situa-

tions and environments. It abounds in the debris of North American cities, resisting all attempts to control it. The Norway rat actually reached this country on the ships of many nations.

The final sentence is out of place, disrupting the continuity of the paragraph. It adds defining information about the Norway rat, but the focus of the paragraph is on the pest's adaptability, not on its origin. Making the final sentence into a relative clause modifying the term **Norway rat** will lessen its importance and tighten the structure of the paragraph, keeping it focused on one central point:

The Norway rat, **which actually reached this country on the ships of many nations,** is regarded by experts as the most destructive mammal on earth and the most adaptive to changing situations and environments. It abounds in the debris of North American cities, resisting all attempts to control it.

You can, of course, add more than one relative clause to a sentence:

The Cro Magnons developed a spear-throwing device **which improved the range of their weapons by 30 yards and which extended the limit of humanity's destructive power.**

Relative clauses can often be simplified to other, more concise and perhaps more effective structures:

Jupiter has 11 moons.
Jupiter is the largest planet in the solar system.

↓

Jupiter, **which is the largest planet in the solar system,** has 11 moons.

OR

Jupiter, **the largest planet in the solar system,** has 11 moons.

For some exercises in this unit write two versions and compare them to decide which is best.

Basic Pattern Exercise

Combine each sequence of sentences below into a single sentence with at least one relative clause.

Example
1. Walden Pond is now the site of many tourist stands.
2. Walden Pond was onee praised by Thoreau for its natural beauty.

↓

Walden Pond, **which was once praised by Thoreau for its natural beauty,** is now the site of many tourist stands.

OR

Walden Pond, **which is now the site of many tourist stands,** was once praised by Thoreau for its natural beauty.

A. 1. The Chinese character *hau* combines the symbol for "woman" with the symbol for "boy."
   2. The Chinese character *hau* means "good."

B. 1. The Autobahn was built by Hitler to transport tanks and troops to Germany's borders in World War II.
   2. The Autobahn is still one of the world's finest highway systems.

C. 1. Paul Newman is a vegetarian.
   2. Paul Newman drinks a case of Coors beer a day.

D. 1. Kwanza has taken root as an Afro-American alternative to Christmas.
   2. Kwanza originated as an African harvest festival.

E. 1. Ralph Nader claims the American consumer needs a voice in the decisions of government.

2. Ralph Nader attacked General Motors in *Unsafe at Any Speed.*

F. 1. The tests do not measure genuine intellectual ability.
   2. Colleges use the tests to screen applicants for admission.

G. 1. The Gypsies are really a nomadic people from India.
   2. The Gypsies migrated into Europe.
   3. The Gypsies were once thought to be Egyptian.

H. 1. Human blood is red, white nautilus blood is blue.
   2. Human blood has an iron base.
   3. Nautilus blood has a copper base.

I. 1. The Sundance Kid's girl friend was actually a prostitute in Fanny Porter's Sporting House.
   2. Hollywood portrayed the Sundance Kid's girl friend as a schoolteacher.

J. 1. Alcohol, a drying agent, is frequently used in cosmetics.
   2. The drying agent evaporates rapidly.
   3. The drying agent therefore has a cooling effect.

Sentence Combining Exercise

Combine the following sentences into an effective whole that includes several relative clauses. Eliminate any details which do not develop the point of the story.

TERM PAPER

1. A trash can sat in the corner of the room.
2. The trash can was filled with the pages of a term paper.
3. The pages were crumpled.
4. The pages were rejected.
5. The room was in a dorm.

6. The desk was cluttered with more papers.
7. And the desk was cluttered with books.
8. The desk was old.
9. The desk had initials carved in it.
10. The desk had obscene remarks carved in it.
11. The carving was by two generations of students.
12. The books were piled on top of each other.

13. Some of the books were open to pages.
14. The pages were highlighted by marks.
15. The marks were yellow.

16. Other books were closed.
17. They were forgotten.

18. In the middle of the desk sat a typewriter.
19. The typewriter was portable.
20. Jonathan's father had given him the typewriter.
21. The typewriter was a present.
22. The present was for high school graduation.

23. The light shone overhead.
24. The light was fluorescent.
25. The light was giving off a buzz.
26. The buzz was soft.
27. The buzz was droning.
28. The buzz was like bees in a hive.
29. The hive was far off.

30. Jonathan lay on the bed.
31. Jonathan was fully clothed.
32. Jonathan was asleep after a night of writing.
33. Jonathan was asleep after a night of rejecting.
34. Jonathan was asleep after a night of revising.
35. The night was frantic.

36. Then the alarm clock sent a ring through the room.
37. The alarm clock had been set for 9 A.M.
38. The ring was shivering.

39. The ring was drowning out the buzz of the light.
40. The buzz was soft.

41. Jonathan stirred.
42. Jonathan was flailing his right arm.
43. Jonathan was flailing to shut off the noise.
44. The noise was annoying.

45. He succeeded only in knocking the clock off the stand.

46. "Damn."
47. He mumbled.
48. At the same time he jumped out of bed.
49. He did so to pick up the clock.

50. A taste welled up in his mouth.
51. The taste was foul.

52. He walked over to the desk.
53. And he picked up the ten pages.
54. The ten pages were neatly typed.
55. The ten pages were his night's effort.
56. A box of No-Doz was falling to the floor.

57. There was a knock at the door.
58. And Harry's voice boomed out.

59. "Jon, are you up?"

60. Jonathan opened the door.
61. He didn't want to yell back.

62. Harry asked whether Jonathan finished the paper.
63. Harry stood in the doorway.
64. Harry was clad only in a towel.

65. "Sure."
66. He answered.

67. "It was easy."
68. "It was just like I said it would be."

Creative Pattern Exercise

Add at least one relative clause to the sentences below. Try for variety by adding your relative clauses to different nouns and by occasionally adding more than one relative clause.

Example
      Two astronauts flight-tested the space shuttle *Enterprise*.

↓

      Two astronauts **who someday hope to fly the craft into earth orbit** flight-tested the space shuttle *Enterprise*.

OR

      Two astronauts flight-tested the space shuttle *Enterprise*, **which is named for the star ship in "Star Trek."**

A. The policeman glanced down the street at the limousine.

B. The creator of this ad is a young woman named Marge Greenstorm.

C. At least one rodeo is held each week at the Lonesome Pine Dude Ranch.

D. The cheers were not for the golfer.

E. Kids made *Star Wars* a hit movie.

F. Johnny Cash is back with a new solo album.

G. Three or four hundred people were waiting to catch a glimpse of Sylvester Stallone.

H. The Wright Brothers were the objects of scorn.

I. His neighbors always wondered about those trees.

J. Industry and government officials fear union bickering.

Sentence Combining Exercise

Combine the following sentences into an effective whole that includes several relative clauses.

ROLLER COASTER

1. The roller coaster is still one of the most exciting rides.
2. The rides are in an amusement park.
3. The roller coaster made its appearance in 1884.

4. Even the rides fail to draw the crowds.
5. The rides are newer.
6. The rides are fancier.
7. The rides are like log flumes.
8. The rides are like screaming demons.
9. The crowds line up to ride the roller coaster.

10. The young seem to enjoy the favorite.
11. The old seem to enjoy the favorite.
12. The favorite is traditional.

13. Its cars and inclines combine the simplicity with the plunges and the swirl.
14. Its cars are open.
15. Its inclines are steep.
16. The simplicity is of a railroad.
17. The plunges are of a ski jump.
18. The plunges are sudden.
19. The plunges are stomach churning.
20. The ski jump is Alpine.
21. The swirl is winding.
22. The swirl is of a run.
23. The run is for bobsleds.

24. The coaster starts slowly.
25. At the same time the passengers ready themselves for the hill.
26. The coaster starts like a train.
27. The train is pulling away from a station.
28. The passengers have waited in line for over an hour.
29. The hill is first.

30. The cars jerk as the coaster climbs to the summit.
31. The jerk is hesitant.
32. The cars' wheels are clicking every inch of the way.

33. The passengers are poised at the peak.
34. The passengers brace themselves for the plunge.
35. The plunge is downhill.
36. The passengers have been waiting for this moment.
37. The plunge is exhilarating.

38. The cars dive.
39. The dive is whipping them into a frenzy.
40. The frenzy is of screams and laughter.

41. The coaster sweeps through the valley in a flow of motion.
42. The valley is first.
43. And the coaster races on to the other dips in a flow of motion.
44. And the coaster races on to the other turns in a flow of motion.
45. The flow of motion is continuous.
46. The flow of motion leaves the thrillseekers hanging in midair.
47. Their knuckles are white from gripping the retaining bars.

48. Then the cars glide onto the last straightaway.
49. The glide is smooth.
50. The brakes stop the ride.
51. The stop is gradual.
52. The ride never fails to please riders.
53. And the ride never fails to excite riders.

Relatives in Context

Each of the paragraphs below has at least one sentence that can be made into a relative clause. Strengthen the focus of the paragraph by making those sentences into clauses and moving them where they belong.

Example

The antiestablishment youth movement of the sixties sowed the seeds of a movement in the seventies to embrace history. The antiestablishment youth movement of the sixties denied the past. The blacks in the movement confronted the establishment with pride in their own origins, and thus began the ethnic-awareness movement of the seventies.

The antiestablishment youth movement of the sixties, **which denied the past,** sowed the seeds of a movement in the seventies to embrace history. The blacks in the movement confronted the establishment with pride in their own origins, and thus began the ethnic-awareness movement of the seventies.

A. Most Americans have become accustomed to driving cars with automatic transmissions. Now that small cars have become popular, many of us must learn to drive all over again, learning to put in the clutch at just the right time without killing the engine. Small cars save on gas.

B. One way of measuring time is by returning to the same vacation spot every year. With each passing year, the cottage seems smaller and the beach more crowded. The people have grown older, and some of them have stopped coming. You knew the people as a child. You wonder where they have gone because they were a part of your childhood.

C. The speech given by arresting officers, beginning "You have the right to remain silent," comes from a landmark Supreme Court decision involving a warehouse worker named Miranda. Miranda had never been informed of his right to counsel and to remain silent. Miranda was convicted of kidnapping and rape on the basis of his confession. As a result of the *Miranda* decision, all suspects must be read their rights.

D. Andrew Wyeth's painting *Christina's World* has fascinated viewers for years. The painting is on display at the Museum of Modern Art in New York City. Characterized by Wyeth's use of muted colors, the painting depicts a woman lying in a field of grass, her body turned uphill toward a run-down shack on the horizon.

E. A common misconception about suicide is that most people who take their own lives are old and near death. The truth is that those under 50 are more suicide prone than those over 50. Suicide is now the third leading cause of death among young people between 15 and 25, the second among college students. Suicide is usually the result of severe depression.

Sentence Combining Exercise

Combine the following sentences into an effective whole that includes several relative clauses.

W. C. FIELDS

1. The man shoved the woman into a car.
2. The man was fat.
3. The man had a strange voice.
4. The voice was nasal.
5. And the man had a bulbous nose.
6. The woman was startled.
7. The man mistakenly thought the woman was about to have a baby.

8. Then the man raced to the hospital.
9. The man was destroying the car in the process.
10. The man was destroying part of the town in the process.
11. The man was destroying the woman's sanity in the process.

12. The scene is typical of the scenes.
13. The scenes are in the movies of W. C. Fields.
14. The scenes are comic.
15. W. C. Fields seemed to relish the destruction of institutions.
16. The institutions are society's.

17. Fields was one of the most interesting of the comedians.
18. The comedians were in films.
19. The films were early.
20. Fields' real name was Claude William Dukenfield.

21. His childhood was extraordinary.
22. His childhood probably gave him the basis for his creation.
23. His creation was comic.
24. His creation was his most memorable one.
25. His creation was the fraud.
26. The fraud was colossal.
27. The fraud flaunts virtues and sentiments.
28. The virtues and sentiments are conventional.

29. Fields ran away from his home at the age of 11.
30. His home was in Philadelphia.
31. Fields became a petty thief.
32. And then Fields joined a vaudeville show as a juggler.
33. The juggler was comic.

34. He reached the top of his craft.
35. He starred in the Ziegfeld Follies.
36. The Ziegfeld Follies was the most popular of the vaudeville reviews.
37. And the Ziegfeld Follies was the most glamorous of the vaudeville reviews.

38. Fields left the Follies.
39. And then Fields began a career in films.
40. The films were silent.

41. Most of his films were hailed by the critics.
42. But most of his films were ignored by the public.

43. Acclaim came in "talkies."
44. The acclaim was public.

45. The juggler played Humpty Dumpty in a version of *Alice in Wonderland*.
46. The juggler is the master of balance.

47. Humpty Dumpty is an egg.
48. The egg is off balance.

49. His movies were the classics.
50. The movies were the most famous.
51. The classics starred him as the fraud.
52. The fraud is raspy-voiced.
53. The classics were *My Little Chickadee* and *The Bank Dick.*
54. *My Little Chickadee* and *The Bank Dick* are still favorites on TV.
55. *My Little Chickadee* and *The Bank Dick* are still favorites in college film series.

56. There is no doubt that Fields was a genius.
57. The genius was comic.
58. The genius could write comedy as well as act.

59. But he was difficult to work with.
60. He was frequently drunk.
61. He was constantly improvising.
62. He was depending on his vaudeville skills to carry the day.

63. The fraud had the laugh on the public.
64. And the fraud had the laugh on the public's sentiments.
65. The laugh was last.
66. The fraud was old.

67. The man died on Christmas Day, 1946.
68. The man claimed to hate children.
69. The man claimed to hate Christmas.

70. He turned a celebration into a wake.
71. He would have enjoyed knowing it.

3. Participles

The simple sentences below may be combined, with no change in their meaning, into a more concise sentence simply by dropping the repeated words **he was:**

> The janitor staggered down the stairway.
> He was stunned.
> He was gasping.

↓

> The janitor staggered down the stairway, **stunned and gasping.**

Here we achieved compactness by reducing the full sentences **he was stunned** and **he was gasping** to the participles **stunned** and **gasping. Stunned,** like **caressed, kicked, blown up, sung,** or **hit** is a PAST PARTICIPLE, verb form that you can use in the construction "Somebody (or something) was _____" or "I have _____ it". **Gasping,** like **running, dancing, driving,** or **anticipating,** is a PRESENT PARTICIPLE, always made by adding **ing** to the basic verb form.

A participle is often supported by additional words built around it and adding detail to it. These together form a PARTICIPIAL PHRASE, such as **equipped with a can of throat spray and a Bible** or **singing songs the Beatles had made famous.** Usually, as in these examples, the modifying words directly follow the participle, but they may also precede it, such as in **madly dancing** or **slowly and reluctantly surrendering.**

Although more concise than a sequence of three simple sentences, the sentence

> The janitor staggered down the stairway, **stunned and gasping.**

still gives you only the bare skeleton of an idea. But participial phrases also enable you to work concrete details into your sentences without actually increasing the number of sentences needed. Compare this:

> The janitor staggered down the stairway, **stunned by the bizarre noises he had just heard upstairs and gasping for air as he hesitantly held on to the bannister.**

Here the result is a more substantial and informative sentence with vivid details about where and why the janitor was stunned, and about the circumstances of his gasping. We can almost *see* the poor man stepping down the staircase, shocked, dazed, disbelieving. It is details that make writing interesting. And participial phrases invite detail.

Where should you add participial phrases in a sentence? In general, add them as close as possible to the word they refer to and modify. As a rule of thumb, the participle(s) in a combined sentence such as the last example should have the same understood subject as the main clause to which the participle (or participial phrase) is added. Both **stunned** and **gasping** meet this condition, since they both refer to the janitor. Similarly, the following are properly combined:

> She was driving without a license.
> She was arrested and jailed by the sheriff.

> **Driving without a license,** she was arrested and jailed by
> the sheriff.

If you ignore this rule, you may end up with an awkward and even
obscure sentence:

> Driving without a license, the sheriff arrested and jailed her.

Of course, you will want to do more than just avoid errors.
You want to be able to make informed choices from the options
available to you. For example, you can gradually reduce and con-
dense full sentences to more concise versions, as shown below:

> Evolution is a conservative process.
> Evolution wastes little of value.

> a. Evolution is a conservative process. It wastes little of value.

> b. Evolution is a conservative process which wastes little of
>   value.

> c. Evolution is a conservative process, **wasting little of
>   value.**

You may choose either to replace a repeated noun by an appropriate pronoun, while keeping the sentences separate (as in a) or to
combine the sentences into a main clause and a relative clause (as
in b). But you also have the option to eliminate the relative pronoun **which** and turn the verb **waste** into the participle **wasting,** thus achieving even more economy (as in c).

Participial phrases can often be moved from one position to
another within a sentence. Just when such movement is possible or
effective is sometimes difficult to decide. Read your versions aloud
and try to hear the differences among them.

Consider the following possibilities:

> His sons lie in cemeteries in France.
> His sons were killed on D-Day.

$$\downarrow$$

a. His sons, who were killed on D-Day, lie in cemeteries in France.

OR

b. His sons, **killed on D-Day,** lie in cemeteries in France.

OR

c. **Killed on D-Day,** his sons lie in cemeteries in France.

OR

d. His sons lie in cemeteries in France , **killed on D-Day.**

Since none of these versions are "wrong," your choice must ultimately be guided by your purpose. If you want more of a conversational style, (a) might be the best choice. In (c) the first word, **killed,** immediately catches the reader's attention and puts the reason for the sons being where they are into sharper focus. In (b) just the opposite is the case—the participial phrase is stashed away within the main clause, calling little attention to itself and allowing the end of the main clause, **in cemeteries in France,** to get the emphasis in the sentence. In contrast, (d) emphasizes the participial phrase **killed on D-Day,** by placing it in the strongest sentence position at the end; but it does so somewhat awkwardly, perhaps, by separating it from the word it modifies, **sons.**

Or, for another example, look again at the sentence about the janitor:

> The janitor staggered down the stairway, **stunned by the bizarre noises he had just heard upstairs and gasping for air as he hesitantly held on to the bannister.**

Here the main clause is followed by the **stunned**-phrase and then by the **gasping**-phrase. Is this the most effective order? Examine the logic of the sentence: the janitor is stunned; *therefore* he staggers downstairs *while* he is gasping. In other words, **stunned** describes the cause of his staggering, whereas **gasping** refers to an action simultaneous to the staggering. Often the ordering of phrases and clauses according to the logical sequencing of events described in the sentence is stylistically the most satisfying option:

> **Stunned by the bizarre noises he had just heard upstairs,** the janitor staggered down the stairway, **gasping for air as he hesitantly held on to the bannister.**

Notice that in this example the cause of an action is expressed by a *past* participial phrase, while a simultaneous action, one that occurs at the same time, is described by a *present* participial phrase. This is often so. In the combined version below, for example, **jolted** tells us what caused Harry's injuries:

Harry was jolted by the collision.
Harry suffered a sprained back.
Harry suffered a broken knee.

↓

> **Jolted by the collision,** Harry suffered a sprained back and a broken knee.

Sometimes present participial phrases can also suggest the cause of an event:

> **Driving through the busy streets like a madman,** he was stopped by the police.

We sense that he was stopped *because* of his reckless driving. But the sentence also suggests that he was stopped *while* in the process of driving. Participial **ing** phrases are especially suitable for suggesting live, animated action, as well as for describing events that take place simultaneously. We have seen the janitor **gasping** as he staggers down the stairway, and someone being stopped while **driving.** Can you sense the difference in these two sentences?

> Water lifted her body, **caressed it,** and carried her out into a misty sea.

Water lifted her body, **caressing it,** and carried her out into
a misty sea.

In the first sentence, the events seem chronological, one following
the other in sequence: **lifted,** then **caressed,** then **carried.** But
in the second one the participial phrase **caressing it** makes the
water's lifting and caressing simultaneous and, more subtly, makes
the caress seem longer, even more affectionate.

One further use of the participle lies in its ability to create
coherence by joining sentences which, if left separate, might seem
disjointed. Using the participial construction, you can combine two
full sentences into a single sentence which more clearly reflects the
relationship between them:

I carried the cumbersome bass drum in front of me. I burrowed
and jostled my way through the stubborn crowd to the
bandstand.

↓

Carrying the cumbersome bass drum in front of me,
I burrowed and jostled my way through the stubborn crowd
to the bandstand.

OR

I carried the cumbersome bass drum in front of me, **burrow-
ing and jostling my way through the stubborn
crowd to the bandstand.**

Basic Pattern Exercise

Combine each sequence of sentences below into a single sentence with at least one participial phrase.

Example

1. The new storm swept from North Dakota through Ohio.
2. It sent temperatures plummeting.
3. It piled drifts high across roads.

The new storm swept from North Dakota through Ohio, **sending temperatures plummeting and piling drifts high across roads.**

OR

Sweeping from North Dakota through Ohio, the new storm sent temperatures plummeting and piled drifts high across roads.

A. 1. It was a battered face.
    2. But it was a noble face.
    3. It commanded immediate respect.

B. 1. Prosecutor, judge, and jury were convinced of the defendant's guilt.
    2. They twisted the facts to support their prejudgment.

C. 1. She was born in Atlanta, Georgia.
    2. She now serves as the corporation's chief legal officer.
    3. She was educated at Duke University.

D. 1. Mandy was mud covered.
    2. Mandy was shivering.
    3. Mandy sat hunched over a bowl of hot broth.
    4. Her father had prepared the broth to drive off the chill.

E. 1. Policemen and firemen combed the smoking rubble.
    2. They found guns.
    3. They found spent cartridges.
    4. They found a charred corpse.

F. 1. Joey was depressed.
   2. He was depressed by his betting losses.
   3. He sat alone on the beach.
   4. He drank a pint of good bourbon.

G. 1. Strip mining completely alters the topography.
   2. It destroys all original vegetation.
   3. It also destroys most of the animal life.
   4. It leaves barren rubble behind.

H. 1. An IQ score is stamped on a permanent school record.
   2. An IQ score can literally determine a child's future.
   3. An IQ score influences teacher expectations.
   4. An IQ score affects many educational and job options.

I. 1. The locomotive lumbered into Grand Central Station.
   2. It skidded along the tracks.
   3. It splashed sparks onto the passenger platform.
   4. It discharged gray puffs of steam.
   5. It finally screeched to a halt.

J. 1. Roy White broke forward with the sound of the bat.
   2. He raced into short left-center field.
   3. He flicked down his sunglasses.
   4. He shouted off the shortstop.
   5. He caught the pop fly.
   6. His catching the pop fly ended the game.

Sentence Combining Exercise

Combine the following sentences into an effective whole that includes several participial phrases.

THE COLONEL

1. Shells boomed.
2. The shells were artillery.
3. The booming was in the distance.
4. The shells shook the ground.
5. The shaking was slight.

6. The shell made bursts of light.
7. The bursts were on the horizon.
8. The horizon was dark.

9. The colonel walked away from headquarters.
10. The colonel was tired of looking at maps.
11. The colonel was exhausted from planning the attack.
12. The attack would be on the next day.

13. The colonel passed a group of soldiers.
14. The soldiers were lying under a tree.
15. The soldiers were lying in the dark.
16. The soldiers were young.

17. One of the soldiers was playing a harmonica.
18. Its sounds were a counterpoint to the boom.
19. The boom was in the distance.
20. The counterpoint was strangely cheerful.
21. The boom was ugly.
22. The boom was menacing.

23. The other soldiers lay around him.
24. They were like the spokes on a wheel.
25. They were silent.
26. They were half asleep.

27. The colonel walked quickly by them.
28. He did not wish to interrupt their rest.

29. He stopped farther down the road.
30. He sat on a rock.
31. And he listened to the tunes.
32. The tunes were interrupted by the booming.
33. The tunes were cheerful.
34. The tunes were high pitched.
35. The booming was distant.
36. The booming was sporadic.

Creative Pattern Exercise

Add at least one participial phrase to each of the sentences below. Try for variety by using both past and present participial phrases, by placing the participial phrase in different positions within your sentence, and by occasionally using more than one participial phrase in a single sentence.

Example

At the far end of the bar sat Riley.

At the far end of the bar sat Riley, **holding his head in his hands.**

OR

At the far end of the bar, **holding his head in his hands,** sat Riley, **so depressed that not even 100 proof scotch could cheer him up.**

A. Grandma stared at him for a moment.

B. The door creaked open.

C. They tentatively reached out their hands toward each other.

D. Franklin and Eleanor were two enormously energetic people.

E. Half of all Americans watch television at least six hours a day.

F. Members of the postwar baby boom are now in the labor market.

G. America is dependent on oil and gas for most of its energy needs.

H. Ellen started to walk slowly and then quickened her pace to a trot.

I. The second baseman took the throw from the shortstop and fired to first for a double play.

J. Karen met Jerry during Christmas vacation and a week later agreed to marry him.

Sentence Combining Exercise

Combine the following sentences into an effective essay that includes several participial phrases.

BLIND DATE

1. The man knocked on the door.
2. The man was young.
3. The man was well dressed.
4. The door was large.
5. The door was white.
6. The knocking was hesitant.

7. He waited a moment.
8. He took a deep breath.
9. Then he knocked again.
10. He knocked louder.
11. He knocked with more self-assurance.

12. He heard sounds on the other side.
13. He heard footsteps.
14. The footsteps were sharp.

15. And the door was opened by a woman.
16. The woman was owl-eyed.
17. The woman was in a bathrobe.
18. The bathrobe was of terry cloth.
19. Her hair was in a towel.
20. She was dripping water.

21. He was taken aback.
22. He said, "I'm Larry Baldwin."
23. "I'm supposed to pick up Rose Ann."
24. He was almost stuttering.

25. The woman mumbled something.
26. She turned her frame.
27. Her frame was huge.
28. And she pointed toward a couch.
29. The couch was in the living room.
30. The living room was untidy.

31. He sat down on the couch.
32. He moved the morning paper to make room.
33. And he turned in time to see the bathrobe disappear around a corner.
34. He heard the clop, clop of Wedgies against the stairs.

35. Larry looked at the puddle.
36. The puddle was small.
37. The woman left the puddle.
38. He wondered what her daughter would look like.
39. He feared the worst.
40. He feared a girl.
41. The girl was fat.
42. The girl was untidy.

43. Footsteps almost startled him.
44. The footsteps were softer.
45. The footsteps came from the stairs.

46. Rose Ann appeared.
47. The appearance was almost instant.
48. She was a girl.
49. She was small.
50. She was dark haired.
51. She had eyes.
52. Her eyes were bright.
53. Her eyes were dancing.
54. She was not at all like the older woman.
55. The older woman was dripping.
56. The older woman was bathrobed.

57. Larry was smiling.
58. Larry got up.
59. And Larry blurted out.
60. "I'm Barry Laldlin."
61. Larry felt foolish for his slip of the tongue.
62. His slip of the tongue was untidy.

Judging Sentences

Choose from each set of four sentences the one you find most effective, and be prepared to explain why. If you find two or more sentences equally effective, be ready to justify that judgment. If you don't like any of the four sentences, create a better version of your own.

A. 1. Trying to stub out her cigarette, she was fiddling with the ashtray in the back seat.
  2. She was fiddling with the ashtray in the back seat, trying to stub out her cigarette.
  3. Fiddling with the ashtray in the back seat and trying to stub out her cigarette.
  4. She fiddled with the ashtray in the back seat, and tried to stub out her cigarette in it.

B. 1. Unnerved by the freak accident she had just seen, Sue was banging on the door, sobbing.
  2. As she was unnerved by the freak accident she had just seen, Sue was banging on the door while sobbing.
  3. Sobbing, Sue kept banging on the door, having been unnerved by the freak accident she had just seen.
  4. Sue was banging on the door, sobbing, unnerved by the freak accident she had just seen.

C. 1. Trained by the apprentice system like their predecessors, Japanese mask makers employ an eclectic array of brushes, knives, and jars of paint to create a finished product.
  2. Japanese mask makers, trained by the apprentice system like their predecessors, employ an eclectic array of brushes, knives, and jars of paint to create a finished product.
  3. Employing an eclectic array of brushes, knives, and jars of paint and trained by the apprentice system like their predecessors, Japanese mask makers create a finished product.
  4. Japanese mask makers are trained by the apprentice system like their predecessors, and they employ an eclectic array of brushes, knives, and jars of paint to create a finished product.

D. 1. Here the valley was wide because the magnificent and slow-flowing river cut down a way for itself between dense banks of trees.
  2. The river, magnificent and flowing slowly, cut a way down for itself between dense banks of trees, making the valley wide here.

3. Here the valley was wide, with the river, magnificent and flowing slowly, cutting a way down for itself between dense banks of trees.
4. Here the valley was wide; the river was magnificent, and it flowed slowly and cut down a way for itself between dense banks of trees.

E. 1. Burdened by cynicism, the aging Mark Twain often retreated with friends for hours at billiards, a long-time source of recreation.
2. Billiards with friends for hours was a long-time source of recreation for the aging Mark Twain, burdened by cynicism.
3. Mark Twain, who was burdened by cynicism as he was aging, often retreated with friends for hours to play billiards, which was a long-time source of recreation for him.
4. Burdened by cynicism, the aging Mark Twain often retreated to his long-time source of recreation, playing billiards with friends for hours.

Sentence Combining Exercise

Combine the following sentences into an effective essay that includes several participial phrases.

THE SUBWAY

1. The train pulled out of the station.
2. The station was grimy.
3. The station was covered with graffiti.

4. The train entered the darkness of the tunnel.
5. The train hissed.
6. The train screamed.
7. The train headed downtown.

8. The third car held five people.
9. The third car held a woman.
10. The woman was old.
11. The third car held the woman's granddaughter.
12. The third car held a man.

13. The man was middle aged.
14. The third car held two men.
15. The two men were young.

16. The people were strangers.
17. The people were thrown into a situation.
18. The situation was suddenly intimate.

19. The woman clutched the pocketbook in her lap.
20. The woman was old.
21. The pocketbook was monogrammed.
22. The clutching was tight.

23. She glanced from time to time at the two men.
24. The two men were across from her.
25. The men were young.
26. The men looked tough.
27. At the same time she listened to her granddaughter.
28. Her granddaughter talked of their outing.
29. The talk was excited.

30. One of the young men stared.
31. The staring was at the darkness.
32. The darkness was outside.
33. He was amused by the movements of the girl.
34. Her movements were staccato.
35. But he tried to avoid her grandmother's glances.

36. The other man read the ads.
37. The ads were familiar.
38. The ads were above the windows.
39. His head bobbed to the rhythm of the train.

40. The man held a newspaper open to the business section.
41. The man was middle aged.
42. The man paid little attention to the others.
43. The man tried to concentrate on the print of the report.
44. The print was small.
45. The report was of the stock market.
46. The man crossed his legs.
47. And the man uncrossed his legs.

48. The crossing and uncrossing was to the movement of the car.
49. The movements were jerking.
50. The man was uncomfortable.
51. The uncomfortableness was obvious.

52. The scene outside brightened when the train pulled into the next station.
53. The train screeched to a halt.
54. The screeching was with the sound of metal resisting metal.
55. The sound was high pitched.

56. The people were pleased when the car filled.
57. It made them all anonymous again.

4. Appositives

The usual way to define or identify something is by saying what it is:

> Mr. Howe is my favorite professor.
>
> Sharks are streamlined swimmers and bloodhounds of the sea.
>
> The Fresh Air Fund is a nonprofit organization.

Often full sentences such as these are appropriate. But sometimes definitionlike details about a noun are more effectively and economically expressed by APPOSITIVES:

> Mr. Howe, **my favorite professor,** has received a Distinguished Teacher Award.
>
> **Streamlined swimmers and bloodhounds of the sea,** sharks are equipped with an extraordinary sense of smell.

The Fresh Air Fund, **a nonprofit organization,** gives impoverished New York City kids the chance to enjoy hills,
animals, and trees.

Appositives clarify and expand the meaning of nouns by supplying
defining details about them. But they do so *within* the same clause,
not as separate sentences or clauses. In other words, appositives
help cut down the number of clauses and at the same time make
the remaining clauses fuller, more substantial, more compact.
    Two of the many options for combining the following three
simple sentences are given below. Which one do you prefer?

She is an excellent, all-around student with a congenial personality.
She is a promising candidate for WOW.
WOW is an international scholarship program for outstanding
women around the world.

↓

Since she is an excellent, all-around student with a congenial
personality, she is a promising candidate for WOW, which
is an international scholarship program for outstanding
women around the world.

OR

**An excellent, all-around student with a congenial
personality,** she is a promising candidate for WOW, **an
international scholarship program for outstanding women around the world.**

In this last sentence, **an excellent, all-around student with a
congenial personality** is an appositive to **she,** and **an international scholarship program for outstanding women
around the world** is an appositive to **WOW.** The second revised sentence is five words shorter than the first; it states more
concisely the very same idea that in the first sentence requires the
connectives **since** and **which,** as well as the repetition of **she**
and **is**. By replacing whole clauses, the appositives seem to make
the second sentence move more briskly.
    Without appositives, **my favorite professor** in the
sentence

Mr. Howe, **my favorite professor,** has received a Distinguished Teacher Award.

might be included in a relative clause:

Mr. Howe, who is my favorite professor, has received a Distinguished Teacher Award.

Don't worry if you can't decide whether one of these sentences is "better" than the other. Both are perfectly good sentences. But it *is* important to be aware of your options; sound them out, listen to them, weigh them. Increasingly, your final choice will be the "right" one. Test your ears and eyes on sentences (a) and (b) below to decide which is more effective:

a. Even a brief visit to Greece, which is a modern gateway to the glory of the past, gives you a profound sense of the roots of our civilization.

b. Even a brief visit to Greece, **a modern gateway to the glory of the past,** gives you a profound sense of the roots of our civilization.

Clearly, **which is** in (a) is unnecessary, and it could even cause momentary confusion as you read the sentence, **even a brief visit to Greece, which is. . . .** At this point, can you be sure that **which** refers to **Greece** and not to **visit?** Using an appositive instead of **which** can be a smart way of avoiding possible confusion.

"Appositive" simply means being "positioned" *next to* something, generally a noun. It does not make any difference where the noun, such as **Joe Pippin** in the following examples, happens to be located in the sentence:

The university has repeatedly denied a speaking permit to Joe Pippin, **a free-lance preacher from the West Coast.**

OR

Joe Pippin, **a free-lance preacher from the West Coast,** has been repeatedly denied a speaking permit by the university.

OR

> A speaking permit to Joe Pippin, **a free-lance preacher from the West Coast,** has been repeatedly denied by the university.

The most common sentence position for the appositive is immediately *after* the noun that it expands. But the appositive can also *precede* the noun, often at the head of the sentence:

> **A free-lance preacher from the West Coast,** Joe Pippin has been repeatedly denied a speaking permit by the university.

By beginning with an unusual detail about the identity of Joe Pippin, you can arouse the reader's interest in what you have to say about him. Sometimes the larger context will call for or encourage an appositive in this spot. For instance, if you mentioned Joe Pippin in the preceding sentence, then an initial appositive referring to him can serve as a link between the two sentences:

> Joe Pippin is another addition to the recent list of unwelcome visitors on campus. **A free-lance preacher from the West Coast,** he has been repeatedly denied a speaking permit by the university.

Short appositives placed at the end can be striking—and remembered for their "punch line" effect:

> Half an hour later, the second diver returned with the same report—**nothing.**

> Incorporated in humanistic programs in our schools is one of the most dehumanizing practices in education—**standardized testing.**

> But there was one court order the neighborhood would refuse to accept—**busing.**

On the other hand, writers often pack a wealth of detail into appositives, making these modifiers carry the bulk of the message, with the details often being given in a SERIES:

Most area residents are likely to talk for the rest of their lives about the drama of that winter—**the record temperatures and snowfall, the school closings, the impassable streets, the cold homes and offices, the idle factories.**

It's precisely to keep young runaways from becoming street people—**to house, feed, and protect them and to help them with their problems**—that runaway houses have been established.

Just about anything that can function as a noun can be an appositive, even full clauses:

The America of the South and West—**what one politician long ago called "the great Baptist subculture of the United States"**—has at last outnumbered and overpowered the America of the long-dominant Northeast.

Appositives can also take a negative form:

Less than 50 feet past the intersection, the car started making unusual noises, **not the familiar rattles and knocks.**

An appositive often restates a noun by repeating it, especially when the noun is separated from the appositive:

We must realize our dependence on facilities and **services** over which we have no personal control—**services that we accept unthinkingly from dozens of nameless men and women every day.**

Literally hundreds of heart-warming **stories** unfolded in every corner of the county—**stories of neighbor helping neighbor, of young helping old, of rich helping poor.**

But when the appositive immediately follows the noun to be repeated, you may use a pronoun such as **one, that, the latter, something,** or **the kind** instead of repeating the noun:

Yesterday I went skating—**something I hadn't done in years.**

The team has hired Bill Simon and Ed Macklin—**the latter to coordinate recruiting efforts.**

Although appositives are normally nouns or nounlike structures, adjectives used in the appositive position can be just as effective in conveying descriptive details:

He revealed himself to be just what he seemed to be—**low-key, honest, and loving.**

Unhappy with their lives, defiant of authority, eager to find a sense of "family" in communal settings, a giant wave of counterculture youth rolled across the North American continent.

Often appositives are introduced and made more specific by CONNECTIVES such as **namely, in other words, for example, including, especially, particularly, notably,** or **mainly:**

A number of American presidents—**including McKinley, Harding, Roosevelt, and Kennedy in the twentieth century**—have died in office.

Some black leaders, **especially the more conservative,** viewed *Roots* as the most significant civil rights event since the 1965 march on Selma.

Whether or not they are preceded by a connective, appositives are usually set off by punctuation marks such as commas, dashes, and colons. These punctuation marks may create different effects. Compare the following:

I bought the flowers for my best friend, **my mother.**

I bought the flowers for my best friend—**my mother.**

I bought the flowers for my best friend: **my mother.**

Of these three versions, the first is perhaps the most matter-of-fact statement, giving the feeling that it should not be particularly surprising for the writer's mother to be his or her best friend. In the second sentence, the dash suggests a bit longer pause, which allows a somewhat greater emphasis on **my mother.** The colon in the last sentence creates an even longer pause, lending the appositive a formal, almost solemn quality.

Basic Pattern Exercise

Combine each sequences of sentences below into a single sentence with at least one appositive.

Example
1. One of the most controversial public school issues is "mainstreaming."
2. "Mainstreaming" is the growing practice of integrating physically and mentally handicapped children into regular classes.

↓

One of the most controversial public school issues is "mainstreaming," **the growing practice of integrating physically and mentally handicapped children into regular classes.**

OR

"Mainstreaming," **one of the most controversial public school issues,** is the growing practice of integrating physically and mentally handicapped children into regular classes.

A. 1. Pet owners upset by soaring veterinary costs can now register for Medipet.
   2. Medipet is a prepaid insurance plan for dogs and cats.

B. 1. A psychological autopsy is the attempt to describe a person's state of mind during the period leading up to death.
   2. A psychological autopsy is usually performed to determine whether death occurred by suicide or accident.

C. 1. Nairobi's railroad station is the starting point for East Africa's most traveled passenger train.
   2. East Africa's most traveled passenger train is the overnight express to Kenya's port on the Indian Ocean.
   3. Kenya's port on the Indian Ocean is Mombasa.

D. 1. Joe Morgan was the National League's Most Valuable Player in 1975.

2. Joe Morgan was the National League's Most Valuable Player in 1976.
3. Joe Morgan led the Cincinnati Reds to two consecutive world championships.

E. 1. Avignon is a walled city of 93,000 inhabitants.
2. Avignon is enclosed by ramparts.
3. The ramparts stretch a circumference of three miles.

F. 1. When a victim suffers a major burn, damage usually extends far beyond the burn site.
2. A major burn is one in which at least 20 percent of the skin is lost.

G. 1. If you are curious about the real South, read a book by historian C. Vann Woodward.
2. The real South is the South you didn't see in *Gone With the Wind*.

H. 1. Murphy's Law is that if anything can go wrong, it will.
2. Murphy's Law is known to schoolchildren the world over as "Jellybread always falls jelly-side down."

I. 1. Casanova was a seducer.
2. Casanova was a charlatan.
3. Casanova was a scribbler.
4. Casanova was a dabbler in Black Magic.
5. Casanova was that most magnetic of figures.
6. Casanova was a legend with nothing lofty about him.

J. 1. The ancient Chinese were a people of inventors and discoverers.
2. The ancient Chinese were a people of philosophers and soldiers.
3. The ancient Chinese were a people of poets and craftsmen.
4. The ancient Chinese gave the world many of its most useful things.
5. Its most useful things are the compass and the mechanical clock.
6. Its most useful things are paper and poetry.
7. Its most useful things are gunpowder and the wheelbarrow.

Sentence Combining Exercise

Combine the following sentences into an effective essay that includes several appositives.

THE LIFE AND DEATH OF A CELL

1. The bacteria cell is like a fortress.
2. The fortress is self-contained.
3. The cell is an organism.
4. The organism has parts.
5. The parts function for protection.
6. The parts function for nourishment and waste disposal.
7. The parts function for reproduction.

8. Outside the wall of the bacteria cell is a capsule.
9. The capsule is a layer.
10. The layer is slimy.
11. The layer is jellylike.
12. The layer helps protect the cell from chemicals.
13. The chemicals are in its surroundings.

14. The cell wall is another layer.
15. The layer is protective.
16. The layer encloses the organism.
17. The layer keeps food molecules out.
18. The food molecules are large.

19. A bacteria cell secretes enzymes.
20. Enzymes are chemicals.
21. The chemicals break down the molecules so that they can enter the cell.
22. The molecules are large.
23. The molecules are of starches.
24. The molecules are of proteins.

25. Just inside the cell wall is a layer.
26. The layer is thin.
27. The layer is fatty.
28. The layer is the membrane.

29. The membrane is of the cell.

30. The membrane contains carrier molecules.
31. The carrier molecules eliminate products.
32. The products are waste.

33. The membrane also helps make DNA.
34. DNA is the substance.
35. The substance contains the information.
36. The information is genetic.
37. The information is necessary for all things to reproduce.
38. The things are living.

39. The cell wall normally protects the life of the bacteria cell.
40. And the cell wall normally supports the life of the bacteria cell.
41. Animal cells lack a cell wall.

42. But penicillin can interfere with the development of the cell wall.
43. Other antibiotics can interfere with the development of the cell wall.
44. Penicillin and other antibiotics upset the systems of the bacteria cell.
45. The systems are digestive.
46. The systems are reproductive.
47. Penicillin and other antibiotics kill the cell.
48. Penicillin and other antibiotics are chemicals.
49. The chemicals are harmless to animal cells.

50. So the strength of the bacteria cell is also its weakness.
51. The strength of the bacteria cell is the cell wall.

Creative Pattern Exercise

Add at least one detail in the form of an appositive to each of the sentences below. Try for variety by placing your appositives in different positions within the sentence, and by occasionally adding more than one appositive.

Example
   The United States Senate consists of 100 members.

↓

   The United States Senate consists of 100 members, **two from each of the 50 states.**

OR

   The United States Senate, **one-half the legislative branch of government,** consists of 100 members.

OR

   A legislative body whose members serve six-year terms, the United States Senate consists of two representatives from each of the 50 states.

A. Jimmy Carter is our first president from the deep South since the Civil War.

B. College life is a series of shocks.

C. Some women feel threatened by the feminist movement.

D. There are advantages in attending a small college.

E. She expected to find a world filled with glamour.

F. These are the characteristics of an effective teacher.

G. Ugly violence characterizes our society.

H. There were only three people in the reading room.

 I. She remembered how thoughts of the dark cellar had always filled her with numb excitement.

J. Gossip serves a useful purpose in society.

Sentence Combining Exercise

Combine the following sentences into an effective essay that includes several appositives.

THE PEPSI GENERATION

1. They were slim.
2. They were tanned.
3. They were Levi-clad.
4. They rode motorcycles while swigging their colas.
5. They rode surfboards while swigging their colas.
6. They were the Pepsi generation.
7. They were the flower children of the sixties.

8. They were affluent.
9. They were numerous.
10. Manufacturers catered to their whims.
11. Advertisers pandered to their fancies.

12. They are grown up.
13. They are filled out.
14. They have swapped their motorcycles for station wagons.
15. They have swapped their surfboards for sedans.

16. The Pepsi generation changed the life-style of America.
17. The change was profound.
18. The Pepsi generation was the product of the baby boom.
19. The baby boom was postwar.

20. They gave us motorcycles.
21. And they gave us surfboards.
22. They gave us rock music.
23. And they gave us disco music.
24. They gave us revolution.
25. And they gave us pot.
26. They gave us peace marches.
27. And they gave us open classrooms.
28. These were the characteristics of a culture.
29. The culture was youth oriented.

30. The median age of the population was 28 in 1970.
31. The population was in America.
32. Twenty-eight is youthful.
33. 1970 was the height of flower power.

34. But the median age will pass 35.
35. The passing will be by 2005.
36. The passing will be when the Pepsi generation begins to think about retirement.

37. The total number of people is 23 million today.
38. The people are over 65 years old.
39. But the total number will swell to 41 million by the end of the century.
40. Sixty-five is retirement age.

41. Manufacturers are beginning to react to this change.
42. And advertisers are beginning to react to this change.
43. This change is demographic.
44. Manufacturers react by moving into areas.
45. The areas are new.
46. Advertisers react by changing their appeal.
47. The reaction is understandable.

48. Gerbers has stopped claiming that babies are its only business.

49. In fact, Gerbers now sells life insurance.
50. The life insurance is for the set.
51. The set is over 50 years old.
52. And Levi's are cut.
53. The cut is fuller.
54. The cut is for the flower children.
55. The flower children's stalks have thickened.

56. Maybe by 2000, colas will be hawked by golden agers.
57. The golden agers will be in bermuda shorts.
58. The golden agers will be riding golf carts.
59. The golden agers will be the Pepsi generation in retirement.

Judging Sentences

Choose from each set of four sentences below the one you find most effective, and be prepared to explain why. If you find two or more sentences equally acceptable, be ready to justify that judgment. If you don't like any of the four sentences, write a better version of your own.

A. 1. The three men, all in their twenties, pleaded not guilty.
   2. All in their twenties, the three men pleaded not guilty.
   3. All three men were in their twenties, and they pleaded not guilty.
   4. Pleading not guilty, all three men were in their twenties.

B. 1. A thunderstorm without rain, a dry lightning storm started a fire in a remote part of the forest in August.
   2. In August a dry lightning storm, a thunderstorm without rain, started a fire in a remote part of the forest.
   3. A fire was started in August in a remote part of the forest by a dry lightning storm—a thunderstorm without rain.
   4. In a remote part of the forest a dry lightning storm started a fire in August—a thunderstorm without rain.

C. 1. *The* American drink ever since the Boston Tea Party, the popularity of coffee had been in decline long before the boycott got under way.
   2. The popularity of coffee had been in decline long before the boycott of *the* American drink ever since the Boston Tea Party got under way.
   3. The popularity of coffee, *the* American drink ever since the Boston Tea Party, had been in decline long before the boycott got under way.
   4. Long before the boycott got under way, its popularity had already been in decline: of *the* American drink ever since the Boston Tea Party—coffee.

D. 1. A grandfatherly old man with a pair of old-fashioned glasses slipping down his nose, the judge looked harmless and ready to believe us from the beginning.
   2. The judge looked harmless and ready to believe us from the beginning—a grandfatherly old man with a pair of old-fashioned glasses slipping down his nose.
   3. From the beginning, the judge, who was a grandfatherly old man and his pair of old-fashioned glasses slipping down his nose, looked harmless and was ready to believe us.
   4. The judge was a grandfatherly old man, with a pair of old-fashioned glasses slipping down his nose, and from the beginning he looked harmless and he was ready to believe us.

E. 1. Some readers—especially student readers—look for a "moral" in everything they read—some rule of conduct which they regard as applicable to their lives.
 2. Some readers look for a "moral" in everything they read, especially student readers—some rule of conduct which they regard as applicable to their lives.
 3. A "moral," some rule of conduct which readers regard as applicable to their lives, is what some of them look for, especially student readers.
 4. In everything they read, some readers—especially student readers—look for some rule of conduct they regard as applicable to their lives, a "moral."

Sentence Combining Exercise

Combine the kernel sentences below into an effective whole that includes several appositives. You will not only need to combine sentences but to rearrange groups of sentences (A through D) by placing them in logical sequence.

THE CHILDREN'S CRUSADE

A. 1. Bands of children assembled under the leadership of Stephen of Cloyes.
 2. The assembling was in northern France.
 3. Stephen of Cloyes was a shepherd boy.
 4. Stephen of Cloyes promised to lead them across the sea to the Holy Land.

 5. They wandered through the French countryside to Marseilles.
 6. Marseilles is a port on the Mediterranean.
 7. They found that the sea did not open to let them pass.

 8. Some of the children returned home.
 9. Some of the children fell into the hands of sea captains.
 10. The sea captains were unscrupulous.
 11. The sea captains sold them into slavery.
 12. The slavery was in North Africa.

B. 13. The Children's Crusade began in 1212.
 14. The Children's Crusade ended in 1212.

15. The Children's Crusade was a movement of children.
16. The children were from France.
17. The children were from Germany.
18. The children were led to believe that they could recover the Holy Land.
19. The recovery would be miraculous.
20. The children were led to believe that they would be like the children of Israel before them.

C. 21. Not a single child from either country ever reached the Holy Land.

D. 22. Twenty thousand children left their homes to follow Nicholas.
23. This happened in Germany.
24. The children were mostly from the lower classes.
25. Nicholas was a visionary.
26. Nicholas was a peasant boy.
27. Nicholas was from Cologne.

28. Nicholas believed that the Holy Sepulchre could be rescued from the Muslims.
29. The Holy Sepulchre is Christ's tomb.
30. Nicholas believed that the rescuing could only be by crusaders who were innocent and pure of heart.

31. Nicholas and his followers struggled up the Rhine Valley.
32. Nicholas and his followers struggled through southern Germany.
33. Nicholas and his followers struggled across the Alps.
34. Nicholas and his followers struggled into Italy.
35. Nicholas and his followers finally arrived at Genoa.

36. Only one-third of the children survived the march.
37. Some died of disease.
38. Some died of hunger.
39. Some were kidnapped by slave merchants.

40. Some survived the march.
41. They failed to find passage across the Mediterranean Sea.
42. Or they were shipwrecked during their journey.

5. Absolutes

Suppose in a paper on the study habits of college students you are describing your roommate as she studies late one night. You begin by writing

> Marie was sitting at her desk.
> Her head was slightly lowered over a pile of chemistry notes.

You like your opening sentences, but you want the fact that Marie is sitting at her desk more closely connected to the detail of her lowered head. At first, you try to make this connection by simply joining the two sentences:

> Marie was sitting at her desk, and her head was slightly lowered over a pile of chemistry notes.

You're not altogether happy with this version either, so you try again. Eventually you write something like this:

Marie was sitting at her desk, **her head slightly lowered over a pile of chemistry notes.**

You may like this version best, both because it is concise and because it clearly connects Marie's sitting at her desk to her lowered head. The phrase **her head slightly lowered over a pile of chemistry notes** is called an ABSOLUTE, a group of words that is almost but not quite a complete sentence. An absolute has a full subject but only part of a predicate, often only a participle. Absolutes are useful for adding narrative and descriptive detail to your sentences. They are especially appropriate for focusing on parts of a whole, in this case for shifting from a general description of Marie to specific details about her—her head, her feet, her hands:

Marie was sitting at her desk, **her head slightly lowered over a pile of chemistry notes, her hands clasped, her feet tapping the floor gently.**

Although the name may not be familiar, you've probably used absolutes without knowing what they were:

Everything considered, New York is the world's most exciting city.
All months have either 30 or 31 days, **February excepted.**
There are, **all told,** 144 countries in the United Nations.

This unit encourages you to practice constructing absolutes so that you will have the option of using them knowingly and purposely in your writing.
  Let's say you are trying to communicate the sense of fear you once felt when a storm arose. At one point in your paper you write

The evening grew more menacing.
The breeze became gustier.
Whitecaps gave the lake a frothy, sinister appearance.

Perhaps these three blunt sentences are exactly what you want to convey your fear. But if not, you will want to experiment with various ways of combining them. Remembering that absolutes are particularly appropriate for adding details, for making a general statement like "the evening grew more menacing" more specific and concrete, you may decide to transform your second and third sentences into absolutes. There are two ways of making a full sentence into an absolute. One is by omitting a form of the verb **to be**—such as **is, are, was,** or **were.** In this way, the full sentence "Her head **was** slightly lowered over a pile of chemistry notes" was made into the absolute "her head slightly lowered over a pile of chemistry notes." The second way of turning a full sentence into an absolute involves changing the main verb into its **-ing** form. In the sentences about the menacing evening, this means changing **became** into **becoming** and **gave** into **giving:**

> The evening grew more menacing, **the breeze becoming gustier, whitecaps giving the lake a frothy, sinister appearance.**

Absolutes often work most effectively at the middle or end of sentences, where they provide supporting detail for a more general previous statement.

Now see if you can make the next two sentences into a single sentence with an absolute:

> The accountant sat quietly in the office.
> His eyes were closed.

You can create a sentence with an absolute by dropping the word **were** from the second full sentence and attaching **his eyes closed** to the first:

> The accountant sat quietly in the office, **his eyes closed.**

If you choose, you may also eliminate "his":

> The accountant sat quietly in the office, **eyes closed.**

The absolute is especially useful because of its flexibility. To the sentence about the accountant, for example, you have the option of adding still further detail following the absolute. You might add such detail in the form of a participial phrase, an appositive, or even another absolute:

> The accountant sat quietly in the office, **eyes closed,** waiting for the telephone to ring.

The accountant sat quietly in the office, **eyes closed,** a defeated man.

The accountant sat quietly in the office, **eyes closed, four tickets to the Cheyenne rodeo in his hands.**

Aside from carrying details, absolutes can be used to suggest a relationship of cause and effect, especially at the beginning of a sentence. Suppose, for example, you wanted to combine the following two sentences in order to imply that one action was the cause of another:

The stern of the battleship was torn apart by torpedoes. The battleship slowly sank into the Pacific.

Your first impulse might be to write,

Because its stern was torn apart by torpedoes, the battleship slowly sank into the Pacific.

This sentence is perfectly acceptable, but the same cause-effect relationship can be suggested, more concisely, with an absolute:

Its stern torn apart by torpedoes, the battleship slowly sank into the Pacific.

If there had been a second cause of the ship's sinking—let's say that its interior had been gutted by fire—that fact could also be added in the form of an absolute:

Its stern torn apart by torpedoes, its interior gutted by fire, the battleship slowly sank into the Pacific.

You also have the option of omitting **its** from each of the absolutes:

Stern torn apart by torpedoes, interior gutted by fire, the battleship slowly sank into the Pacific.

What cannot be omitted is the comma, or sometimes the dash, which always accompanies an absolute. When absolutes occur in the middle of a sentence, they are punctuated by two commas or, less frequently, two dashes.

How would you combine the following sentences?

His homework was done.
His English composition was written.
Larry decided to go see *One Flew Over the Cuckoo's Nest.*

You have, as always, a number of options:

His homework was done and his English composition was written, so Larry decided to go see *One Flew Over the Cuckoo's Nest.*

OR

Since his homework was done and his English composition was written, Larry decided to go see *One Flew Over the Cuckoo's Nest.*

OR

After his homework was done and his English composition was written, Larry decided to go see *One Flew Over the Cuckoo's Nest.*

Another workable option is the absolute, here constructed by omitting the verb **was** from each of the first two sentences:

His homework done, his English composition written, Larry decided to go see *One Flew Over the Cuckoo's Nest.*

But notice that moving the absolutes to the end of the sentence produces some confusion:

Larry decided to go see *One Flew Over the Cuckoo's Nest,* his homework done, his English composition written.

Confusion is created because the time relationships expressed in the sentence are unclear. Since Larry completed his homework and wrote his composition before deciding to take in a movie, those facts should logically be expressed first, not last, in the sentence. In general, absolutes work best at the middle or end of a

sentence, but absolutes that either suggest a cause-effect relationship or refer to an earlier event work best at its beginning.

Like participles and appositives, absolutes may be used in a
series, which can be particularly forceful when building toward a
climax:

> The arrested woman was slammed against a wall, **her body
> frisked, her wrists handcuffed, her dignity lost.**

In this example the final absolute **her dignity lost** both gen-
eralizes from the two earlier absolutes and broadens their meaning.
The sentence would lose impact if **her dignity lost** did not occur
as the final series item. To hear the difference, try reading the
sentence out loud with **her dignity lost** as the first or second
item.

Knowing that an absolute series gains power when its items
are placed in order of increasing importance, how would you combine these sentences?

> The room was in chaos.
> Empty soda bottles and beer cans were everywhere.
> Soiled clothes were strewn on the floor.
> Cosmetics were scattered over the dresser.

Since the sentence with the bottles and cans "everywhere" comes
closest to describing the room's complete disorder, it should probably be positioned at the end of the series:

> The room was in chaos—**soiled clothes strewn on the
> floor, cosmetics scattered over the dresser,
> empty soda bottles and beer cans everywhere.**

Basic Pattern Exercise

Combine each of the groups of sentences below into a single sentence containing at least one absolute.

Example
   1. When I walked in, Grandpa was sitting at the kitchen table.
   2. The newspaper was spread before him.

↓

When I walked in, Grandpa was sitting at the kitchen table, **the newspaper spread before him.**

A. 1. Jimmy walked slowly to the corner of the playground.
    2. His face was streaked with tears.

B. 1. The station wagon sped away.
    2. The taillights disappeared into the distance.

C. 1. *Rocky* is a slum fairy tale.
    2. Its plot is simple even by Hollywood standards.

D. 1. Imagine yourself on top of a long, steep, snowy-white hill.
    2. The sky is burning blue around you.

E. 1. His opponent had gained a lead of almost 100,000 votes.
    2. The senator publicly conceded that he had lost his reelection bid.

F. 1. Waiting for Matt Dillon in the center of Dodge City is the bad guy.
    2. His black hat casts a dark shadow upon the town.

G. 1. The women up and down the alley swatted flies.
    2. They fussed with their unruly hair.
    3. Their mouths were full of clothespins.

H. 1. The photographer sits, compact, on the 30-yard line.
    2. One knee is folded under his body.
    3. The other knee is upright to support his elbow.

I. 1. A few minutes later I made my way to the Chevy pickup.
    2. Packages were under my arm.
    3. Crudely drawn maps were in my hand.
    4. The pickup was parked in front of the store.

J. 1. The professor rested against the blackboard.
    2. Chalk was in one hand.
    3. A look of profound discouragement was in her eyes.
    4. A textbook was in the other hand.

Sentence Combining Exercise

Combine the following sentences into an effective whole that includes several absolutes. Add a detail or two of your own to the story.

FISHING

1. The boys leaned against the willow tree.
2. The tree grew next to the stream.
3. Their fishing poles rested on sticks.
4. Their eyes gazed at the bobbers.
5. The bobbers floated on the ripples.

6. The morning had been cool.
7. It had been comfortable.
8. The afternoon was growing sultry.

9. Both boys had taken great pleasure.
10. The pleasure was in planning the trip.
11. Both had looked forward to Friday.
12. Friday was their only day off from school all spring.

13. The bass hadn't been biting.
14. The boys spent most of the morning.
15. They spent it talking.
16. They spent it occasionally dozing off.
17. They dozed off to dream.
18. They dreamed of catching fish.

19. The fish didn't take the lines.
20. They periodically teased the boys.

21. They nibbled at the bait.
22. They jumped.
23. The jumping was within arms' reach of the boys.
24. The boys were on the bank.

25. The boys tried changing bait.
26. They tried changing rods.
27. They tried changing places.
28. Nothing worked.

29. One bluegill did strike.
30. It was tiny.
31. It struck late in the afternoon.
32. It fell off just as it was drawn near the bank.

33. That was the end.

34. Their stomachs were crying.
35. The crying was for food.
36. Their backs were burning.
37. The burning was from too much sun.
38. Their legs were stiff.
39. The stiffness was from sitting.
40. Both boys gathered their gear.
41. They headed for home.

Creative Pattern Exercise

To each of the following sentences add one fact or detail in the form of an absolute. Add some of the absolutes at the beginning of the sentence, some in the middle, and some at the end. For any two sentences add a series of three absolutes.

Example

Diane stood motionless at the end of the diving board.

↓

Diane stood motionless at the end of the diving board, **tears streaming down her cheeks.**

OR

Diane stood notionless at the end of the diving board, **hands at her side, heels slightly raised, every muscle anticipating action.**

A. The passengers waited patiently inside the bus terminal.

B. He spoke to her gently, soothingly.

C. Johnny tumbled down the grassy slope.

D. The cast left the theater for home.

E. Barbara sat alone on the basement floor playing solitaire.

F. I finally reached Interstate 70.

G. From across the street the house looked deserted.

H. The dog barked once and then twice more before settling back to sleep.

I. A full-color ad featuring a beautiful woman is likely to sell more cigarettes than one listing tar and nicotine levels.

J. By the time the rescue squad arrived, firemen had already stretched a ladder from the street to the fourth-floor window.

Sentence Combining Exercise

Combine the following sentences into a short essay that includes several absolutes.

EASY SELL

1. The cowboy dominates the pages of many magazines.
2. He is tanned and rugged.
3. His hair is dark and curly.
4. His broad shoulders are sloping yet powerful.
5. His expression is calm and confident.

6. One hand grasps a pack of Marlboros.
7. The hand is weather-worn.

8. The cowboy catches our interest.
9. But the cigarettes sell.

10. We might expect advertisers to emphasize their product.
11. We don't expect them to emphasize the cowboy.
12. But modern ads deemphasize the product.
13. They rely instead on the idyllic context for the big sell.

14. We are impressed with the magnificence of the people and places.
15. We don't actually buy the product.
16. We buy the sex appeal and the tantalizing scenes.

17. Sex never fails to sell.

18. A Ford pickup becomes more attractive when a woman is draped across the hood.
19. The truck is large and clumsy.
20. The woman is gorgeous.
21. She is clad in a bikini.
22. Her hair is a bit wind-blown.
23. Her mouth is open in awe.

24. Johnny Walker's taste improves.
25. It improves when two young lovers linger over their scotch.
26. They are in romantic surroundings.

27. Lustrous hair can turn even Midas mufflers into sex symbols.
28. Vic Tanny physiques can, too.
29. So can the latest fashions.

30. The ad's setting also provides a visual feast.

31. In the summer, refreshing scenes cool us off.
32. The scenes are wintry.

33. A cozy fireside setting makes us desire Harvey's Bristol Cream sherry.
34. Snow is falling gently outside.
35. A happy couple lounges inside.

36. A ski lodge captures us with its appeal.
37. The lodge is jammed with dancing students.
38. They are all wearing Levi's.
39. It has "winter wonderland" appeal.

40. In the winter, the ads offer us summertime.

41. Coca-Cola is drunk by sunbathers.
42. A healthy family enjoys Wheaties.
43. The family is on the patio.
44. The patio is under cloudless summer skies.
45. Friendly United Airlines flies us to tropical Jamaica.

46. The ads change with the weather.
47. They always tempt us with the elusive comfort.
48. The comfort is provided only by their product.

49. The products are ordinary.
50. The products are sometimes dull.
51. The ad execs know just what to do.

52. The ad execs give us a voluptuous body.
53. They hope we will buy the Chevrolet.
54. The body just happens to be sitting in the Chevrolet.

Judging Sentences

Choose from each group of four sentences below the one you find most effective, and be prepared to explain why. If you find two or more sentences equally acceptable, be ready to justify that judgment. If you don't like any of the four sentences, create a better version of your own.

A. 1. The evening growing more menacing, the breeze becoming gustier, whitecaps giving the lake a frothy, sinister appearance.

2. The breeze becoming gustier, whitecaps giving the lake a frothy, sinister appearance, the evening grew more menacing.
3. The evening grew more menacing, the breeze becoming gustier, whitecaps giving the lake a frothy, sinister appearance.
4. Whitecaps giving the lake a frothy, sinister appearance, the evening grew more menacing, the breeze becoming gustier.

B. 1. When the police arrived, sirens blaring, blue and red lights flashing, the accident scene took on the atmosphere of a carnival.
2. The accident scene took on the atmosphere of a carnival, sirens blaring, blue and red lights flashing, when the police arrived.
3. When the police, sirens blaring, blue and red lights flashing, arrived, the accident scene took on the atmosphere of a carnival.
4. Sirens blaring, blue and red lights flashing, when the police arrived, the accident scene took on the atmosphere of a carnival.

C. 1. Unable to say a word, her mouth twitching, her eyes unfocused, Brenda just lay there.
2. Brenda just lay there, her mouth twitching, her eyes unfocused, unable to say a word.
3. Brenda just lay there with her mouth twitching and her eyes were unfocused, unable to say a word.
4. Her mouth twitching, her eyes unfocused, unable to say a word, Brenda just lay there.

D. 1. A small cotton bag over his face, hands tied behind his back, a noose fixed securely about his neck, the prisoner stood quietly on the wooden platform.
2. The prisoner stood quietly on the wooden platform, a noose fixed securely about his neck, a small cotton bag over his face, hands tied behind his back.
3. His hands tied behind his back, a small cotton bag over his face, the prisoner stood quietly on the wooden platform, a noose fixed securely about his neck.
4. The prisoner stood quietly on the wooden platform, hands

tied behind his back, a small cotton bag over his face, a noose fixed securely about his neck.

E. 1. Then the two players let him fall to the track, his chest landing first, his head following, bouncing, and finally lying still.
   2. Then the two players letting him fall to the track, his chest landed first, then his head, which bounced and finally lay still.
   3. Then the two players let him fall to the track, and his chest landed first and his head followed and it bounced and finally lay still.
   4. Then the two players let him fall to the track, his chest landing first, his head followed, bounced, and finally lay still.

Sentence Combining Exercise

Rearrange the following sentences into a well-organized essay that defines karate and explains its appeal. You may change the structure as well as the order of the sentences whenever such changes make your essay more effective.

KARATE

1. Karate, which means "empty hand" in Japanese, differs from ju-jitsu, judo, and sumo wrestling, all Oriental forms of self-defense.

2. There are 50,000 American students of karate, ranging from mild-mannered teachers to burly construction workers.

3. Karate appeals to people for various reasons.

4. For most people, their bodies flabby and their muscles weak, karate is a way to get in shape.

5. While ju-jitsu, judo, and sumo wrestling rely on close personal contact, karate technique involves quick blows delivered with the hands, knees, and feet from a safe distance.

6. Karate is like a mixture of boxing and foot fighting.

7. The two-by-four rests solidly on two cinder blocks placed three feet apart.

8. Suddenly, a piercing cry destroys the silence as a hand descends, fingers together and extended, swiftly and surely shattering the board.

9. The setting for this scene is a *dojo,* a karate training school.

10. For other people, especially those concerned with protecting themselves against muggers, karate provides effective fighting skills.

11. For many college students, karate means two credit hours toward graduation.

12. Whether their initial interest is exercise, protection, or credit hours, karate students quickly realize the other benefits offered by the sport.

13. With more students seeking more *dojos,* karate seems here to stay.

14. Whatever its appeal, karate is gaining in popularity.

15. Karate devotees flock to practice their kicks and blows, called *kumite,* and their graceful and deceivingly fast delivery, called a *kata.*

16. Karate is an ancient Oriental art of self-defense.

6. Summing Up

Putting It Together I

Combine each of the following groups of sentences into a single, more effective sentence. Use whatever constructions work best—relative clauses, participles, appositives, absolutes, or any others.

Example
1. Tennis doubles is a game of maneuver.
2. It is a game of feints and finesse.
3. It is a game of unexpected advances and sudden retreats.
4. All these maneuvers are designed to win points.
5. The points are won by surprising the opposition.

↓

Tennis doubles is a game of maneuver, of feints and finesse, unexpected advances and sudden retreats—all designed to win points by surprising the opposition.

OR

In the game of tennis doubles, maneuvers like feints and finesses, sudden retreats and unexpected advances, are designed to surprise the opposition and to win points.

A. 1. Almost every summer night the cooling northeast wind swept through our bedroom windows.
   2. It made air conditioning unnecessary.
   3. It made a light blanket welcome.

B. 1. Television news people are pawns in the rating game.
   2. They are hired and fired in some instances on the basis of skin tests.
   3. The skin tests are given to viewers to measure their emotional reactions.

C. 1. The steep surrounding slopes were capped with snow.
   2. The snow fed two streams.
   3. The streams plunged down to join in the valley below.

D. 1. The last ticket for the Frampton concert had been sold.
   2. The Music Hall closed its doors.
   3. A crowd was left outside.
   4. The crowd was angry.
   5. The crowd was disappointed.
   6. The crowd threatened to burn down the building.

E. 1. Justice has always been the most elusive of human principles.
   2. Justice has always been a utopian goal.
   3. The goal was never fully clear in theory.
   4. The goal was rarely approximated in practice.

F. 1. The New Jersey referendum on gambling was one of the hottest issues in the state.
   2. It aroused the strong opposition of church leaders.
   3. It aroused the strong opposition of law-enforcement officials.
   4. They warned that turning Atlantic City into a giant casino would attract not only tourists.
   5. They warned it would also attract organized crime.

6. They warned it would also attract prostitution.
7. They warned it would also attract loan sharks.

G. 1. A Minnesota Viking player was proficient in karate.
   2. He hit a rookie linebacker's neck hard.
   3. He hit it so hard that the linebacker fell to the turf.
   4. The linebacker was unconscious.
   5. The linebacker was choking in blood and vomit.

H. 1. The grueling race was finally over.
   2. The distance runner collapsed onto the cinders.
   3. She was gasping for breath.
   4. Her chest was heaving.
   5. Her face was a splotchy red and gray.

I. 1. "Ten Who Dared" was a television series.
   2. It chronicled the journeys of Pizarro and Columbus.
   3. It chronicled the journeys of Amundsen and Cook.
   4. It recaptured the very feel of exploration.
   5. The very feel of exploration is the determination and the doubt.
   6. The very feel of exploration is the fear and the triumph.

J. 1. He is nearing the top.
   2. His eyes are already glowing with triumph.
   3. He climbs faster and faster.
   4. He climbs recklessly fast.
   5. He suddenly slips and falls.
   6. He tumbles to the ground.
   7. He lies motionless there.
   8. He is a crumpled pile of arms and legs.

Sentence Combining Exercise

Combine the following sentences into an effective essay.

SNOWBOY

1. Ricky heard his mother.
2. She was calling him in.
3. Her voice sounded colder than the winter wind.

4. He turned from the frozen white walls.
5. The turning was reluctant.
6. He had made the walls.
7. He looked to the back door.
8. The looking was hopeful.
9. His cheeks were red.
10. The redness was from hours of play.
11. His nylon snow suit was a shade darker.
12. The darkness was from the melted snow.

13. No reprieve came.
14. He waved to his day-long companion.
15. His companion was the snowman.
16. He began the trek to his house.
17. The distance was 50 feet.
18. He prolonged every step.
19. He took last glimpses of his empire.

20. He dragged his black galoshes through the snow.
21. The dragging was heavy.
22. He thought only of the day's fun.
23. He thought of the snowballs thrown.
24. He thought of the new territories conquered.
25. The warm dinner seemed less inviting than the many mouthfuls of snow.
26. His mother would insist the warm dinner was good for him.
27. He had swallowed snow while crawling.
28. He crawled through his network of tunnels.

29. His only comfort was one last wild plunge.
30. He plunged over the snowy yard.
31. He plunged through an enemy fort.
32. The fort was already weak.
33. The weakness was from his earlier barrage of iceballs.

34. Ricky's day was ending.

35. It had seemed to go on forever.
36. Now the games were gone.
37. The friends were gone.
38. The runny noses were gone.

39. Ricky lingered awhile on the porch.
40. He stomped his boots clean.
41. He clapped his mittens free of the snow.
42. Snow was frozen in every crease.
43. He wished to return to his real home.
44. The yard was his real home.

45. His mother finally hurried him into the house.
46. She was growing impatient.
47. The house swallowed him for the evening.

Taking It Apart

Make each of the long, unwieldy sentences below into a more effective short paragraph of two or more sentences.

Example

Ski resorts were once deserted during the summer months when it doesn't snow, but now they have created a new sport to entice visitors when not a trace of snow can be found on the ski slopes, a ride called the Alpine Slide which lasts about four minutes, covers anywhere from 2000 to 4000 feet of mountainside, costs about $3, and reaches speeds up to 25 miles an hour, with the rider, who sits in a fiberglass sled, regulating speed by pushing a control stick forward to accelerate or pulling it backward to stop or slow down as the sled moves along curving chutes made from asbestos cement.

↓

Once deserted during the snowless summer months, ski resorts now attract visitors with a new sport—the Alpine Slide. Riders cruise down curving chutes of asbestos cement in a fiberglass sled whose speeds, reaching 25 miles an hour, are regulated by a control stick which can be pushed forward to accelerate or pulled backward to brake. Covering anywhere from 2000 to 4000 feet of mountainside, the ride lasts four minutes and costs only $3.

OR

Ski resorts that were once deserted during the snowless summer months have now created a new sport to entice visitors— the Alpine Slide. The slide covers 2000 to 4000 feet of mountainside, lasts a full four minutes, and costs only $3. In cruising down curving chutes of asbestos cement, riders regulate their own speed, pulling a control stick backward to brake or pushing it forward to accelerate to speeds as high as 25 miles an hour.

A. Educators report that high school seniors of the 1970s are primarily interested in grades and economic success, can be expected to cheat and plagiarize more frequently than those who graduated ten years earlier, are far less concerned with the problems of society than with their own personal future, are characterized by passivity, conformity, and materialism, and seem to organize their lives about what others expect of them.

B. When former attorney general John N. Mitchell, the "iron man" of the Nixon administration, the "Big Enchilada" of the Watergate affair according to co-conspirator John Erlichman, and the first attorney general in history to be convicted of criminal acts, surrendered himself to Alabama prison authorities in June 1977, thereby making himself a prisoner of the federal justice system he once ran as the nation's chief law enforcement officer, he became the 25th—and probably the last—person sent to jail for Watergate crimes.

C. Because the highly regarded Nevada-Las Vegas basketball team, ranked third in the national polls, was the last of the four squads to arrive at the NCAA regional tournament site, thereby missing the opportunity for a scheduled early morning work-out, its coach explaining that his players had to attend classes, there were immediate questions about which classes his players attended—remedial roulette? principles of blackjack?

D. Each spring, during what has become known as "College Weeks," some 250,000 college students crowd into Daytona Beach, another 100,000 invade Ft. Lauderdale, and still another 10,000 fly on to Bermuda, with resort owners welcoming the business that college students bring, those in Bermuda, for example, seeking to attract vacationing students and to keep them happy and occupied once they arrive by offering free harbor cruises, free lunches, limbo contests, volleyball matches, and get-acquainted dances, but with the same resort owners breathing sighs of relief when the invasion is over.

E. Psychologists who have studied children in Northern Ireland, scene of a long, bitter, and bloody civil war, tell us that 75 percent of the ten-year-olds believe that any unknown object found in the street—a cigarette pack, a letter, a package—is likely to be a bomb, and that 80 percent of the children believe that shooting and killing are acceptable ways of achieving political goals, clear evidence that the use of violence leads to further violence.

Sentence Combining Exercise

Combine the sentences below into an effective essay.

TATTOOING

1. The arm of a seaman is decorated with a cobra.
2. The arm is sweaty and muscular.
3. The arm glistens with salt spray.
4. The cobra is red and green.
5. The cobra is coiled.
6. The cobra is ready to strike.

7. A well-dressed gentleman slyly raises his pant cuff.
8. He is in a smoke-filled bar.
9. A sleazy trumpet moans in the background.
10. He reveals a blue infinity sign.
11. The sign identifies him as a member of a secret gang.

12. Three high school students gawk at the design book.
13. They decide on the naked bust of a sultry brunette.
14. The bust will be emblazoned on their upper leg.
15. The bust will be safely hidden from their parents' gaze.

16. The practice of tattooing has appealed to various people.
17. It has appealed for various reasons.
18. It apparently derives much of its appeal from an aura.
19. Its aura is of mystery.
20. Its aura is of evil.

21. In primitive societies tattooing was used as magic.

22. A tattoo of a snake supposedly protected a warrior from his enemies.
23. A tattoo of a cat supposedly increased a warrior's cunning and agility.

24. In modern societies, however, tattooing has usually been associated with evil.
25. Tattooing has usually not been associated with magic.

26. In modern societies, the practice of tattooing has always been frowned upon.
27. The practice of tattooing has sometimes been banned.

28. Tattooing was forbidden in Europe.
29. It was forbidden after the introduction of Christianity.
30. But it maintained its popularity in underworld circles.

31. Convicts in prison were identified by tattoos.
32. This occurred as late as the nineteenth and early twentieth centuries.
33. The tattoos were in conspicuous places.
34. Conspicuous places are the back of the hand and the cheek.

35. Today, tattoos are most common among military personnel, motorcycle gangs, and criminals.
36. The criminals now use tattoos to identify themselves as gang members.
37. The criminals now use tattoos to indicate their rank within the gang.

38. It is with these values that most people associate the innocent practice of tattooing.
39. These values are a life of violence or a life of crime.

40. Most recently, tattooing's shadowy aura of evil and mystery has been amplified.
41. Tattoo parlors have been banned in major cities.
42. One such city is New York.
43. Health authorities fear that tattooing may lead to hepatitis and cancer.

44. But even today young people are fond of tattoos.
45. The young people are of both sexes.
46. Perhaps their fondness is because there is glamour in being marked.

47. The most popular style for women is a finely sketched flower.
48. The flower is tattooed on a shoulder, thigh, or breast.

49. The most popular style for men is a large dragon.
50. The body of the dragon is wrapped around the arm.
51. Or the most popular style for men is a heart.
52. A woman's name is enclosed within the heart.

53. Tattooing may one day shed its associations with the underworld.
54. This may occur if there are more talented artists.
55. This may occur if there are safer methods.
56. This may occur if there are less painful methods.

57. Tattooing may even become a legitimate art form.
58. Tattooing may not be just a means of identifying criminals.

59. Tattooing may not be just a means of identifying members of secret gangs.

60. Tattooing may gain acceptance by society at large.
61. If so, it will have lost its special aura of mystery and evil.

Putting It Together II

Combine each of the following groups of sentences into a single effective sentence. Use any constructions that work—relative clauses, participles, appositives, absolutes, or anything else.

Example
1. We arrived by plane from Denver.
2. It was a 16-minute flight.
3. The flight culminated in a breathtaking touchdown.
4. The flight culminated in a smooth touchdown.
5. The touchdown was at a tiny airport.
6. The airport was tucked in among the Rocky Mountains.

We arrived by plane from Denver, a 16-minute flight that culminated in a breathtaking but smooth touchdown at a tiny airport tucked in among the Rocky Mountains.

OR

We arrived by plane from Denver, a 16-minute flight culminating in a smooth yet breathtaking touchdown at a tiny airport that was tucked in among the Rocky Mountains.

A. 1. Only two kinds of people read novels nowadays.
   2. The first kind is the insomniacs.
   3. The insomniacs are in pink plastic curlers.
   4. The insomniacs would rather be watching TV quiz shows.
   5. The second kind is the college students.
   6. The college students' professors make them do it.

B. 1. His central idea is that the South has produced the outstanding minds in American political history.
   2. His central idea is that this is a contribution unrecognized by the nation.

3. It is unrecognized because conquerors write history.
4. It is unrecognized because losers do not write history.

C. 1. I could see her lying on her couch.
2. Her couch was across from the dining room table.
3. She was a pink-cheeked Russian peasant.
4. She had bouquets in her brown eyes.

D. 1. There is a touch of arrogance in the way Jimmy Connors moves around the tennis court.
2. His shoulders are hunched.
3. His head is sinking down to his chest.
4. His eyes are focused on himself.

E. 1. Gordie Howe is charging at full speed.
2. Gordie Howe calculates how to outwit the goaltender.
3. The goaltender's body is swollen with nearly 40 pounds of equipment.
4. The goaltender's body is crouching to block much of the net.
5. The net is 4 × 6.
6. The net is cagelike.

F. 1. The mighty Mississippi lies at the heart of a large river-freighting system.
2. The system carries some 600 million tons of cargo each year.
3. 600 million tons of cargo is 15 percent of domestic commerce.

G. 1. The U.S. government came up with a project.
2. The project was designed to make play out of work.
3. At least for tourists it would make play out of work.
4. The government issued a directory.
5. The directory is of more than 1500 businesses and factories.
6. The businesses and factories offer free tours to visitors.

H. 1. His suit was rumpled.
2. His thinning hair was combed.
3. The combing was in a vain attempt to camouflage a bald spot.
4. The man sat clutching a shabby briefcase.

    5. He sat staring at his shoes.
    6. His shoes were equally as shabby as his briefcase.
    7. He never once looked up.

I. 1. There was a coordinated American and French offensive.
    2. It was combined with pressure on Turkey to cut off its supply of opium.
    3. The offensive and the pressure virtually shut down "The French Connection."
    4. It forced drug dealers to look elsewhere.

J. 1. We liked what we saw from the beginning.
    2. We saw thick foliage.
    3. The foliage was carpeting the jagged pinnacles.
    4. The foliage was shading the road.
    5. We saw rows of banana trees.
    6. The banana trees were bearing clusters of tiny yellow fruit.
    7. We saw tidy villages.
    8. The villages were with pastel concrete houses.
    9. The houses were clinging to the hillsides.

Sentence Combining Exercise

Combine the following sentences into an effective essay.

THE HOME FRONT

    1. "Rosie the Riveter" was the symbol for the civilians.
    2. The civilians worked for the war effort.
    3. The work was during World War II.

    4. She was like all of them.
    5. All of them rode to work at a war factory.
    6. The riding was in a '38 Studebaker.
    7. The Studebaker had bald tires.
    8. The car was filled to capacity.
    9. But the car was short on gas.

   10. She put up blackout curtains at night before she did this.
   11. She turned on the lights.

12. And she tuned in the radio.
13. She wanted to hear Gabriel Heater or H. V. Kaltenborn.
14. They had the latest reports from the European Theater of Operations.
15. They had the latest reports from the Pacific Theater of Operations.

16. She made supper.
17. At the same time, she was listening to "Amos 'n Andy" or "The Hit Parade."
18. She was listening to "Gangbusters" or "Lux Radio Theater."

19. But mostly she thought about her husband.
20. Her husband was "somewhere in the Pacific."
21. The censored letters always said "somewhere in the Pacific."

22. This was it.
23. Millions of Americans spent the war years somehow.
24. They were waiting for loved ones in uniform.
25. They were listening to the news on the radio.
26. And they were taking part in this.
27. It was the greatest production effort a people have ever made.

28. Women like Rosie learned how to do this.
29. They soldered.
30. They ran lathes.
31. They drove buses for this reason.
32. They wanted to replace men.
33. Men were needed for combat.

34. High school kids worked evenings.
35. They worked in tank factories.
36. They worked at steel mills.

37. Old people took up trades.
38. The old people were in retirement.
39. The trades were half-forgotten.

40. They produced the weapons.
41. The weapons fought the Axis powers.
42. They produced 296,029 airplanes.
43. They produced 86,333 tanks.
44. They produced 319,000 artillery pieces.

45. They raised steel production by 70 percent over prewar years.
46. They increased the production of aluminum by 429 percent.
47. They increased the production of magnesium by 3358 percent.

48. They saved tin cans.
49. They brushed their teeth with half brushfuls of toothpaste.
50. They worked at the local U.S.O.

51. They walked the darkened streets in the evenings.
52. They were air raid wardens.

53. Or they strained their eyes.
54. They were peering through the night skies.
55. They were aircraft-warning watchers.

56. They waited.
57. They worked.
58. They lined up.
59. The lining up was for hard-to-get items.
60. Sugar was a hard-to-get item.
61. Nylons were a hard-to-get item.
62. Tires were hard-to-get items.
63. Coffee was a hard-to-get item.
64. Their ration coupons were in hand.

65. They were a people.
66. The people were united against totalitarianism.
67. The people were united in their desire.
68. They wanted to win a war.
69. They believed in the war.

7. Prepositional Phrases

It's a good bet that you won't keep on speaking or writing very long—perhaps not beyond a sentence or two—without using a preposition. Whether you tell **about** your trip **to** Alaska **with** some friends **during** the summer, argue **for** or **against** the Panama Canal Treaty, or explain how to turn salt water **into** fuel **by** a new process—you are bound to use prepositions to form your ideas and to relate them to one another. The most common simple prepositions are **of, to, for, at, from, on, with, by,** and **as;** others include **after, before, in, over, through, under, until,** and **without.** Many prepositions are more complex, such as **according to, because of, except for, rather than, contrary to, in the absence of, in compliance with,** and **in addition to.**

A preposition does not occur by itself, but—as its name implies—it is "positioned before" something, usually a noun or noun phrase, which serves as its object. A preposition and its object together form a PREPOSITIONAL PHRASE, such as **with us, against the neutron bomb, because of favorable experience**

with coeducational dorms over the past several years.
This unit is intended to help you become aware of the options that
prepositional phrases provide.

One option is to substitute prepositional phrases for full
clauses. In revising your first draft, you may decide that a full clause
either makes your sentence wordy or does not precisely convey the
intended relationship between two ideas. In such a case, a prepositional phrase gives you a handy option for rewording the
sentence:

> Although they have a menacing appearance, most reptiles
> aren't really vicious if you leave them alone.

> ↓

> **Despite their menacing appearance,** most reptiles
> aren't really vicious if you leave them alone.

> Even though it is a popular belief that leprosy is a thing of the
> past, there are at least 12 million leprosy victims in the
> world today.

> ↓

> **Contrary to the popular belief that leprosy is a
> thing of the past,** there are at least 12 million leprosy
> victims in the world today.

> Now that urethane wheels have been invented, today's
> skateboarding knows no limits.

> ↓

> **With**
> **Thanks to** } **the invention of urethane wheels,**
> today's skateboarding knows no limits.

You often have the option of moving a prepositional phrase
to other sentence positions. Its mobility depends on the preposition
itself or on the role of the phrase in the sentence. In the skateboarding sentence above, the phrase beginning with **thanks to** can be
moved to the end, but the phrase introduced by **with** cannot:

> Today's skateboarding knows no limits, **thanks to the in-
> vention of urethane wheels.**

BUT NOT

Today's skateboarding knows no limits, with the invention of
urethane wheels.

In the next example the prepositional phrase is closely linked to the
phrase **summarize accurately** and cannot be moved:

The ability to summarize accurately, **with due care for
proportion as well as fact,** is a necessary quality in a
research paper.

BUT NOT

With due care for proportion as well as fact, the ability to
summarize accurately is a necessary quality in a research
paper.

OR NOT

The ability to summarize accurately is a necessary quality in a
research paper, with due care for proportion as well as fact.

On the other hand, when the prepositional phrase modifies a short
subject noun, for example, then the phrase can occur on either side
of the noun:

Calder's art has exuberant simplicity.
Calder's art represents a complex fusion of many elements.

↓

For all its exuberant simplicity, Calder's art represents a
complex fusion of many elements.

OR

Calder's art, **for all its exuberant simplicity,** represents a
complex fusion of many elements.

Italy has vast treasures of Etruscan pottery, old Roman ruins,
and baroque palaces.
Italy is a 600-mile long art gallery.

↓

With its vast treasures of Etruscan pottery, old

Roman ruins, and baroque palaces, Italy is a 600-mile long art gallery.

OR

Italy, **with its vast treasures of Etruscan pottery, old Roman ruins, and baroque palaces,** is a 600-mile long art gallery.

Women have increasing representation in the work force. Women have failed to approach the income of men.

↓

Despite their increasing representation in the work force, women have failed to approach the income of men.

OR

Women, **despite their increasing representation in the work force,** have failed to approach the income of men.

A similar pattern involves a preposition—usually **after, aside from, before, besides, by, for, in,** or **without**—followed by the present participle **ing** form:

Virginia Woolf wrote a lovely suicide note to her husband. Then she drowned herself.

↓

Before drowning herself, Virginia Woolf wrote a lovely suicide note to her husband.

OR

Virginia Woolf, **before drowning herself,** wrote a lovely suicide note to her husband.

Bruce Wayne made cryptic allusions to Batman's identity. Bruce Wayne did not give any clue to his dual role.

↓

Without giving any clue to his dual role, Bruce Wayne made cryptic allusions to Batman's identity.

OR

Bruce Wayne, **without giving any clue to his dual role,** made cryptic allusions to Batman's identity.

The preposition **with** is sometimes used to introduce absolutes:

We crossed the river by ferry.
The bus accompanied us.

↓

We crossed the river by ferry, **with the bus accompanying us.**

The coal supply was rapidly diminishing.
The governor was forced to close all the schools.

↓

With the coal supply rapidly diminishing, the governor was forced to close all the schools.

Prepositional phrases can also be used to create parallel structures either with paired prepositions or by repetition of the same preposition in a series. The use of paired prepositions such as **from-to, with-without,** or **for-against** creates the effect of balancing opposites:

The mad dancing epidemics of southern Europe in the Middle Ages have been blamed on everything **from** mildew in the rye meal **to** religious fanaticism.

A series, on the other hand, enumerates parallel points:

The Chinese have built a society **with** an educational system radically different from ours, **with** aspirations challenging some of our most cherished values, and **with** a strong sense of mission at times enviable, at times frightening.

Similar in appearance to prepositional phrases are adverbial INFINITIVES. Such infinitives are always introduced by the preposition **to** or **in order to,** followed by a simple verb form as their object: **to see, to write, to daydream.** An adverbial infinitive generally implies an intention, goal, or purpose, something that a person "wants" to do:

> Your purpose is becoming a liberated woman.
> You don't have to act as a man is supposed to act, according to outdated stereotypes.

↓

> **To become a liberated woman,** you don't have to act as a man is supposed to act, according to outdated stereotypes.

> Cowpunchers want to soften a new rope.
> Cowpunchers will spend hours pulling it, stretching it, and twisting it.

↓

> **To soften a new rope,** cowpunchers will spend hours pulling it, stretching it, and twisting it.

Ordinarily, the infinitive is understood to have the same subject as the rest of the sentence—**you** and **cowpunchers** in the last two examples. This is true of many short infinitive phrases that are frequently used to introduce sentences, such as **to make certain, to be on the safe side, to prove the point, not to be outdone.** For example,

> The Shah wanted to be on the safe side.
> The Shah brought along 200 body guards.

↓

> **To be on the safe side,** the Shah brought along 200 body guards.

But the rule is often ignored, especially with common idiomatic expressions such as **to be sure, to tell you the truth, to put it differently, to begin with, to give an example:**

> I want to tell you the truth.
> Melvin is incompetent.

↓

To tell you the truth, Melvin is incompetent.

Adverbial infinitives may occur at the end as well as at the beginning of the sentence:

> Medical students serve an internship **in order to gain first-hand experience before they officially enter into a medical career.**
> One raccoon family took over part of the old house, with the female commandeering an old sofa on the third floor **to raise her brood of four young.**

Or they can occur in the middle of the sentence, between commas, sometimes creating the effect of an important afterthought:

> Repeaters are given study materials designed especially for them, and, **to avoid the stigma of studying with younger children,** placed in classes with children their own age.

Sometimes an interrupting infinitive adds special emphasis to the following words by forcing the reader to pause before them. In the next sentence the pause after **term** helps emphasize the words **a superprimate:**

> Man is, **to use the author's own term,** a superprimate.

Infinitives can also occur in a series, either preceding or following the main clause. After the first infinitive in the series, the preposition **to** may be omitted:

> **To meet our energy needs, compete with foreign industry, build a projected 30 million new homes, and maintain our standard of living,** we need staggering amounts of new capital.

The final example illustrates the simplicity and elegance of an adverbial infinitive in comparison to other options:

The Reverend Elisabeth Jans wants to erase the traditional
   image of God as a man.
The Reverend Elisabeth Jans refers to God as a woman.

↓

Because she wants to erase the traditional image of God as a
   man, the Reverend Elisabeth Jans refers to God as a
   woman.

OR

To erase the traditional image of God as a man, the
   Reverend Elisabeth Jans refers to God as a woman.

Basic Pattern Exercise

Combine each set of sentences below into a single sentence using one or more prepositional phrases (Example I) or infinitive phrases (Example II).

Example I

1. GOP affiliation is at its lowest point ever.
2. Republican leaders have launched "Operation Grassroots."
3. This was an effort to rebuild the party at the local level.

With GOP affiliation at its lowest point ever, Republican leaders have launched "Operation Grassroots" **in an effort to rebuild the party at the local level.**

A. 1. There was no second to the motion.
   2. The motion died.

B. 1. We complied with local law.
   2. We paid a $5 fine.
   3. The reason was that we had eaten a bag of peanuts in a public street.

C. 1. Some 50 million Americans have become the legal owners of one-third of corporate America.
   2. Their pension funds made this possible.

D. 1. There are traffic jams.
   2. There is a lack of parking space.
   3. The administration has banned all cars.
   4. You can no longer drive into the central campus area.

E. 1. Pygmies do not grow to full adult height.
   2. Pygmies inherit their stunted stature.
   3. Pygmies are not like children born to dwarf parents.
   4. Children born to dwarf parents almost always grow to full adult height.

Example II
1. You want to keep your transportation costs down.
2. Fill your gas tank at a self-serve pump.

↓

To keep your transportation costs down, fill your gas tank at a self-serve pump.

F. 1. The campaign wanted to reach large numbers of people quickly.
2. The campaign focused on mass immunization techniques.

G. 1. The hijackers wanted to attract the attention of the American public.
2. The hijackers tried to force a major network.
3. The network was to broadcast the hijackers' political demands.

H. 1. You want to be approved for a proficiency examination.
2. You must convince the department.
3. You have a reasonable chance of passing the examination.

I. 1. The aim of the school was helping students understand death as the natural end of a life cycle.
2. The school introduced a noncredit course.
3. The title of the course was Death.

J. 1. The purpose of many Americans is overcoming their fear of unknown assailants.
2. The unknown assailants stalk city streets.
3. Many Americans take instruction.
4. They are instructed in some sort of Oriental self-defense.

Sentence Combining Exercise

Combine the following sentences into an effective essay. Create several sentences with prepositional or infinitive phrases.

MOUNT RUSHMORE

1. They stand far above the waters of the Belle Fourche River.
2. They stand over the tops of the tall conifers.
3. The conifers grow on the steep slopes.
4. The slopes are of the Black Hills.

5. They stare out with sightless eyes.
6. They stare out from Mount Rushmore.
7. They stare out at the unfathomable follies of men.

8. They are statues.
9. The statues are of Presidents Washington, Jefferson, Lincoln, and Theodore Roosevelt.
10. And the statues themselves are not the least unfathomable.
11. Men's follies are unfathomable.

12. The aim of the National Park Service was a gigantic memorial.
13. The gigantic memorial was to these four presidents.
14. The memorial was to be gnawed out of the mountain's natural granite.
15. The National Park Service commissioned Gutaon Borglum.
16. Borglum was a sculptor of some fame in his time.

17. From its inception in 1927 the project has never been free from controversy.
18. Until its completion in 1941 the project has never been free from controversy.
19. And for years afterwards the project has never been free from controversy.

20. This was a memorial designed to overwhelm.

21. The purpose was to tell the world about the fervent patriotism of America.
22. The purpose was to tell the world about the superiority of America's technological power.

23. The sculpture was meant to exceed the pyramids in height.
24. The sculpture was meant to surpass the grandeur of all other modern wonders.

25. Perhaps it has achieved these ends.

26. But some in Borglum's day wondered about the price.
27. And some in our own day have wondered about the price.
28. The price was a loss of the mountain's natural splendor.

29. The Mount Rushmore Memorial is only a forbidding example.
30. It is a forbidding example to many of its critics.
31. It is an example of legalized vandalism.
32. It is an example of graffiti.
33. The graffiti is written on a magnificent scale.

Creative Pattern Exercise

Type A. To each of the sentences given below, add at least one further detail in the form of a prepositional phrase (Example I) or an infinitive phrase (Example II). Experiment with different positions for each phrase within the sentence. Adjust the punctuation as necessary.

Example I
Elvis Presley couldn't walk the street alone.

↓

With all his success, Elvis Presley couldn't walk the street alone.

OR

Because of his enormous popularity, Elvis Presley couldn't walk the street alone **without a disguise.**

A. "Peanuts" is probably the most widely read comic strip in the world.

B. How would you like to get stranded in the middle of Death Valley?

C. People need time out to relax.

D. A war with modern weapons cannot serve the purposes of any government in the world.

E. Smoking has never been proven to cause cancer.

Example II

After three days of powwow and dance, the elders of the Comanche tribe and the Ute nation gathered before sunrise.

After three days of powwow and dance, the elders of the Comanche tribe and the Ute nation gathered before sunrise **to seal a peace and officially end their two centuries of war.**

OR

To seal a peace and to celebrate the end of their two centuries of war with a handshake, the exchange of scrolls, and the smoking of peace pipes, the elders of the Comanche tribe and the Ute nation gathered last Sunday after three days of powwow and dance.

F. An instant chocolate drink should look brown, not gray.

G. The dispatcher keeps a computer terminal near his desk.

H. The town's tornado sirens sounded an ominous alarm at 2:33 P.M.

I. The president gave the visiting prime minister the red-carpet treatment.

J. Increasingly, persons are doubling up and becoming roommates.

Type B. Construct complete sentences by adding a main clause to each of the following prepositional phrases (Example III) and infinitive phrases (Example IV). Decide whether the added clause is more effective before or after the phrase. If you wish, you may supply further details through additional phrases. Adjust the punctuation as necessary.

Example III
> rather than taking a chance on being grounded at the airport
>
> ↓
>
> Rather than taking a chance on being grounded at the airport, **we decided to drive to Kansas City.**
>
> OR
>
> Rather than taking a chance on being grounded at the airport **because of the impending strike, we decided to take the slower but surer route and drive to Kansas City.**

K. with malpractice suits against schools and teachers on the rise

L. despite widespread publicity about unemployed college graduates

M. in response to the flood of angry telegrams pouring into the president's office

N much to the surprise of everyone in the class

O. in comparison to other countries in the Western hemisphere

Example IV
> to stay physically and mentally vigorous
>
> ↓
>
> To stay physically and mentally vigorous, **you must give as much time and thought to keeping your energy sheet in balance as to balancing your financial budget.**
>
> OR

To stay physically and mentally vigorous, **take Geritol every day and don't worry about the cost.**

P. to get the most pleasure out of parachuting

Q. to comprehend the agony of loneliness

R. to protect the rights of airline passengers "bumped" in the last minute because of overbooking or flight cancellation

S. to free yourself from the grasp of the inevitable party bore who traps you in a corner

T. in order not to jeapordize my chances for getting the job

Sentence Combining Exercise

Combine the following sentences into an effective essay. Create several sentences with prepositional or infinitive phrases.

DRESSED TO KILL

1. It was easy.
2. You could tell the good guys from the bad guys.
3. The good guys were like Gene Autry.
4. The good guys were like Roy Rogers.
5. This was in the old cowboy movies.

6. The good guys looked good.
7. The bad guys looked bad.

8. The good guys never lost their hats in fights.
9. The good guys perspired little.
10. Or the good guys perspired not at all.
11. And the good guys wore light-colored clothing.

12. On the other hand, the bad guys perspired a lot.
13. The bad guys lost their hats frequently.
14. And the bad guys always wore black.

15. You might laugh at the Hollywood stereotypes.
16. But some psychologists agree about this.
17. People do reveal their personalities by their clothing.

18. Police uniforms signal authority.
19. Clown costumes indicate silliness.

20. In the same way, the everyday clothes tell others who we are.
21. We wear the clothes.

22. People wear loud clothes.
23. The people have loud personalities.

24. Optimists tend toward bright clothing.
25. The bright clothing is happy.
26. And pessimists prefer grey clothing.
27. The grey clothing is neutral.

28. One whole generation of youth signaled this.
29. They were rebelling against their parents' values.
30. They signaled by adopting a new form of dress.
31. The new form of dress was highlighted by blue jeans.
32. The blue jeans were faded.

33. Not all those agree with this.
34. All those study clothing and personality.
35. You can analyze people by their clothing.

36. Most do agree with this.
37. The clothes you wear identify your social status.
38. The clothes you wear identify your authority.
39. The clothes you wear identify your sophistication.

40. For instance, ties with big pictures identify males.
41. The males are lower class.
42. Paisley ties mark upper-class gentlemen.
43. Paisley ties are neat.

44. One survey reveals this.
45. The survey is of clothing shops.

46. Men's stores in fancy neighborhoods sell beige raincoats.
47. The sales are at a rate of four to one over black raincoats.

48. Black raincoats outsell beige.
49. This is in stores that cater to the lower middle class.

50. Another study indicates this.
51. Students apparently react to symbols of authority.
52. Students work harder for some teachers than for others.
53. Students work harder for teachers who dress in suits.
54. Students don't work so hard for teachers in shirt-sleeves.

55. And you may want to move up the corporate ladder.
56. Then be prepared for this.
57. Dress properly in suits.
58. The suits are dark.
59. The suits are pinstriped.

60. Forget about bow ties.

61. Bow ties indicate this.
62. A man is a crook.

63. And never wear green.

64. People are judged.
65. People wear green.
66. They are less honest.
67. They are less likable.
68. This is for some reason.

69. It seems true.
70. Gene Autry had the right idea.
71. Roy Rogers had the right idea.

Rewriting Exercise

Rewrite each of the following sentences by making the most effective use of prepositional phrases and infinitives. Rearrange parts of the sentence where you think it's necessary.

Example

> Some countries have strong religious laws, because women are not allowed in the streets except when they have a male chaperone.

↓

Because of strong religious laws, women in some countries are not allowed in the streets **without a male chaperone.**

OR

In some countries **with strong religious laws,** women must have a male chaperone **to be allowed** in the streets.

A. French meals are incomplete if there is no cheese between salad and dessert.

B. Cattle farmers shot dozens of calves in front of network TV cameras, because they wanted to dramatize their serious economic problems and hoped to make you choke on your steak dinner while watching the six o'clock news.

C. The late nineteenth century saw the advent of the railroad and the telegraph, and, as a result of this, our world shrank more in a single generation than in the preceding 5000 years.

D. The Bermuda Triangle mystery is not reinforced by eyewitness reports, but similar controversies, like UFOs, Bigfoot, the Loch Ness Monster, and the Abominable Snowman, are.

E. The aim of the editors was learning how college students feel about clothing, so they interviewed over 1000 students on 50 campuses across the country.

Sentence Combining Exercise

Combine the sentences below into an effective essay that includes several prepositional or infinitive phrases. Add two or three of your own examples of graffiti at appropriate places in your essay.

FOR A GOOD TIME, CALL. . . .

1. You make your third or fourth bathroom trip.
2. It is during a hard night of drinking.
3. It is your first night of hard drinking since final exams.
4. You notice "Sex kills—Come here and live forever."
5. It is written in purple crayon on the wall.

6. You are at the library.
7. You see "God is dead—Nietzsche" scrawled on the side of a study carrel.
8. "Nietzsche is dead—God" appears below that.
9. The final word on the debate is at the bottom.
10. The final word is, "Yeah, but Nietzsche published six books."

11. You are at the zoo.
12. You see an elephant lumbering away.
13. Her trunk reaches for one last peanut.
14. A scarlet peace sign is sprayed on her flanks.

15. Graffiti decorates empty places everywhere.
16. The places may be on elephants.
17. The places may be on john walls.

18. Public restrooms offer literature.
19. Desks offer literature.
20. Buildings offer literature.
21. They offer nearly as much literature as the public library reading rooms.
22. They frequently draw larger crowds.
23. Librarians are dismayed by the larger crowds.

24. The most popular topics on any wall inform us how to have a "good time."
25. They tell us how someone's lover turned out to be a rat.
26. They related the newest joke.
27. The most popular topics are sex, anger, and humor.

28. Sociologists have offered explanations for graffiti.
29. Psychologists have offered explanations for graffiti.

30. Explanations for graffiti have also been offered by anthropologists.
31. Explanations for graffiti have even been offered by some drunks.
32. Most agree that people feel a strong need.
33. The need is for artistic expression.
34. The need is for prestige.
35. The need is for recognition.
36. Their creativity is often stifled.
37. Their existence is ignored.
38. They have few chances to get things off their chest.

39. Graffiti is the result.

40. Graffiti is like most forms of expression.
41. Graffiti changes with the times.

42. Graffiti still retains much of the "Pete Loves Cathy" flavor.
43. Graffiti still retains much of the "Flaming Skulls Rule" flavor.
44. The new graffiti has become more contemporary.
45. The new graffiti has become more concerned with social and political issues.
46. The new graffiti reflects a new awareness among bathroom philosophers.

47. Much modern graffiti goes beyond self-indulgence.
48. It expresses people's concern with their world.
49. It attempts to communicate information.
50. The information is more relevant than who has the best equipment.
51. The equipment is for those "good times."

52. This modern sociopolitical graffiti encompasses drugs.
53. It encompasses religion.
54. It encompasses politics.
55. It encompasses sexuality.
56. Currently, feminism enjoys the most popularity.

57. "God is better than drugs" and "Religion is for those who can't take drugs" exist side by side.

58. They express polar attitudes.
59. The attitudes are toward religion and drugs.

60. Politics has generated graffiti worldwide.
61. It has been popular since the Vietnam War.
62. The Vietnam War aroused public hostility.

63. "Hell no, we won't go" expressed strong feelings.
64. "P.O.W.s never have a nice day" expressed strong feelings.

65. The Vietnam War was over.
66. Then the Panama Canal Treaty became the most controversial issue.
67. "Don't give *our* canal away" voiced one political position.
68. "I didn't know Canada wanted the Erie Canal" voiced the opposite political position.

69. Feminism has recently become the primary topic.
70. It is on bathroom walls.
71. It is also in more obvious places.

72. One artist managed to decorate a billboard.
73. The artist was particularly bold.
74. The billboard overlooks a major Texas highway.
75. The artist wrote "Dismember rapists!"

76. Other feminist slogans can also be found.
77. They are tamer.
78. They include "You've come a long way."
79. They include "Sisters—Unite."
80. They are scribbled.
81. They are carved.
82. They are lipsticked.
83. They are nearly everywhere.
84. They appear on subway cars.
85. They appear on "For Sale" signs.
86. The signs are on middle-class lawns.

87. Masters and Johnson can't offer more information than the average restroom.

88. The Hite Report can't offer more information either.

89. Graffiti is no longer confined to revealing who loves whom.
90. It is no longer confined to revealing who beat up whom.
91. It has evolved into a nationwide "Dear Abby" column.
92. It offers advice.
93. The advice is of all kinds.

94. You may want to score some dope.
95. You may want to learn how to make a Molotov cocktail.
96. You may want to find out how to ditch a bummer blind date.
97. Just open your eyes.

98. The handwriting is on the wall.
99. It is also on the floor.
100. It is on the billboards.
101. It is even on the elephants.

8. Subordination

The same two sentences combined differently can make different points. Suppose you want to make these two observations:

a. Some species of whales are nearing extinction.
b. Many countries refuse to accept even a partial ban on whale hunting.

To suggest that these two sentences are logically related but that neither has more weight than the other, you can combine them with a connective such as **and yet** or **so:**

> Some species of whales are nearing extinction, **and yet** many countries refuse to accept even a partial ban on whale hunting.

OR

> Many countries refuse to accept even a partial ban on whale hunting, **so** some species of whales are nearing extinction.

Suppose, however, that you want to emphasize one statement more than the other. If, for example, you're writing an essay about the lack of international cooperation in environmental protection, the point to make—as an illustration of your thesis—is that many countries are unwilling to accept a ban on whaling. Main points generally go into main clauses. Thus sentence (b) becomes the main clause of the combined sentence, and the observation about the predicament of some species of whales is changed into a SUB-ORDINATE CLAUSE to supplement or qualify the main statement.

> **Although**
> **Though** } **some species of whales are nearing**
> **Even though** | **extinction,**
> **While**
>> many countries refuse to accept even a partial ban on whale hunting.

The subordinate clause is generally introduced by a SUBORDINATOR, which expresses a specific relationship between the meaning of the subordinate clause and that of the main clause. In our first example, sentence (a) appears to contrast with (b), but it is precisely this contrast that gives force to the combined sentence: the ban on whale hunting takes on more significance in view of the impending doom of some species of whales.

But now let's suppose that your paper is not about protecting the whales but about the whales themselves or the growing threat to many species. Perhaps your paper attempts to identify some causes of this threat. In this context, you will want to focus on sentence (a), the threat itself, and point to the lack of a ban as a factor that may be responsible for it:

> **Because** } **many countries refuse to**
> **Since** } **accept even a partial ban**
> **In view of the fact that** } **on whale hunting,**
>> some species of whales are nearing extinction.

Contrast and cause, shown by these examples, are among the basic adverbial relationships between one statement and another that subordinate clauses can express. Others will be illustrated below. Remember that you can make a subordinate clause out of *any* simple sentence, as long as you can link its meaning in some logical way to the meaning of another sentence. Sometimes either one or the other of two given sentences can be subordinated—the choice must be guided by your purpose:

The students were protesting.
The lecture was canceled.

↓

The students were protesting **because the lecture was canceled.**

OR

The lecture was canceled **because the students were protesting.**

In trying different options for subordination, you can often choose among several subordinators. To make a clause expressing time, for example, you can use **when, whenever, before, after, until, till, while, as, since, as long as, as soon as,** or **no sooner . . . than:**

The Mongol hordes threatened to conquer all Europe.
Genghis Khan's death forced them to return to Asia.

↓

The Mongol hordes threatened to conquer all Europe **until Genghis Khan's death forced them to return to Asia.**

OR

Before Genghis Khan's death forced them to return to Asia, the Mongol hordes threatened to conquer all Europe.

OR

Just when the Mongol hordes threatened to conquer all Europe, Genghis Khan's death forced them to return to Asia.

Even when the meaning commits you to subordinating one sentence and not the other, you may still have a choice among subordinators:

Michelangelo's *Pieta* was damaged by a madman recently.
Michelangelo's *Pieta* is now displayed only behind a protective glass shield.

↓

Because
Since } **Michelangelo's *Pieta* was damaged by a**
After   **madman recently,**

it is now displayed only behind a protective glass shield.

OR

Because
Since } **it was damaged by a madman recently,**
After

Michelangelo's *Pieta* is now displayed only behind a protective glass shield.

Any one of these subordinators is appropriate in this sentence, because each logically links the step taken to protect the sculpture (the effect) to the madman's act (the cause). But there is a difference between the subordinators. **Because,** for example, suggests only the cause, whereas **after** also implies the time sequence of the events: first the damage, then the protection. Adverbial relationships expressed by different subordinators often overlap in such subtle ways. Study the various shades of meaning among the subordinate clauses in the next example:

Air traffic is closely controlled.
Flying is relatively { safe / unsafe } .

↓

CONDITION: **If**
Provided that
In case
Assuming that

DEGREE: **Inasmuch as**
Insofar as
To the extent that

REASON: **Because**
Since
Considering that

air traffic is closely controlled, flying is relatively safe.

TIME: **When**
Whenever
As long as
While
Once

PLACE: **Where**
Wherever

OR

CONDITION:
(negative) **Unless**

CONTRAST: **Although**
Even though

air traffic is closely controlled, flying is relatively unsafe.

CONDITION:
(alternative) **Whether or not**

In this last series of examples each of the subordinate clauses precedes the main clause. This is often but not always the case: you will find clauses at the end and even in the middle of a sentence as well. Varying the position of the subordinate clause in the sentence can be an effective way of controlling emphasis and of letting your readers know how you really feel about what you're saying. Read

the next two sentences carefully and see if they give you the same
impression:

> **If local residents are willing to put up with them,**
> nuclear plants are a clean and economical way of produc-
> ing vast amounts of much-needed energy.

OR

> Nuclear plants are a clean and economical way of producing
> vast amounts of much-needed energy, **if local residents
> are willing to put up with them.**

Reading the first sentence, you are likely to respond to nuclear
plants as something desirable, despite the suggestion that residents
may have reason to be uneasy about them; but the second version
implies a grimmer view, directing attention more to the residents'
concern about safety than to the plants' economic advantages. A
sentence tends to impress on the reader what it says toward the
end, where the stress naturally falls; but in the second version the
emphasis is increased by the slight pause at the comma before the
subordinate clause, which helps put more emphasis on **if** and adds
to the reader's uneasiness.

The position of the subordinate clause within a sentence is
also related to the broader context. For example, an if-clause at the
end will make you anticipate a sentence that further focuses on the
disadvantage of nuclear plants. Thus

> Nuclear plants are a clean and economical way of producing
> vast amounts of much-needed energy, if local residents are
> willing to put up with them.

is much more likely to be followed by something like

> In fact, many of them aren't.

than by the sentence

> Diminishing oil supplies make plans for a number of such
> plants especially urgent.

This last sentence, on the other hand, would fit well after a statement that implies the advantages of nuclear plants:

> If local residents are willing to put up with them, nuclear plants are a clean and economical way of producing vast amounts of much-needed energy. Diminishing oil supplies make plans for a number of such plants especially urgent.

Clearly, no sentence exists in a vacuum: your combining options are always limited by what precedes and what follows in your developing paragraph.

One more note on order: in a special type of emphatic construction the subordinate clause always occurs at the beginning of the sentence and is followed by the verb. This pattern is especially effective when the subordinate clause should receive unusual emphasis:

> **Only if my safety is guaranteed in writing** am I willing to join the experiment.

> **Not unless they institute sweeping reforms** can southern European governments cope with the growing power of Communist parties.

Writing is a process of building up and then cutting down. In revising your paper, you can often get rid of words that, on second thought, are unnecessary. For example, when it has the same subject as the main clause, a subordinate clause can often be simplified to an adverbial *phrase,* which is more concise than a clause. The verbs **is, are, was,** and **were** in a subordinate clause should encourage you to simplify:

> When you are in doubt about deductions on your tax return, call the IRS collect.

> ↓

> **When in doubt** about deductions on your tax return, call the IRS collect.

> Although they were common a hundred years ago, red wolves are now increasingly rare.

> ↓

Although common a hundred years ago, red wolves are now increasingly rare.

Vitamin C tablets, if they are taken regularly, may reduce your chances of getting a cold.

↓

Vitamin C tablets, **if taken** regularly, may reduce your chances of getting a cold.

While it was cruising at 33,000 feet, the plane suddenly fell apart.

↓

While cruising at 33,000 feet, the plane suddenly fell apart.

Basic Pattern Exercise

In each set below, combine the sentences into a single sentence that contains at least one subordinate clause, as shown in the example. Try to place the subordinate clause in different positions in the sentence. Where possible, try out different connectives and decide which one gives the clearest meaning.

Example
> Cities like New York and Detroit can survive.
> They can overcome serious problems like crime and pollution.

↓

Cities like New York and Detroit can survive **if they can overcome serious problems like crime and pollution.**

OR

Provided (that) they can overcome serious problems like crime and pollution, cities like New York and Detroit can survive.

A. 1. You may like it.
   2. You may not like it.
   3. The metric system is on its way.

B. 1. The murderer admitted his guilt.
   2. The innocent man was executed.

C. 1. Many liberal arts graduates will have difficulty finding employment.
   2. They are willing to accept work outside their major interests.
   3. The economic situation becomes more favorable.

D. 1. The mayor and his wife were attending a conference on penal reform.
   2. Their house was ransacked by a juvenile gang.

E. 1. Congressmen can ill afford to support a new pay raise for themselves.
   2. The public remains suspicious of them.

F. 1. Aerosol cans are banned from the market.
   2. The ozone layer may be permanently damaged.

G. 1. The new law is enacted.
   2. It will increase social security taxes by 30 percent.

H. 1. Kamikaze pilots flew their missions.
   2. They cut off a finger or a lock of hair.
   3. They sent it as a memento to their mothers or wives or lovers.

I. 1. The Warren Report has been accepted by most Americans.
   2. The Warren Report has left many questions unanswered.

J. 1. Advertising in magazines is becoming less profitable.
   2. There is increased competition for advertising time on television and radio.

Sentence Combining Exercise

Combine the following sentences into an effective persuasive essay. Use several subordinate clauses.

NO MORE BURGERS?

1. Suppose there aren't any burgers.
2. Suppose there aren't any hot dogs.
3. Can a picnic really be fun?
4. The picnic is on the Fourth of July.

5. Can eggplant casseroles ever replace lamb chops?
6. Can cheese soufflés ever replace filet mignon?

7. Suppose most Americans shudder.
8. Most Americans are to contemplate such alternatives.
9. The alternatives are distasteful.
10. The reason is that most Americans have been raised on meat.
11. The idea of meatless meals is gradually gaining popularity.

12. There are sound reasons that it is gaining popularity.

13. Certainly, the idea of meatless meals is not a new one.

14. Many peoples have refrained from eating flesh at all.
15. Millions do not touch at least some forms of meat.
16. This might be for religious reasons.
17. This might be for nutritional reasons.
18. This has been true since ancient times.

19. Vegetarians may seem like emaciated fanatics.
20. The fanatics slobber over a few nuts and berries.
21. The vegetarians seem like this to meat eaters.
22. Yet these nut and berry eaters may already know something.
23. Most Americans do not yet want to hear it.

24. Populations continue to grow.
25. Available land rapidly dwindles before our eyes.
26. Soon there won't be enough food.
27. The food is to feed the world's mouths.
28. The mouths are hungry.

29. Suppose we don't shift to mainly vegetarian diets.
30. The purpose is to use land resources more wisely.
31. The purpose is to use animal resources more wisely.
32. Then we may face a hunger.
33. The hunger will be colossal.
34. The hunger will be global.

35. A rural countryside may be a beautiful sight.
36. The countryside is dotted with cows and sheep.
37. The cows and sheep graze peacefully.
38. The methods waste vast areas of land.
39. We use the methods.
40. The methods are for raising livestock.

41. In contrast, vegetarian practice has the immediate advantage.
42. The advantage is land conservation.

43. We can reap from five to 15 times more protein.
44. We grow wheat or beans.
45. We do this to nourish ourselves.
46. We don't do this to fatten some Black Angus.
47. This is according to the Department of Agricultural Economics.
48. The department is of Cornell University.

49. An 1100-pound steer eats over 5500 pounds of nutrients.
50. It does this during its lifetime.
51. The steer yields only 460 pounds of meat.

52. This means that the steer gobbles up 12 pounds of food.
53. The food is for every pound of edible meat.
54. The steer supplies the edible meat.

55. We could get more and better protein.
56. We grow corn, lentils, and spinach.
57. We do not produce porkchops and porterhouses.

58. Such figures can't be ignored.
59. We want to use our land more wisely.

60. Land conservation isn't the only advantage.
61. The advantage is of a meatless diet.

62. Nutrition experts used to chuckle.
63. The chuckling was at radical vegetarians.
64. Even the World Health Organization now admits the values.
65. The organization is conservative.
66. Nuts and berries have values.

67. Meatless meals easily supply all the essential nutrients.
68. Meatless meals can include almost anything.
69. Anything ranges from crisp fruit salads and creamy vegetable soups.
70. Anything ranges to trout filets and cheese fondue.
71. The meatless meals must be properly combined.

72. It is no less important.
73. Meatless meals cost only 20 to 30 percent as much.
74. The cost is compared to a meat-centered diet.

75. This is to summarize.
76. Meatless meals provide more nutrition.
77. Meatless meals require less money.
78. Meatless meals require much less land.

79. The day is coming.
80. Famines will force us to sacrifice.
81. We are to sacrifice spareribs for squash.
82. We are to leave all the meatballs out of the spaghetti sauce.

83. Start retraining your taste buds right now!

Creative Pattern Exercise

Add at least one subordinate clause to each of the sentences below. Try for variety by placing the subordinate clauses in different positions within the sentence and by occasionally adding more than one clause.

Example

The Western world continues to regard acupuncture with suspicion.

Although the Chinese have successfully used it for thousands of years to cure a variety of maladies, the Western world continues to regard acupuncture with suspicion.

OR

The Western world continues to regard acupuncture with suspicion, **perhaps because the method is so alien to our concept of medical treatment.**

OR

As long as no more than a handful of Westerners have profited from its benevolent effects, the Western world will continue to regard acupuncture with suspicion, **even though the Chinese have had great success with it.**

A. There is an urgent national need for more green land.

B. A professional theater can contribute to a community's prosperity.

C. Within the next 100 years, dozens of animal species will die out.

D. Some atheists have argued that the motto, "In God We Trust," violates their civil rights.

E. I was ten years old that lazy July afternoon.

F. No part of America is immune from tornadoes.

G. The United States once had an emperor.

H. Our national leaders have consistently lied to the people.

I. The threat of a long-range nationwide water shortage is serious.

J. The addiction to TV stifles creativity.

Sentence Combining Exercise

Combine the following sentences into an effective essay that includes several subordinate clauses. Eliminate any details which do not contribute to the central idea of the essay.

NURSING HOME POETS

1. Sam Rainey recalls two of his most memorable moments.
2. One was this.
3. He made love to a woman.

4. He loved the woman.
5. The other was this.
6. He had his leg amputated.

7. Mary T. Kalec goes to church.
8. She likes to hear the beating of her heart.
9. Then she likes to go home.
10. She is happy.

11. Perhaps these are not the sort of trivia.
12. The trivia inspire many people.
13. They are inspired to poetic expression.
14. These experiences have in fact touched off responsive emotions.

15. The experiences were sung about in poems.
16. The poems were written by pupils.
17. The pupils were between the ages of 70 and 90.
18. The pupils were residents in a nursing home.

19. Poet Kenneth Koch wanted to teach poetry to old people.
20. He had been moved by his many visits.
21. The visits were among the walls of such homes.
22. The walls were cryptlike.

23. Koch found dullness.
24. Koch found sterility.
25. He found an atmosphere.
26. The atmosphere was more like death.
27. The atmosphere was less like life.
28. He found this everywhere he went.

29. Something occurred to Koch.
30. He might be able to revitalize the dreary existence.
31. The existence was of these old folks.
32. Suppose he found a way to stimulate their minds.
33. Suppose he found a way to stimulate their hearts.

34. Koch would teach the old folks poetry.
35. He hoped to free them from the bonds.

36. The bonds were cruel.
37. The bonds were of growing old.
38. He hoped to free them for moments, at least.

39. Koch wasted no time.
40. He started.
41. He encouraged the old folks.
42. The old folks were to express their strongest feelings.

43. At first the students were encouraged.
44. The students were to utter just one sentence.
45. This was a task.
46. The task was not so simple for many of them.
47. The sentence might be about that first mutt.
48. They befriended the mutt.
49. The sentence might be about the brightest red ever seen.
50. The brightest red was seen by the students.
51. The sentence might be about some flowers or records.
52. Koch brought along the flowers or records.

53. Leroy, Selena, and the other pupils had all spent a lifetime.
54. They pressed clothes.
55. The pressing was for some dry cleaner.
56. They flipped pancakes.
57. The flipping was at the corner grill.
58. The pupils had never imagined this.
59. Their lives could be subjects for poetry.

60. Now many spent their last few years.
61. They were suffering from seeing defects.
62. They were suffering from hearing defects.
63. They were in constant pain.
64. They were in constant depression.
65. The seeds of poetry seemed too dormant.
66. The seeds of poetry were to sprout.

67. The task seemed difficult.
68. Koch refused.
69. Koch was not discouraged.

70. Soon his students began to respond.
71. The response was to violets.
72. The response was to Vivaldi.
73. Now he helped them open up their hearts.
74. Now he helped them express their deepest memories.

75. Laura, Eric, and 14 more budding poets marveled at their own work.
76. Laura, Eric, and 14 more budding poets were eager.
77. The eagerness was to write more.
78. This was after a class or two.

79. Koch sometimes read examples of talky poetry.
80. The poetry was written about red sunsets.
81. The poetry was written about dirty dishes.
82. He did this to stimulate them.
83. Most of the time Koch searched their past.
84. The search was for the biggest trout.
85. The search was for the frilliest dress.
86. The search was for the meanest teacher.

87. The students brimmed with ideas.
88. The students brimmed with a fresh love for life.
89. The students were now poets.
90. This was after the 16-week program.

91. Koch had reminded them.
92. They were alive.

93. They learned to write poetry.
94. This was so important for the students.
95. They continued writing.
96. They continued helping each other.
97. They were growing all the while even after that.
98. Classes were already completed.

99. So utterly were their lives transformed.
100. Leroy, Laura, Selena, and Sam no longer considered themselves useless, unwanted old people.
101. The old people's heads droop.
102. The drooping is out of boredom.

103. They considered themselves poets.
104. They were full of ideas.
105. They were full of life.

Rewriting Exercise

Most of the sentences in this exercise will sound better if you rewrite them with subordinators. Change those sentences that you think need revision. Whether or not you decide to make a change, try to explain your decision.

Example

Public schools can be improved, but the colleges of education must work seriously to upgrade their advanced degree programs.

↓

Before public schools can be improved, the colleges of education must work seriously to upgrade their advanced degree programs.

OR

If the colleges of education work seriously to upgrade their advanced degree programs, the public schools can be improved.

A. Automakers plan to make only a few gas guzzlers by the early 1980s, but the market will still be flooded with them.

B. Thomas Edison's most productive year came at the age of 35, and he remained active and creative into his 80s.

C. It may seem ridiculous to worry about the Black Plague—the disease that in a single year in the 1600s wiped out more than a quarter of Europe's population—but in one recent year more than 90 cases occurred in the United States, many of them fatal.

D. You want to succeed in the impersonal and competitive world of a large city: you have to watch out for your own interests.

E. Oriental religions seem to be attracting thousands of American youth, and traditional churches are rapidly losing members.

F. TV's prime time could be filled with high quality programs, but such programs couldn't sell detergent and beer.

G. Men may deny it but, even so, women will soon be able to compete with them in most sporting events.

H. A country remains militarily strong, and it need not worry about being attacked.

I. Quebec may choose to remain a part of Canada, but its decision alone won't solve the deep-rooted problems that gave rise to the Separatist movement.

J. You need not be a professional masseur to administer an effective massage, but you can't just begin rubbing without some idea of what it will do to a body.

Sentence Combining Exercise

Combine the following sentences so as to develop either the thesis that (1) the appeal of the Dracula legend lies in its implied sexuality or (2) the appeal of the Dracula legend stems from its veiled promise of eternal life. Exclude from your essay any facts or details which do not help develop the thesis you choose.

DRACULA

1. "Good evening. I am Count Dracula."

2. Bela Lugosi's voice chilled theater goers.
3. His voice is now famous.
4. Then it ushered in the modern Dracula era.
5. It did this 50 years ago.

6. The blood-sucking count has walked the night.
7. He has walked since the days of ancient Egypt.
8. He has walked since the days of ancient Greece.

9. And now he lurks in the rock group Kiss.
10. And now he lurks in the Vampire Research Society of America.

11. Some of this interest is devoted to the historical Vlad the Impaler.
12. Vlad was a fifteenth-century Romanian prince.
13. He was nicknamed Dracula.
14. Dracula means "son of the devil."

15. Vlad was famous for torturing to death 30,000 Turks.
16. He did this in one day.
17. Dracula's appeal transcends a mere historical interest.
18. The interest is in one otherwise obscure prince.

19. What makes the infamous Prince of Evil so potent a monster?

20. What explains the endurance of the count?
21. The endurance is from one generation to the next.

22. It is for a reason.
23. We see in him the hope for immortality.

24. Dracula's latent sexual appeal fascinates us.
25. It draws us into his deadly arms.
26. It may sound morbid.

27. A vampire's existence may not appeal to many people.
28. The appeal is conscious.
29. But the all-important promise of life after death strikes a chord.
30. The chord is deep in our unconscious.
31. The chord is the powerful will to live.
32. This is despite the cost.

33. It is this sexual magnetism of Dracula.
34. The sexual magnetism makes the count the ultimate sexual partner.
35. It is his lurid machismo.

36. He is so polite.
37. He is so aristocratic.

38. Death has traditionally been a metaphor.
39. The metaphor is for the moment of sexual ecstasy.
40. Who but Count Dracula can make one "die" so thoroughly?
41. Dracula roams only at night.

42. The horror of seeing Dracula's victims collapse in death is offset.
43. The vision of their resurrection offsets it.
44. Their resurrection is in a new existence.

45. His awful bite holds the promise of a ghoulish paradise.
46. It is a paradise of perpetual youth.

47. Dracula's own immortality in myths reinforces his appeal.
48. Dracula's own immortality in history books reinforces his appeal.
49. Dracula's own immortality in novels reinforces his appeal.
50. And Dracula's own immortality in movies reinforces his appeal.

51. Movie heroines and devotees have never been able to resist.
52. They can't resist his bedroom voice.
53. He seduces them with his kiss.

54. The count's passion for virgins contributes to his reputation.
55. He devours them with his steady gaze.
56. He evokes their deepest passion.

57. The most engrossing moments are always the ultimate moments of passion.
58. The moments are in Dracula stories.
59. The young, innocent woman submits to the count's charm.

60. She collapses with him.
61. They are in a passionate embrace.
62. Her desire and blood are drained together.

63. Audiences grow quiet.
64. Dracula wins another convert.
65. They don't grow quiet for the horror.
66. They grow quiet for the passion of the moment.

67. Bela Lugosi stays young in the old movies.
68. The old movies are on TV.
69. And the character Dracula is given a new resurrection.
70. Christopher Lee resurrected the character.

71. Suppose we look hard enough.
72. Then we can always find Dracula alive.
73. And we can always find Dracula ageless.

74. The phallic image is an appropriate symbolic end.
75. The image is of a stake.
76. The stake is driven deep into the vampire's heart.
77. It is the appropriate symbolic end for a creature.
78. The creature's fangs have drained the blood.
79. The blood is from many a virgin.

80. We find him.
81. Then we can submit to his bite.
82. We submit to it in our minds.
83. And we can hope to live on.
84. We will live on as one of his disciples.
85. One of his disciples is able to enjoy the immortality forever.
86. Only a vampire's bite can grant the immortality.

87. We may not realize the sexual passion on one level.
88. The passion is latent in Dracula's character.
89. But the next time you meet him in a book see this.
90. The next time you meet him on the screen see this.
91. The next time you meet him around the corner see this.
92. What wins Dracula a place in your heart?
93. Is it the castle and bats?
94. Is it the gruesome seduction?

9. Coordination

In everyday talking and writing, in ordering lunch at the Pizza Hut or in sending off a postcard, we use coordination more frequently than any other pattern. Coordination is so simple and so basic that all of us were coordinating almost as soon as we began to talk. Since you already use coordination in your writing—you may even over-use it—you obviously don't need instruction in how to coordinate or encouragement to coordinate more frequently. What may be helpful, however, and what this unit offers is practice with various patterns of coordination.

The simplest sort of coordination occurs when a word called a COORDINATOR—a word like **or, and,** or **but**—connects one element in a sentence to another. The elements joined by a coordinator may be single words

walks **or** runs

students **and** teachers

happy **but** tired

or phrases

> walking down the street **or** running through an alley
>
> students from Stanford **and** teachers from Berkeley
>
> happy with her achievement **but** tired from the struggle

or clauses

> boys who walk down the street **or** who run through an alley
>
> if the students are from Stanford **and** the teachers are from Berkeley
>
> since she is happy **but** he is tired

Simple coordination is surely the most common and often the most effective way of joining two similar elements within a sentence. But occasionally you may prefer a somewhat more subtle pattern of coordination. One such pattern involves deliberately interrupting coordinated elements with a modifying word, phrase, or clause:

> The conference on nuclear energy was attended by students from Stanford and teachers from Berkeley.
> The attendance of the teachers from Berkeley was predictable.

$$\downarrow$$

> The conference on nuclear energy was attended by students from Stanford and, **predictably,** teachers from Berkeley.
>
> Donna was happy with her achievement but tired from the struggle.
> She was tired after three days of intense competition.

$$\downarrow$$

> Donna was happy with her achievement but, **after three days of intense competition,** tired from the struggle.
>
> Keith spends Saturday nights walking down the street or running through alleys.

He runs through alleys when the cops are after him.

Keith spends Saturday nights walking down the street or, **when the cops are after him,** running through alleys.

The interrupting word, phrase, or clause normally follows the coordinator and is usually set off by commas. The occasional interruption of coordinated elements enables you to add details smoothly and concisely while at the same time varying the structure and sound of your sentences.

A second pattern of coordination makes use of PAIRED COORDINATORS to strengthen the connection between two coordinated elements. There are about six paired coordinators in the English language:

both . . . and

either . . . or

neither . . . nor

whether . . . or

not . . . but (only)

not only . . . but (also)

Because each pair includes two coordinators, its connecting power is roughly twice that of a single coordinator. Paired coordinators therefore help both to emphasize the relatedness of the elements they join and to make writing tighter, more coherent:

Keith spends Saturday night and all day Sunday running through alleys.

Keith spends **both** Saturday night **and** all day Sunday running through alleys.

Donna was not satisfied with her own achievement or with the team's performance.

Donna was satisfied **neither** with her own achievement **nor** with the team's performance.

The conference on nuclear energy was attended by Berkeley teachers and also by Stanford students.

↓

The conference on nuclear energy was attended **not only** by Berkeley teachers **but** also by Stanford students.

As with simple coordination, sentences with paired coordinators may be interrupted by a word or phrase that adds detail or that more precisely reflects the writer's attitude:

Keith spends Saturday nights **either** walking down the street **or, when the cops are chasing him,** running through alleys.

Donna was satisfied **neither** with her own achievement **nor, despite a second-place finish,** with the team's performance.

The conference on nuclear energy was attended **not** by students **but, much to our disappointment, only** by teachers.

A great deal of simple coordination will tend to make your writing seem relaxed and casual, sometimes even innocent and childlike. Conversely, using paired coordinators and interrupting coordinated elements will tend to make your writing seem more formal, serious, and sophisticated. For any writing situation, then, you have choices to make. Do you want to sound off-handed in asking Mom and Dad to send extra money for your Christmas skiing vacation at Squaw Valley? Then use lots of simple coordination in your letter, and you will come across as just an innocent and lovable kid. But if you want to impress either a prospective employer or a distant lover with both your maturity and sophistication, then your letter should include not only paired coordinators but, when appropriate, coordinated elements interrupted by modifiers.

A third pattern of coordination involves the SERIES, a list of three or more items. A series is usually written with commas following each item except the last, and with a coordinator—**and** or **or**—connecting the final two items:

> The Triple Crown of thoroughbred racing consists of **the Kentucky Derby, the Preakness, and the Belmont Stakes.**

> At diploma mills throughout the country you can buy **a bachelor's degree for about $1500, a master's degree for $1600, or a doctorate for $1700.**

> There are five types of discharge from military service: **honorable, general, undesirable, bad conduct, and dishonorable.**

But the series, like other constructions, offers a number of options. To make the series move slowly and seem lengthy and drawn out and perhaps even tired, try repeating the coordinator:

> At weekend tournaments in California, skateboarding contestants demonstrate all sorts of feats—wheelies **and** kick flips **and** revolutions **and** hand stands.

> Raising vegetables presents endless opportunities for weeding **and** thinning **and** hoeing **and** watering.

To make the series more rapid, to create a suggestion of urgency, excitement, anger, fear, try eliminating all coordinators:

> Individuals are less troubled by feelings of guilt when they share responsibility for killings with a group—**a street gang, lynch mob, terrorist organization.**

> Vietnam differed from all earlier American wars in **the elusiveness of the enemy, the widespread use of drugs, the American soldier's sense of outrage.**

It is even possible to combine in a single sentence a series that repeats coordinators with one that eliminates them completely:

> There is **no pattern, no meaning, no larger significance** in last week's outbreak of crime except what is weary **and** obvious **and** painful: ours is an era of ugly violence.

Here, the opening series with coordinators eliminated suggests a sense of frustration, even anger, but the repeated coordinators of the second series indicate that the initial anger has given way to fatigue and resignation. In the sentence below, the eliminated coordinators of the opening series contrast with the repeated coordinators of the second to help emphasize the differences between city and country life:

> In the country there are **no honking horns, no diesel trucks, no pollution**—just the sounds of wind rustling the tree leaves **and** red squirrels chattering in the distant oaks **and** cool creek water rushing down its endless course.

Just as two coordinated elements may be interrupted by a modifier—

> Willie Mays played for the Giants and, **during his final years,** the Mets.

so can the three or more items of a series:

> Raising vegetables presents endless opportunities for weeding, thinning, hoeing, watering, and, **one always hopes,** harvesting and eating.

> John Frankenheimer has directed action movies such as *The Manchurian Candidate, Seven Days in May, Grand Prix,* and, **more recently,** *Black Sunday* and *Brinks.*

> The filming of *Black Sunday,* a movie in which an Israeli agent chases a blimp into the Super Bowl, required permission from the Super Bowl, the city of Miami, and, **most importantly,** Goodyear.

Inserting a modifier before the final item of a series is one way of emphasizing the item's importance.

When the series contains over three items, there are more options than just repeating or eliminating coordinators and interrupting the coordinated items. Instead of items listed one after the other, such as in

> Only a few cities are known as "good baseball towns"—
> Cincinnati, Detroit, Chicago, Boston, Los Angeles, and
> New York.

they can be grouped into pairs:

> Only a few cities are known as "good baseball towns"—
> Cincinnati **and** Detroit, Chicago **and** Boston, Los Angeles
> **and** New York.

And rather than write

> Black American writers like Frederick Douglass, W. E. B.
> DuBois, Malcolm X, and Eldridge Cleaver have found au-
> tobiography an especially congenial form.

you can pair the items:

> Black American writers **from** Frederick Douglass **and**
> W. E. B. DuBois **to** Malcolm X **and** Eldridge Cleaver have
> found autobiography an especially congenial form.

However the series is coordinated and arranged, try to order it so
that the most important item, if there is one, comes last.

As well as joining words, phrases, and clauses, coordination
also functions to connect sentences. Two separate sentences can be
made into one through coordination if a comma and then a
coordinator—**and, or, but, for, so, yet**—are placed between
the two original sentences.

> The bicentennial year of 1976 is over**, yet** the bicentennial
> era goes on and on.

> Every Friday morning in Green Bay, Wisconsin, a buzzer
> sounds at 10 o'clock**, and** the National Cheese Exchange
> opens for business.

> George C. Scott thinks of acting as a form of prostitution**, but**
> Al Pacino honors acting as a noble profession.

A second, more formal way to coordinate sentences is by replacing
the comma, and often the coordinator as well, with a semicolon:

The bicentennial year of 1976 is over; the bicentennial era goes on and on.

George C. Scott thinks of acting as a form of prostitution; Al Pacino honors acting as a noble profession.

Coordination is usually most appropriate when the two coordinated sentences are equal or nearly equal in importance. If two sentences to be combined are not equally important to the purpose of your paper, you should probably make the less important sentence into a subordinate clause or a phrase. But if the two sentences are roughly equal, their equality will be emphasized through coordination:

The Columbia Phonograph Broadcasting Company sold for $400,000 in 1928, **but** its annual sales now approach $1 billion.

This sentence suggests through coordination that its two elements—"The Columbia Phonograph Broadcasting Company sold for $400,000 in 1928" and "its annual sales now approach $1 billion"—are equally important. Should you want to suggest, instead, that the latter part of the sentence is more important, you would probably reduce the first part to a subordinate clause or a phrase:

Although the Columbia Phonograph Broadcasting Company sold for $400,000 in 1928, its annual sales now approach $1 billion.

OR

The Columbia Phonograph Broadcasting Company, which sold for $400,000 in 1928, now has annual sales approaching $1 billion.

OR

Sold for $400,000 in 1928, the Columbia Phonograph Broadcasting Company now has annual sales approaching $1 billion.

Like coordinated words, phrases, or clauses, coordinated sentences lend themselves to interrupting modifiers:

> The Columbia Phonograph Broadcasting Company sold for $400,000 in 1928, but—**known as CBS**—it now has annual sales that approach $1 billion.

Without interrupters, coordinated sentences are particularly effective for reinforcing a sense of informality and spontaneity:

> Toss a pop bottle out of any college dorm, and it will probably hit somebody struggling to get into law school.

Coordination becomes more informal as the coordinated sentences become shorter and more numerous and if commas are omitted. Here is an umpire explaining why players have more fun:

> A player can strike out twice **and** make three errors **and** then hit a single in the ninth **and** win a ball game **and** he's a hero. But an ump can get ten plays right in a row **and** nobody says anything **and** then miss one **and** everybody's mad.

Basic Pattern Exercise

Combine each of the following groups of sentences into a single sentence by using one or more of the patterns of coordination—interrupted coordination, paired coordinators, or series variation.

Example

1. New Hampshire does not have a general sales tax.
2. New Hampshire does not have an income tax.
3. New Hampshire is the only state that doesn't have at least one of the two taxes.

New Hampshire is the only state without **either** a general sales **or** an income tax.

OR

New Hampshire is the only state with **neither** a general sales **nor** an income tax.

A. 1. For the first time I saw my father not as the giant of my childhood.
   2. I saw my father simply as a lonely man.

B. 1. More and more universities are creating loan plans to aid middle-income families.
   2. Middle-income families are not rich enough to pay rising college costs.
   3. Middle-income families are not poor enough to qualify for assistance.

C. 1. The four largest hotel companies in the United States are Hilton, Sheraton, Hyatt, and Western International.
   2. Western International is the fastest growing hotel company.

D. 1. Above all, lawyers should be committed to the operation of justice.
   2. Lawyers should also be committed to their clients.
   3. Lawyers should be committed to the judicial process as well.

E. 1. The drug PCP is a substitute for heroin.
   2. It is a cheap substitute.
   3. But it is a deadly substitute.
   4. California high school students have recently learned that it is a deadly substitute.

F. 1. PCP is known in the streets as angel dust.
   2. PCP is known in the streets as hog.
   3. PCP is known in the streets as peace pills.
   4. PCP is known in the streets as superjoint.
   5. PCP is known in the streets as magic mist.
   6. PCP is known in the streets as wobble weed.

G. 1. No matter how you measure it, education is the largest "industry" in the nation.
   2. You can measure it in terms of dollars spent.
   3. You can measure it in terms of people involved.

H. 1. Methodists set out for the Oregon Territory in the 1830s.
   2. They went to convert the Indians.
   3. They went to support American government claims to the area.
   4. Most of them did not know that they went to support American government claims to the area.

I. 1. Fewer blacks are leaving the rural South these days.
   2. They are staying not because farming has become more popular.
   3. They are staying because industry is moving in.

J. Pantomime cannot convey a complicated story line or deep philosophical reasoning, but for the creation of certain moods or scenes, its effectiveness is unparalleled.
   1. The audience is unhampered by stage properties.
   2. The audience is aided by the supple mind of the actor.
   3. The audience is aided by the supple body of the actor.
   4. The audience can see what is not there.
   5. The audience can hear what is not said.
   6. The audience can believe the impossible.
   7. The believing will be for a short while at least.

Sentence Combining Exercise

Combine the following sentences into an effective essay using several patterns of coordination. Eliminate any details which do not help develop its central idea.

THE UNBEATABLE BUG

1. An ambiguous shape approaches in the opposite lane.

2. From a distance it vaguely resembles a huge Easter egg.
3. It resembles an orange.
4. But up close it resembles some monstrous insect.
5. The insect's eyes are bright.
6. Its body is hard and metallic.

7. Barring the fantastic, it's probably just a Volkswagen Beetle.
8. There are many Beetles remaining.
9. They are chalking up more miles on an odometer.
10. The odometer has already turned over once or twice.

11. The VW has provided popular and practical transportation for millions.
12. Adolph Hitler commissioned Porsche to design and build a "people's car" in 1936.
13. Porsche is a sports car manufacturer.

14. Americans buy the bug because of its economy and durability.
15. They also buy it because the tiny Beetle suits the owners' personalities.
16. Or it can be made to suit their personalities.

17. Americans do love Volkswagens.

18. Over five million have been sold here since 1952.
19. Some "collectors" hoard as many as ten specimens.

20. The Beetle's main appeal in the early days was its practicality.

21. Many Americans realized the economy of a car.
22. The car got over 30 miles per gallon.
23. Even the backyard mechanic could service it.
24. He fooled around with a few bolts and wires.

25. The bug lured many away from American cars.
26. It could outmaneuver those tail-finned and hood-ornamented monstrosities.
27. It outmaneuvered them on a winding road.
28. It outmaneuvered them into a tight parking space.

29. This practical car still appeals to the new generation of buggers.
30. It is cheap to buy and maintain.
31. It especially appeals when gas prices have even the wealthy on their knees.

32. The VW's simplicity also serves another purpose.

33. It allows bug owners to go wild with their cars.
34. They add a few strokes of paint here.
35. They exchange a fender or two there.
36. They create a work of art on wheels.
37. They express their own personalities.

38. Peggy Childs added eyelashes around the headlights.
39. She souped up her VW with a hot-pink paint job.
40. She is a state representative from Georgia.
41. She wanted to let people know she was energetic.
42. She wanted to let them know she was outgoing.

43. Several years ago a Chicago student created a poor man's Rolls Royce.
44. He chopped off his bug's hood.
45. He replaced it with an exact replica.
46. The replica was of the luxury car's front end.

47. VWs now scoot around America's roads.
48. They have wind-up keys.
49. The keys are attached to the rear end.
50. They resemble children's toys more than adult cars.

51. Few people would dare to paint facial features on a Lincoln.
52. Few would weld a key onto a Ferrari.
53. The humble bug obediently allows its owner to dress it up at will.

54. There are thousands of vehicles swarming over the roads.
55. They are all nearly identical.
56. Car owners appreciate the chance to distinguish themselves.
57. They can distinguish themselves even with a hot-pink VW.

58. A switch helps drivers ward off psychological dangers.
59. The dangers are of that 30th, 40th, or 50th birthday.
60. The drivers are age-conscious.
61. The switch is from a Chrysler to a VW.
62. A daring racing stripe turns their bug into a Lemans racer.

63. A book has even been written about the Volkswagen.
64. The book says the Volkswagen is a sex symbol.

65. The bug has all that going for it.
66. How could the bug be stopped?

67. The Beetle has only one drawback.
68. The drawback is its supposed frailty.
69. The drawback has aroused the fears of some.

70. Its engine is in the back.
71. The Beetle's front end is light.
72. It is hollow.
73. It is dangerous.

74. Smashed VWs don't exactly encourage many drivers.
75. They are smashed accordion-style.

76. Neither do hospital emergency rooms.
77. The rooms are dubbed "Volkswagen Wards."

78. The weak of heart do tend to shy away.

79. The Beetle consistently outsold all other imports until 1974.
80. VW production was cut back in 1974.

81. People continued to appreciate a car.
82. The car's looks remained simple.
83. Its quality was constantly improved.
84. The improvement may have been as simple as a better doorlock.

85. Higher production costs resulted in the Beetle's giving way.
86. Higher import taxes resulted in its giving way.
87. So did greater competition.
88. The Beetle gave way to the Rabbit and the Dasher.
89. The Rabbit and the Dasher are more expensive VWs.

90. Serious buglovers keep their Beetles on the road.

91. Beetles by the thousands can still be seen.
92. They sardine into impossible places.
93. They park in driveways of even Beverly Hills homes.
94. They bug around America's highways.

95. They have sound bodies.
96. They have flawless paint jobs.
97. They have enthusiastic owners.

98. Who knows how long they will remain?

Rewriting Exercise

Make each of the following sentences more effective by changing the patterns of coordination.

Example

> For decades FBI agents wiretapped the phones of American citizens with the attorney general's approval, and they didn't have warrants.
>
> ↓
>
> For decades FBI agents wiretapped the phones of American citizens **with** the attorney general's approval and **without** warrants.

A. More people live by themselves and more women work and more money is available, and for these reasons one of every three American food dollars now goes to restaurants or fast-food shops.

B. A small percentage of the Mexican population is comfortably rich; a large portion is poor, and their being poor is distressing.

C. Marijuana smuggling has become a multibillion dollar industry, and the American government and the Mexican government do not collect any taxes from it.

D. Rugby is played with no substitutions, no regard for life and limb, and no pads.

E. The elementary school teacher teaches the "three R's" of reading, 'riting, and 'rithmetic, and the industrial psychologist deals with alcoholism, absenteeism, and accidents, which are known as the "three A's."

F. Journalists do not usually select stories that appear on local television newscasts, but they are usually selected by "consultants" who search for stories the public will find least objectionable.

G. Television has been called a source of information, a means of entertainment, and a "plug-in" drug; especially its severest critics call it a "plug-in" drug.

H. Many people hope that the Irish Republican Army won't turn out to be the most powerful force in Northern Ireland and that the Ulster Defense Association won't, but that the Women's Peace Movement will.

I. Every year the United States admits 400,000 legal immigrants, and this is more than all other nations combined, but an even greater number of illegal immigrants manages to get into the country every year.

J. In frisbee golf, the "tee" is likely to be a small rock, and the "hole" will probably be a drinking fountain, or it might be a lamp post.

Sentence Combining Exercise

Combine the following sentences into a persuasive essay using several patterns of coordination.

LAST CALL

1. A 9-year-old arrested for drunken driving in a stolen Mustang?

2. It sounds incredible.
3. In 1975, 51 children were arrested for drunken driving.
4. The children were age 10 and under.

5. Thousands of others were charged with related offenses.
6. This also occurred in 1975.
7. A related offense is theft.
8. A related offense is assault.
9. A related offense is rape.
10. All these offenses were committed by children.
11. The children were drunk.

12. Drunkenness among teens and preteens continues to spread.
13. Alcoholism among teens and preteens continues to spread.
14. Most people regard such behavior as mere child's play.

15. Actually, alcoholism among the young poses a deadly problem.
16. Only sustained efforts can solve the problem.
17. Only concerted efforts can solve the problem.

18. Alcohol abuse among youths is by no means child's play.

19. Eleven- and 12-year-olds frequently come to school drunk.
20. This occurs in Boston and in New York.
21. Sometimes they even bring their bottles along.

22. Gangs of friends regularly huddle in the john.
23. They take quick swigs from a pint of Southern Comfort.
24. A buddy plays lookout.
25. The buddy is already inebriated.

26. Forty percent of the students admit to drinking.
27. They drink before they are 15.
28. The students are on the West Coast.

29. Nationwide, high school and even junior high school students gather for drunken parties.
30. They gather weekly.
31. Many of the students have excellent academic records.
32. Drunken gangs clash at local McDonalds or Burger Kings.

33. Drinking has increased.
34. There are now an estimated 500,000 alcoholics.
35. They are under age 21.
36. There are over 25 special Alcoholics Anonymous chapters.
37. Their activities are geared solely to teens and preteens.

38. The crimes are even worse than the statistics indicate.
39. The crimes are committed by these young alcoholics.

40. More and more teens and preteens are drinking.
41. Alcohol-related arrests have tripled in the last ten years.

42. Arrests cause suffering for the family.
43. Arrests mark the youths with a criminal record.
44. Statistics predict the record will probably grow.

45. Teenage drinkers also hurt other people.

46. Teenage drinking causes at least 8000 traffic fatalities.
47. Teenage drinking causes over 40,000 serious injuries.
48. This happens each year.

49. Young people are pressured by school work.
50. Young people are encouraged by their peers.
51. Young people often resort to drinking like adults.
52. Young people often resort to committing crimes like adults.
53. Young people often resort to dying like adults.
54. Dying like adults is saddest of all.

55. Most people still shrug off teen and preteen drinking.
56. They do this despite the sobering facts.
57. They think drinking is simply a way of blowing off steam.

58. Most parents are thankful that their kids crave booze.
59. Most parents are thankful that their kids do not crave pot, acid, or heroin.
60. Most parents casually encourage drinking at home and social gatherings.

61. Teen drinking becomes a regular habit.
62. When this happens, parents tend to regard their child's drinking as a ritual of initiation into adulthood.
63. Their Steven or Joan comes home blind drunk.
64. When this happens, the parents laugh it off.

65. But Steven or Joan gets expelled for drunkenness.
66. Or Steven or Joan dies in a grinding, head-on collision.
67. Then the laughing stops.

68. It usually takes a catastrophe.
69. The problem's gravity is dramatized by the catastrophe.
70. This is unfortunate.

71. Everyone must accept the responsibility.
72. The responsibility is combating teen and preteen alcoholism.
73. Especially parents must accept the responsibility.

74. Parents can help.
75. They can teach their children about the dangers of alcohol.
76. They can set good examples at home.
77. Children demonstrate interest in drinking.
78. Then the parents can listen and respond like a friend.

79. Schools should attempt to educate students.
80. Schools should sponsor lectures.
81. Schools should establish hot lines.
82. Schools should make the problems of alcoholism and drunken driving a central part of health courses.
83. Schools should make the problems of alcoholism and drunken driving a central part of driver education programs.

84. Beer, wine, and liquor companies must realize the problems they create.
85. They make their products especially appealing to young crowds.
86. They must change their advertising campaigns.

87. Sensible laws must be passed.
88. The laws must deter illegal drinking.

89. These are only a few possible courses of action.
90. Such changes may help hold off the rising tide of alcohol abuse.

91. We must work together.
92. If we don't, the Age of Alcohol will surely drown out the Age of Aquarius.
93. It will destroy many people in the process.

Judging Sentences

Choose from each group of four sentences below the one you find most effective, and be prepared to explain why. If you find two or more sentences equally acceptable, be ready to justify that judgment. If you don't like any of the four sentences, create a better version of your own.

A. 1. Rugby is a game which pits mind against mind, elbow against eyeball, and muscle against muscle.
   2. Rugby is a game which pits mind against mind, muscle against muscle, and, most importantly, elbow against eyeball.
   3. Rugby is a game which pits elbow against eyeball, muscle against muscle, and mind against mind.
   4. Rugby is a game which pits muscle against muscle, mind against mind, and elbow against eyeball.

B. 1. Eurocommunism is the word applied to western European communists who have not chosen the revolutionary but the parliamentary path to power.
   2. Eurocommunism is the word applied to western European communists who have chosen not the revolutionary but the parliamentary path to power.
   3. Eurocommunism is the word applied to western European communists who have chosen not the revolutionary path to power but the parliamentary one.
   4. Eurocommunism is the word applied to western European communists who have not chosen the revolutionary path to power but the parliamentary path to power.

C. 1. Car washes have become popular fund-raising events in junior highs; probably because 13-year-olds are big enough to get the cars clean and young enough so that they enjoy getting wet.
   2. Car washes have become popular fund-raising events in junior highs, probably not only because 13-year-olds are big enough to get the cars clean but also because they are young enough to enjoy getting wet.
   3. Car washes have become popular fund-raising events in

junior highs, probably because 13-year-olds are big enough to get the cars clean and young enough to enjoy getting wet.
4. Car washes have become popular fund-raising events in junior highs, probably because 13-year-olds are big enough to get the cars clean but also because they are sufficiently youthful to enjoy getting wet.

D. 1. At diploma mills throughout the country you can get an academic degree and never have to write a paper or take a test or even open a book.
2. At diploma mills throughout the country you can get an academic degree and never have to write a paper or take a test or even opening a book.
3. At diploma mills throughout the country you can get an academic degree. Without ever having to write a paper, take a test, open a book.
4. At diploma mills throughout the country you can get an academic degree without ever having to write a paper, taking a test, opening a book.

E. 1. New Hampshire is the only state with neither a sales nor an income tax, and this is a major attraction for tax-weary residents of other states, but its teachers' salaries and workers' wages are among the lowest in the country.
2. New Hampshire is the only state with neither a sales nor an income tax, a major attraction for tax-weary residents of other states, but its teachers' salaries and workers' wages are among the lowest in the country.
3. New Hampshire is the only state with neither a sales nor an income tax, a major attraction for tax-weary residents of other states, but both the salaries of its teachers and the wages of its workers are among the lowest in the country.
4. New Hampshire is the only state with neither a sales nor an income tax, a major attraction for tax-weary residents of other states, but not only are its teachers' salaries among the lowest in the country; but so are its workers' wages.

Sentence Combining Exercise

Reorder the 14 groups of sentences below to construct a coherent essay. Develop the thesis that Americans seek "cheap thrills" to escape from the tedium of their everyday existence. You may change the wording of the sentences as well as their order.

CHEAP THRILLS

1. The contemporary American is eminently safe. Modern technology provides so many conveniences and labor-saving devices that no dangers, no challenges remain to relieve a pervasive sense of boredom.

2. Ancient Romans had gladiators and martyrs; even the highly civilized English relished such brutal activities as bear baiting. But we now have more people more bored and more alienated than ever before.

3. The man, dressed like an astronaut just prior to blast-off, leans back nervously in his padded seat. The "All Clear" sign flashes and, once again, Evel Knievel flies down the ramp, soars over a deadly ravine, and lands safely on the other side, thousands of fans screaming their approval as he touches down.

4. Nature no longer threatens to overwhelm civilization with disasters, and job specialization reduces the average person's work to assembling the same part every day, driving the same sales route every week, or teaching the same biology course every year.

5. That many fans view brutal violence and the constant risk of death with morbid pleasure suggests that they enjoy more than the expertise of the performers. But what happens when the standard spectacles lose their potency and we demand newer thrills?

6. Even our meager attempts to "return to nature" are thwarted by restricted, patrolled campgrounds and Winnebagos complete with TV and, of course, air conditioning. Such creeping boredom has everyone yawning, praying for a thrill.

7. Fortunately, entertainment people are already anticipating our problem. One major TV producer predicts that at

least 95 percent of the potential viewing audience would watch a game show in which losing contestants paid with their lives.

8. Millions of people regularly pay ten to hundreds of dollars to witness daredevils risk their lives, daredevils like Knievel, demolition derby drivers, and the Human Fly, who rides atop a Jumbo 747. Why are Americans so fascinated by death-defying acts such as these?

9. Fortunately, we also have faster motorcycles, cars, and jets to satisfy our needs. In the old days, perhaps several thousand spectators enjoyed two slaves battling to death, but now civilization enables millions to thrill to whole teams on a field or scores of Indianapolis drivers, all risking death.

10. Just imagine Charlie's Angels, all armed with high-powered rifles, eagerly awaiting a wrong answer from some nervous contestant.

11. But that's not all. Americans feel increasingly alienated from their fellow inmates. Everyone seeks not only the uniformity granted by conforming to the latest fashions but also the anonymity found in the flashing strobes and pulsing beat of the disco and in the crowds at ball games and concerts.

12. For the most part, modern Americans flock to these bizarre spectacles because it is there that they can vicariously experience the danger and excitement so obviously missing from their ho-hum middle-class lives.

13. Performers ranging from comparatively tame football and hockey players to the real daredevils like Knievel and the Human Fly accept the burden and respond to our cry for action.

14. In these huge groups, we can stomp and scream without distinguishing ourselves at all. Actually, what we seek is the chance to peer out of our padded-cell worlds and witness others doing what we can't do.

10. Noun Substitutes

In everyday conversation and in casual writing, it is natural to state some observation in one sentence or clause and then comment on it in the next:

a. Nuclear waste could be deposited in outer space. **This** could be one way to solve a difficult dilemma.

b. The university insists on controlling the private lives of its students, **which** is a laughable anachronism.

c. Laura was late for her trial, and **it** really made the judge furious.

d. Why don't Americans listen to classical music? **This** is a mystery to Europeans.

There is nothing wrong with these sentences, and one of your options is to keep them as they are. But in revising your writing, you may decide that the words **this, which,** and **it** aren't really necessary, because each of them can be replaced by a version of the sentence preceding it.

In example (a), you can change the verb sequence **could be deposited** into the ING-NOUN **depositing:**

> **Depositing nuclear waste in outer space** could be one way to solve a difficult dilemma.

In example (b), you can convert the verb **insists** into the INFINITIVE **to insist** and add **for** before the subject:

> **For the university to insist on controlling the private lives of its students** is a laughable anachronism.

In example (c), you can make the first sentence into a THAT-CLAUSE, a clause introduced by **that:**

> **That Laura was late for her trial** really made the judge furious.

In example (d), you can transform the question beginning with the question word **why** into a WH-CLAUSE simply by moving the verb **don't** to the other side of the subject, **Americans:**

> **Why Americans don't listen to classical music** is a mystery to Europeans.

These four kinds of structures—**ing**-nouns, infinitives, **that**-clauses, and **wh**-clauses—are NOUN SUBSTITUTES. A noun substitute has the meaning of a complete sentence, but it appears only as a part of another sentence, in a spot normally occupied by a noun or pronoun. In this way, you can integrate the ideas expressed in two or more separate sentences into a single sentence in which noun substitutes play the role of nouns. By joining related ideas more closely, you can often achieve increased precision.

Not only do noun substitutes provide a means for converting sentences into nouns, they also give you alternative ways of making that conversion. Often two, sometimes three, and occasionally even all four types of noun substitutes are possible options for combining, with subtle differences in the resulting meanings. In the next example the **that**-clause states a fact; the **ing**-noun phrase implies a bit more of the act, the "doing"; the infinitive phrase suggests a sense of intent or possibility; and the **wh**-clause makes the statement somewhat more personal:

> You can slight the value of early detection programs for cancer.
> But this invites disaster and defeat.

↓

> **(The fact) that you slight the value of early detection programs for cancer** invites disaster and defeat.

OR

> **Slighting the value of early detection programs for cancer** is inviting disaster and defeat.

OR

> **To slight the value of early detection programs for cancer** is to invite disaster and defeat.

OR

> **Whoever slights the value of early detection programs for cancer** invites disaster and defeat.

Noun substitutes can help you with another ingredient of effective writing—getting movement and vitality into your sentences. It is usually verbs, not nouns, that can provide these qualities, but noun substitutes have a stronger verbal force than ordinary nouns. After all, both **that**-clauses and **wh**-clauses contain verbs, and even **ing**-nouns and infinitives remind us of verbs because they look like verbs. Indeed, infinitives imply a future action, and **ing**-nouns suggest a sense of "doing," "happening," "experiencing." In this respect they are both quite different from real nouns, which are often more abstract. The phrase

> a time **to live** and a time **to die**

loses much of its vitality when its infinitives are replaced by abstract nouns:

> a time for life and a time for death.

In the second sentence we no longer sense the act or process, and perhaps no longer feel as keenly the contrast between the experiences of being alive and being dead. Try to describe the differences among the following:

Death with dignity and grace is an ancient idea.

Dying with dignity and grace is an ancient idea.

To die with dignity and grace is an ancient idea.

The word **death** doesn't move—it suggests an abstract and impersonal event or state. But **dying** evokes the image of a living body's last moments and the course of its passing away, and **to die** almost gives you a sense of the purposefulness of death. Similarly,

Protests will get you nowhere.

lacks the sense of active personal involvement, the sense of your "doing" it, that is conveyed by

Protesting will get you nowhere.

Notice how this quality of **ing**-nouns contrasts with the dryness and heaviness of abstract nouns:

Destroying the tapes ⎫
The destruction of the tapes ⎬ was his worst mistake.

Removing garbage ⎫
The removal of garbage ⎬ costs the city millions of dollars.

The government should stop ⎰ **deporting aliens.**
⎱ the deportation of aliens.

Both **ing**-nouns and infinitives remind us of verbs because they are verbs converted to nouns. We can tell that they are very close to verbs from the fact that, just like verbs, they can have a subject, such as **the dog, aging ballplayers,** and **a man or woman** in the following:

The dog howled and whined all night long.
This kept the whole neighborhood awake.

The dog's howling and whining all night long kept the whole neighborhood awake.

Aging ballplayers can move to Japan, where baseball is popular.
This is a sensible way to extend a career.

For aging ballplayers to move to Japan, where baseball is popular, is a sensible way to extend a career.

A man or woman may live over a hundred years in Soviet Georgia.
This means that yogurt must be somewhere nearby.

For a man or woman to live over a hundred years in Soviet Georgia means that yogurt must be somewhere nearby.

Sometimes the subject is expressed indirectly, as **vacationers, Kissinger,** and **farmer** in the next examples:

The most common mistake vacationers make is this.
Vacationers take too many clothes with them.

The most common mistake vacationers make is **taking too many clothes with them.**

Kissinger had been accused of this.
He prolonged the Vietnam War and meddled into other nations' affairs.
Then Kissinger won the Nobel Prize.
This must have been the highlight of Kissinger's career.

After he had been accused of **prolonging the Vietnam War and meddling into other nations' affairs, winning the Nobel Prize** must have been the highlight of Kissinger's career.

The farmer does not plant any crops.
This is the farmer's best weapon against low prices.

↓

Not to plant any crops is the farmer's best weapon against low prices.

A vague and impersonal subject such as **they, one, someone, a person,** or even **you** need not be stated when it is understood:

They treat disease through the mind.
This is the latest thing in medicine.

↓

Treating disease through the mind is the latest thing in medicine.

You vote Republican.
This means you endorse big business.

↓

Voting Republican means **endorsing big business.**

OR

To vote Republican means **to endorse big business.**

Balanced infinitives of the type "To do this is to do that" are an effective means of implying a definition: the sentence "To vote Republican means to endorse big business" indirectly defines the Republican party as the party of big business. But this kind of definition often implies a comparison as well: the next sentence suggests the greatness of Julius Erving as a basketball player by comparing him to the greatest English poet:

To say that Julius Erving jumps is **to describe** Shakespeare as a guy who wrote poetry.

Infinitives—and indeed other noun substitutes—can also occur in a series. In the following example the last infinitive strengthens the link between the two sides of the sentence without destroying the balance:

> **To believe** that Christianity is concerned only with the after-life is **to ignore** the ethical dimension of Christ's life, **to deprive** the gospel of its earthly and human significance.

A series is a useful organizing principle for any type of information that suggests parallel points. In a first draft you might jot down such information in the form of sentences that obscure the parallelism:

> The new law would require the president to inform American citizens when he had grounds to believe that they were victims of eavesdropping by agents of another country. Then the agents involved must be requested to stop the eavesdropping, and they are to be ordered out of the country if they persist.

But in revising this passage you might realize that the law would require the president not only **to inform** American citizens but also **to request** foreign agents to stop the eavesdropping and **to order** them to leave. Accordingly, you can rewrite the paragraph with an infinitive series to show the parallel points:

> The new law would require the president **to inform** American citizens when he had grounds to believe that they were victims of eavesdropping by agents of another country, **to request** the agents involved to stop the eavesdropping, and **to order** them out of the country if they persist.

Of course, a series can be used with any noun substitute. For a slightly different effect, try **that**-clauses:

> The new law would assure **that** American citizens are informed by the president when he had grounds to believe they were victims of eavesdropping by agents of another country, **that** the agents involved are requested to stop the

eavesdropping, and **that** the violators are ordered out of the country if they persist.

Wh-clauses are slightly different from the other noun substitutes because they are closely related to questions. There are two kinds of questions in English: those that must be answered with "yes" or "no," and those that cannot be. "Did the Giants win yesterday?" is a yes-no question, but "When is payday?" is not; questions introduced by words such as **when** are **wh**-questions.

To make a yes-no question into a noun substitute, convert the question into a statement (where the verb follows the subject), and add **whether** or **whether or not** in front:

Will taxes be raised again this year?
This remains to be seen.

↓

Whether (or not) taxes will be raised again this year remains to be seen.

OR

It remains to be seen **whether (or not) taxes will be raised again this year.**

Does a government employee have the right to strike?
This is a constitutional question.

↓

Whether or not a government employee has the right to strike is a constitutional question.

All other **wh**-clauses come from questions that begin with one of the following question words:

who, whoever	where, wherever
whom, whomever	when, whenever
whose	why
which, whichever	how, however
what, whatever	

The next examples illustrate how a **wh**-question, converted into a noun substitute, can replace **it** or **this:**

>Which airline do you take?
>It doesn't affect the price of the ticket.

$$\downarrow$$

>**Which airline you take** doesn't affect the price of the ticket.

>Psychologists are trying to determine this.
>How much effect does TV have on the reading and writing abilities of young children?

$$\downarrow$$

>Psychologists are trying to determine **how much effect TV has on the reading and writing abilities of young children.**

>Why were the hijackers allowed to go free?
>This puzzled the public.

$$\downarrow$$

>**Why the hijackers were allowed to go free** puzzled the public.

>What amazes many foreigners?
>It is this.
>How easily can Americans switch to a first-name basis even with superficial acquaintances?

$$\downarrow$$

>**What amazes many foreigners** is **how easily Americans can switch to a first-name basis even with superficial acquaintances.**

Often you have the option of simplifying a **wh**-clause into a **wh**-infinitive phrase:

>You learn this.
>How do you write an effective job application?
>This should be a part of everyone's education.

$$\downarrow$$

>Learning **how to write an effective job application** should be a part of everyone's education.

Basic Pattern Exercise

Combine each set of sentences below into a single sentence using at least one noun substitute, as shown in the respective examples below. Note that Example I calls for **ing**-nouns; Example II for infinitive phrases; Example III for **that**-clauses; and Example IV for **wh**-clauses.

Example I
    1. One cheats on tests repeatedly.
    2. This is risky.
    3. This is self-defeating.

↓

    Repeated cheating on tests is risky and self-defeating.

OR

    Cheating on tests repeatedly is risky and self-defeating.

A. 1. She pretended to be one of us.
   2. She took part in all our pranks.
   3. This helped hide her identity.
   4. She was a policewoman.

B. 1. You bury a dead cat at midnight.
   2. Or you rub the spot with grasshopper spit.
   3. This might cure warts as effectively as medical treatment.

C. 1. You reduce your weight.
   2. It is not just a matter of this.
   3. You clip a diet out of a magazine.

D. 1. One tries to bring about changes in education.
   2. This has been compared to a move.
   3. One moves a cemetery.

E. 1. You can gamble legally.
   2. This is one of society's adjustments of its laws.
   3. The adjustments are periodic.

Example II
   1. One is born and raised in the West.
   2. This means one is suspicious and fearful of claus-
      trophobia.
   3. Claustrophobia envelops the East.

   To be born and raised in the West means that you
   are suspicious and fearful of the claustrophobia envelop-
   ing the East.

                              OR

   To be born and raised in the West is **to be suspicious and fearful of the claustrophobia that envelops the East.**

F. 1. You eat Japanese style.
   2. This means you experience a passion.
   3. The passion is almost fanatical.
   4. The passion is for balance and contrast.

G. 1. One says this.
   2. History is a record of dates and battles.
   3. This ignores most of history's significance.
   4. This makes history merely a list of selected events.

H. 1. The Equal Rights Amendment is not ratified by three-
      fourths of the states.
   2. The Equal Rights Amendment does not become law.
   3. This would be a slap in the face to millions of American
      women.

I. 1. A restaurant becomes a five-star restaurant.
   2. This means the restaurant has consistently maintained
      superior standards.
   3. The standards are of quality in food and service.

J. 1. The faculty do not want to have their classes evaluated by
      students.
   2. This is to reject the best kind of advice.
   3. How can the faculty improve and perfect their teaching?

Example III
1. The earth's climate changes.
2. The earth's climate even now may be changing rapidly.
3. This is widely recognized.

It is widely recognized **that the earth's climate changes and even now may be changing rapidly.**

OR

That the earth's climate changes, and even now may be changing rapidly, is widely recognized.

K. 1. Even in some elementary schools, children have easy access to drugs.
   2. This is no longer a secret.

L. 1. Al Capone tried to keep his criminal record clean.
   2. This helped him.
   3. He controlled his underworld empire without police interference.

M. 1. The editors of the *Washington Post* hoped this.
   2. The story would be accepted by the public.
   3. The story would be hailed by the public.
   4. The editors of the *Washington Post* doubted this.
   5. The story would be embraced by the president.

N. 1. The percentage of Americans is increasing dramatically.
   2. The Americans are left-handed.
   3. This shows something.
   4. We're obviously becoming a left-handed nation.

O. 1. The Olympic Games have become prohibitively expensive.
   2. This is one reason for it.
   3. Why do American cities show little interest in hosting the Olympic Games?

Example IV
1. Should a state university invest in stocks?
2. Companies sell the stocks.
3. The companies do business with racist governments.
4. This has been a matter of controversy on several campuses.

It has been a matter of controversy on several campuses **whether a state university should invest in stocks sold by companies that do business with racist governments.**

OR

Whether a state university should invest in stocks sold by companies that do business with racist governments has been a matter of controversy on several campuses.

P. 1. It is this that makes some people reject modern art.
   2. Modern art apparently lacks concern for traditional values.
   3. Traditional values include beauty, proportion, and technical expertise.

Q. 1. Who claims the word of God as his personal domain?
   2. That person is more likely to be a fanatic than a saint.

R. 1. Where did Moriarty make his mistake?
   2. He underestimated the skill of his nemesis.
   3. His nemesis was Sherlock Holmes.

S. 1. How soon is socialized medicine coming to America?
   2. This depends on the time.
   3. When will the majority of Americans get tired of paying astronomical doctor's bills?

T. 1. Should prisoners be used for human experiments?
   2. This is not only a legal question.
   3. This is also a moral question.

Sentence Combining Exercise

Combine the following sentences into a short essay. Use several noun substitutes.

NUCLEAR REACTORS: WHAT'S THE RUSH?

1. The depletion will be a major concern.
2. The depletion will continue.
3. Fossil fuels will be depleted.
4. The concern will be for the rest of the century.
5. This is now a widely accepted fact.

6. This has led government to seek out sources.
7. This has led industry to seek out sources.
8. The sources are alternative.
9. The sources are of energy.
10. The sources offer a dependable supply of power.
11. They offer it at reasonable cost.

12. Nuclear power stations are being developed.
13. This has been put forth as a solution.
14. The solution is at least partial.
15. The solution is to our dilemma.

16. Many people feel this way.
17. Our nuclear technology is still too experimental.
18. The technology is for widespread practical application.

19. They argue.
20. One races ahead with the development.
21. Nuclear reactors are developed.
22. One takes too many risks.
23. The risks involve the environment.
24. The risks involve public health.

25. They point this out.
26. Studies of thermal pollution remain inconclusive.
27. Studies of radioactive pollution remain inconclusive.
28. The safety devices are not well tested.
29. Plant security is lax.

30. Where are we to find energy?
31. We need the energy to sustain our civilization.
32. This is a difficult question.

33. How many compromises will Americans have to make then?
34. How much hardship will Americans have to endure then?
35. Then energy sources begin to dry up.
36. These cannot yet be envisioned.

37. Opponents of quick atomic energy development only urge this.
38. We do not act out of anxiety.
39. We examine all aspects of the question carefully.
40. We take into account long-term results of our decision.

41. One does anything less.
42. This may be dooming future generations.
43. They are doomed to a living hell.

Creative Pattern Exercise

In each of the following sentences replace the pronoun in boldface by a noun substitute phrase or clause. In sentences where this pronoun is **it,** you have the additional option of keeping **it** and inserting the noun substitute elsewhere in the sentence. Experiment with different types of noun substitutes.

Example
    It was a courageous act.

It was a courageous act **for the Egyptian president to visit Israel.**

OR

What he did to end centuries of hatred and hostility was a courageous act.

OR

> **Defying the advice of many of his friends and doing what he believed he had to do** was a courageous act.

> OR

> **It** was a courageous act on the part of the president **that he was willing to risk the wrath of his allies in the interest of peace.**

A. You should have decided **that** before you mailed the letter.

B. **This** is what she would like to have done, had she not been afraid of seeming to be rude.

C. **It** threatened to endanger our relationship.

D. What none of us could understand—and still don't—was **this.**

E. **It** is not to state a general truth but rather to exhibit a personal phobia.

F. **That** is one reason why Americans spend $8 billion a year on weddings, not counting gifts for the young couple.

G. In view of **this,** the Planned Parenthood clinic performs a useful service.

H. **It** is rarely mentioned in arguments about the coed dormitories.

I. To know another culture well and to speak another language mean **this.**

J. **This** is a good example of the American weakness for beef.

Sentence Combining Exercise

Combine the following sentences into an effective essay. Make use of several noun substitutes.

MARGARET SANGER

1. Margaret Sanger was a maternity nurse.
2. She was working on New York's lower east side.
3. She was working in 1912.
4. She decided that something was wrong with the sex education of the day.

5. The women had too many children.
6. She treated the women.
7. The women didn't know this.
8. How do you prevent unwanted pregnancies?

9. She saw one young woman.
10. The woman was near death.
11. It was from self-induced abortion.
12. The woman begged the doctor to tell her how to do it.
13. It was to stop having children.

14. "Tell Jake to sleep on the roof," the doctor said.

15. Three months later she was dead.
16. She died from abortion.
17. The abortion was attempted.

18. These women were so desperate.
19. These women were so ignorant about their bodies.
20. This made Margaret Sanger see it.
21. She saw how much was wrong.
22. This made her decide to do something about it.

23. She invented the term.
24. The term was *birth control.*
25. She set out to wage a war.

26. Sanger was to begin her fight.
27. Sanger first waged a war of information.

28. She published a magazine.
29. The magazine was *The Woman Rebel.*
30. She distributed a pamphlet.

31. The pamphlet was *Family Limitation*.
32. The magazine and the pamphlet were designed to furnish information.
33. The information was about birth control.

34. This information was distributed.
35. But it was a federal offense at the time.
36. It was considered the same thing as using the mail.
37. Obscene material was distributed through the mail.

38. Sanger was arrested.
39. It was one of eight times she was arrested.
40. And it was one of eight times she would stand trial.

41. The charges were eventually dropped.
42. The publicity helped Sanger.
43. It fulfilled her initial purpose.
44. The purpose was to let women know.
45. The women could do something about birth control.
46. The purpose was to let them know.
47. She was fighting.

48. Sanger was to turn information into action.
49. Sanger opened the first clinic in the nation.
50. The opening was in 1916.
51. The clinic was for birth control.
52. The clinic was in Brooklyn, N.Y.

53. On the first day more than 150 women crowded in.
54. Most women were carrying babies.
55. Most women were holding their children by the hand.
56. The women wanted to pay the registration fee.
57. The registration fee was ten cents.

58. Nine days later the police came.
59. The purpose was to close the clinic.
60. The purpose was to arrest Sanger.
61. Sanger "maintained a public nuisance."

62. It was to make matters worse in Sanger's eyes.
63. Among the arresting officers was a policewoman.

64. "You are a traitoress to your sex," Sanger said angrily.

65. Sanger refused to ride in the paddywagon.
66. Sanger marched to jail.
67. The marching was amid shouts of support.
68. The support was from her clinic customers.

69. Sanger served 30 days.
70. She served in the workhouse.
71. She served for her crime.

72. But the people began to see.
73. The people heard about her work.
74. Hers was an idea.
75. The time of the idea had come.
76. It didn't matter what the law said.

77. Her case came up for appeal.
78. Public sympathy was with her.
79. The judge decided.
80. The judge was on the New York Court of Appeals.
81. The judge granted doctors the right.
82. The right was to give advice to their patients.
83. The advice was about birth control.

84. Sanger formed conferences.
85. Sanger formed leagues.
86. She formed them throughout the 1920s and 1930s.
87. The conferences further spread her cause.
88. The leagues further spread her cause.
89. And in 1936 she won her victory.
90. The victory was the most striking.
91. Doctors were granted the right.
92. The right was to import contraceptive devices.
93. The right was to prescribe contraceptive devices.

94. Sanger's idea was worth this to her.
95. It was worth a lifetime of fighting.
96. The idea was that every child should be a wanted child.

97. She fought for birth control.

98. But she also fought for another control.
99. The control was of a broader kind.
100. She wanted to show women this.
101. How could they take control of their bodies?
102. How could they take control of their lives?

Rewriting Exercise

Rewrite each of the following sentences. Try to make the most effective use of noun substitutes. Rearrange parts of the sentence where necessary.

Example

House sparrows are able to build nests, lay eggs, and rear their young on constantly moving objects such as oil pumps, and this has helped make them the most widespread land birds.

Being able to build nests, lay eggs, and rear their young on constantly moving objects such as oil pumps has helped make house sparrows the most widespread land birds.

OR

That house sparrows are able to build nests, lay eggs, and rear their young on constantly moving objects such as oil pumps has helped make them the most widespread land birds.

A. When you think difficult problems through, it requires time, solitude, and relaxation.

B. Studies show when you use the lap-shoulder belt it reduces the chance that you will be killed in a car accident by 60 percent.

C. One can contribute to the Conscience Fund of the U.S. Treasury Department, which is one way that citizens who suffer second thoughts about cheating on their tax return can soothe their conscience.

D. Getting their children into college used to be the goal of millions of Americans; nowadays, with the spiraling costs of higher education, it has become the bigger challenge to pay for college.

E. They must establish safeguards for the privacy of personal records; furthermore, to inform individuals how their files are being used and to let them know what is in the files should be constitutional obligations of every employer.

F. People doze at the wheel, and this is the major reason that motorists run off the road and hit parked vehicles, according to a recent study involving 2000 accidents.

G. Know how to read a map—orienteering is all about this.

H. Perhaps America should have a new national anthem, but the reason for this has never been convincingly demonstrated.

I. It was concluded by the panel that if you search for the causes of the decline in SAT scores, it is an exercise in conjecture.

J. Will the Supreme Court's decision on several cases of "reverse discrimination" affect access by minorities to higher education? It is not yet clear.

Sentence Combining Exercise

Formulate a thesis statement for or against amnesty. Support this thesis in an effective persuasive essay by (1) combining the following sentences into paragraphs, (2) adding details of your own throughout the essay, and (3) continuing with additional sentences to complete the argument. Use noun substitutes where appropriate.

AMNESTY?

1. Jon enjoys the "good life" in Quebec.
2. He has lived in Quebec since 1968.
3. He evaded the draft in 1968.
4. He fled to Canada in 1968.

5. His life seems casual.
6. His life seems carefree.

7. He has a job at a craft shop.
8. He weaves baskets.
9. He decorates candles.

10. He works at his hobbies.
11. Then scores of young people and tourists flock to watch.

12. What does he need?
13. He seems to have it.
14. He has a job.
15. He has an apartment.
16. And he has friends.

17. What does he really want?
18. But he does not have it.
19. He does not have the life he could have led in the United States.

20. Suppose the Vietnam War had not intruded.
21. Then Jon would have finished college.
22. Then Jon would have become an attorney.
23. His father is an attorney.

24. But the war took away his chances for that life.
25. He felt morally bound to resist the war.
26. The war cut him off from his family.
27. The war cut him off from his country.
28. The war cut him off from his dreams.

29. Mike chose a different path.
30. He joined the Marine Corps in 1968.
31. He was fresh out of high school.
32. And he served in Vietnam.
33. He was wounded in Vietnam.

34. His life is anything but carefree.

35. He works eight hours a day.
36. He is a short order cook in a diner.
37. Eight hours a day he stands on one good leg and one artificial one.

38. Mike is like Jon.
39. What had Mike dreamed of?
40. Mike lost this.
41. He had dreamed of a college basketball scholarship.
42. He had dreamed of a chance to coach basketball.
43. Or he had dreamed of maybe even playing pro basketball.

44. But the war took away his chances for that life.
45. The war was damned.
46. He had felt bound to fight the war for his country.
47. His father had fought the Japanese for this reason.

48. Now Jon wants to return to the United States.
49. Now many like Jon want to return also.

50. But the thought of Mike gnaws at our conscience.
51. The thought of thousands of others like Mike gnaws at our conscience.

52. We ponder.
53. Should amnesty be granted to draft dodgers?
54. Should amnesty be granted to deserters?

11. Summing Up

Putting It Together I

Combine each of the following groups of sentences into a single, more effective sentence. Use whatever constructions work best.

Example

1. The small town of Willingboro, New Jersey, was convinced of something.
2. The panic selling of homes was responsible for something.
3. The town's white population was declining.
4. Willingboro adopted a ban on "for sale" signs.

↓

Convinced that the panic selling of homes was responsible for its declining white population, the small town of Willingboro, New Jersey, adopted a ban on "for sale" signs.

OR

The small town of Willingboro, New Jersey, adopted a ban on "for sale" signs when it became convinced that the pan˙ selling of homes was responsible for the decline in its white population.

A. 1. But the United States Supreme Court made a ruling.
   2. The ruling was 8–0.
   3. The ban was illegal.
   4. It violated the guarantee of free speech.
   5. The First Amendment guarantees free speech.

B. 1. Only one American has ever fully recovered from a rabies attack.
   2. He was a boy.
   3. He was 6 years old.
   4. He was from Ohio.
   5. He recovered in 1972.

C. 1. A crime ring developed a booming business in fake art.
   2. The ring was international.
   3. The ring was organized.
   4. The ring was skillful.
   5. The ring counterfeited contemporary paintings expertly.
   6. Even the original artists could sometimes not detect the forgery.

D. 1. Dwight Eisenhower never intended to divorce his wife.
   2. His wife was Mamie.
   3. He once told her something.
   4. She shouldn't worry about gossip.
   5. According to gossip, he was having an affair with his secretary.

E. 1. Extinction is the fate of most species.
   2. Most species fail to adapt rapidly enough.
   3. The adaptation is to conditions of climate and competition that change.

F. 1. The famous factory is located on Chocolate Avenue in the center of Hershey, Pennsylvania.
   2. It is the world's largest factory.

G. 1. Prejudice against old people is stupid.
   2. Even Archie Bunker is smart enough.
   3. He does not direct his bigotry against groups.
   4. He will eventually join those groups.

H. 1. Kittenish actress Brigitte Bardot declared herself bored with making movies.
   2. She made a decision.
   3. She would establish a foundation.
   4. The foundation would protect animals.

I. 1. Suppose orphaned children are placed in the care of a succession of different nurses.
   2. The children suffer severe emotional shocks.
   3. The children eventually refuse something.
   4. They will not form attachments to new nurses.

J. 1. "Sunshine laws" are statutes.
   2. The statutes give citizens greater access to political bodies.
   3. Boards of education are political bodies.
   4. Zoning boards are political bodies.
   5. Town councils are political bodies.
   6. The premise of all "sunshine laws" is this.
   7. Secrecy at all governmental levels is inherently evil.

Sentence Combining Exercise

Combine the following sentences into an effective essay.

THE ORIGIN OF SPEECH

1. We do not know this.
2. How did the first people learn to communicate with language?

3. Linguists have too little knowledge of prehistoric people.
4. Linguists study the matter seriously.
5. Linguists are specialists in language.

6. But they have not kept others from this.
7. Others speculate on the origin of language.

8. Defenders of the "bow wow" theory claimed this.
9. Our ancestors began speaking.
10. They imitated the sounds of animals.

11. This was according to them.
12. Humans walked out of the primordial mist.
13. And humans began barking like dogs.
14. Humans began howling like wolves.
15. Humans began chirping like birds.
16. Humans began clucking like chickens.

17. Others held this.
18. They put their faith in the "pooh pooh" theory.
19. Language derived from instinctive cries.

20. That is, old grandfather Og walked into the cave one day.
21. He was tired from a hunt.
22. He stubbed his toe on a rock.
23. And he cried out "ow"!

24. Of course, suppose this.
25. Your prehistoric grandparent lived in England.
26. He probably muttered "tut tut"!

27. The "ding dong" theorists related language origins to this.
28. There is a mystic harmony between sound and sense.

29. This was according to them.
30. Primitive humans had a peculiar facility to know this.
31. A rock should be called *rock*.

32. After all, rocks give off "rockness."
33. In the same way, bells ring.

34. Yet others believed this.
35. Others were "yo heave ho" theorists.
36. Language derived from the sounds emitted during labor.

37. Supposedly, prehistoric people began speaking.
38. At the same time they grunted and groaned.
39. The grunting and groaning was over their daily tasks.

40. There is a basic fallacy in all these theories.
41. Humans remained mute until this.
42. They "created" language.

43. In other words, they had organs for speech before this.
44. They found a use for them.

45. But biologists know this.
46. Organs are not already perfected at their first use.
47. This happens in the evolution of species.

48. On the contrary, use develops organs.

49. We may never know this.
50. How did humans learn to speak?

51. But we can be sure of this.
52. Humans didn't learn to speak by saying "bow wow."
53. Humans didn't learn to speak by saying "pooh pooh."
54. Humans didn't learn to speak by saying "ding dong."
55. Humans didn't learn to speak by saying "yo heave ho."

Taking It Apart

Make each of the long, unwieldy sentences below into a more effective short paragraph of two or more sentences.

Example

> According to Piet Van de Mark, who conducts ocean tours off the coast of Baja California, grey whales like to watch people, the whales usually observing the boats from afar, then approaching, touching them with their snouts and waiting to be petted by the usually startled tourists—all this convincing de Mark that nature is not necessarily hostile, that if you step on a rattlesnake, you better watch out, but if you smile at a whale, it will smile at you.

↓

> According to Piet Van de Mark, who conducts ocean tours off the coast of Baja California, grey whales like to watch people. The whales will usually observe the boats from afar, then approach, touch them with their snouts and wait to be petted by the usually startled tourists. All this has convinced de Mark that nature is not necessarily hostile, that if you step on a rattlesnake, you better watch out; but if you smile at a whale, it will smile at you.

OR

> Piet Van de Mark, a conductor of ocean tours off the coast of Baja California, claims that grey whales like to watch people, often observing the boats from afar. When boats approach, the whales touch them with their snouts and wait to be petted by the usually startled tourists. This behavior convinces de Mark that nature is not necessarily hostile. In other words, if you step on a rattlesnake, you better watch out. But if you smile at a whale, it will smile at you.

A. Metaphors, words that say other than what is literally true, make poetry lively and interesting and do the same for the street language of the black ghetto, where, in street talk, a *crib* isn't merely a cozy place to bunk a baby but a "nice apartment," and where someone who's *shooting the pill* isn't destroying medicine but "playing basketball," and where *Mother's Day* comes once a month—although it may come once a year as a holiday to honor maternity—when welfare checks arrive, and even dull, throbbing "hangovers" become *headbusters* in the vivid language of the street.

B. When he opened his first restaurant in 1955, Ray Kroc, a milkshake machine salesman, gambled his life savings on the belief that Americans would rather wolf down a meal than linger over it, as the Europeans do, and his gamble paid off because in 1978 Kroc opened the 5000th store in his chain—a chain that sells nearly one billion hamburgers every three months—and Kroc had revolutionized the food industry with food that is hygienic, copious, and quick—the Big Mac.

C. A Michigan State University psychologist confirms what most of us already knew—that romance is going out of our lives—and he claims that the conditions for romantic love no longer exist, that they are replaced in men and women today by a pragmatic cynicism in which they view each other with a cool and objective eye and that casual sex and contraception have killed off romance, so that would-be Dantes can now have affairs with would-be Beatrices rather than mope and pine away in poetry.

D. Folklore celebrates the independent trucker as the cowboy of the twentieth century—the tough, proud rogue of the open road—though the trucker himself will tell you that—folklore be damned—trucking is a business, and not too good a one anymore, because, since the Arab oil embargo, many truckers—their expenses so high—have been forced out of business and only a small number can now clear a reasonable profit and that, moreover, the federal "boo-aucracy" (the ICC) favors the trucking companies, and so it might not be too many years before the independent truckers, like the cowboys before them, will be extinct, left to bite the dust.

E. Americans seem to like their history fictionalized and their fiction laced with history, and this explains the success of novels like *The Confessions of Nat Turner* and *Ragtime* and also explains the success of the television phenomenon called "docudrama," that is, history or biography spiced with enough exaggeration or fabrication to make it fresh and titillating, and so docudramas like "Roots" and "Eleanor and Franklin" are popular because they have both the excitement of fiction and the easy identification of history—and although the critics complain of historical inaccuracies in such TV fare, the public seems more concerned with a good story than with historically accurate details.

Sentence Combining Exercise

Combine the following sentences into an effective essay.

PINK FLOYD

1. The sky is reddened by a typical midwestern sunset.
2. The sky begins clouding over just before dusk.

3. But no threat of rain can stop something.
4. Twenty thousand rock fans flock to Cincinnati's Riverfront Coliseum.
5. They are coming to see and hear Pink Floyd.

6. The concert is still three hours off.
7. The concert has already attracted early birds.
8. There are several thousand of them.
9. They are all decked out.
10. They are all wearing their best rock-concert, faded blue jeans.
11. They are all wearing their best rock-concert, tie-dyed T-shirts.
12. They are all keyed up for the high-energy Pink Floyd show.

13. There are newcomers to the rock scene.
14. Their newness is obvious.
15. They wander around.
16. They gawk at the others.
17. They are conspicuous.
18. They wear neatly pressed checked slacks.
19. They wear expensive shirts.

20. There are groups of "hipper" friends.
21. They have already arranged themselves.
22. The arranging is in tight circles.
23. The circles are around bottles of Boone's Farm.
24. The circles are around joints.
25. It is as though they were conducting some mysterious preconcert ritual.

26. There are loners.
27. Their eyes are barely open.
28. Their arms dangle uselessly at their sides.
29. They weave aimlessly around the circles.
30. They occasionally squint into the sunset.
31. The squinting is so they can steady themselves.

32. There are couples.
33. They cling to each other.
34. They are near fountains or in remote corners.

35. There are real police.
36. They are not the rent-a-cop breed.
37. They stride confidently.
38. They stride in large groups.
39. They stride among the crowd.
40. They twirl their billyclubs.
41. They sweep their eyes over the area.
42. They look for trouble.

43. Hawkers call out.
44. They call wherever there are crowds.
45. They try to unload cheap T-shirts.
46. They try to unload pennants.
47. They draw only laughter from most concert goers.

48. The numbers grow.
49. There are circles of roamers, couples, and cops.
50. Roamers swarm confusedly over the acres of concrete.
51. Couples swarm confusedly over the acres of concrete.
52. Cops swarm confusedly over the acres of concrete.
53. The acres of concrete lead up to the auditorium.

54. The management realizes something.
55. The hordes can no longer be contained peacefully.
56. Then, the doors open.
57. Waves of fans pour into the coliseum.
58. They are already tired from waiting.
59. They are already sweaty from waiting.
60. They are just in time for something.
61. They wait out the final hour before the show.

Putting It Together II

Combine each of the following groups of sentences into a single, more effective sentence. Use whatever constructions work best.

Example

    1. Residents have erected a windmill.
    2. It is on a cooperative apartment building.
    3. It is on the rooftop.
    4. The building is in Manhattan.
    5. The windmill produces two kilowatts of electricity.
    6. The production is during 20-mile-per-hour winds.
    7. Two kilowatts of electricity light twenty 100-watt bulbs.

> On the rooftop of a cooperative apartment building in Manhattan, residents have erected a windmill that during 20-mile-per-hour winds produces two kilowatts of electricity, sufficient to light twenty 100-watt bulbs.

OR

> The residents of a Manhattan cooperative apartment building have erected a windmill on its rooftop, which produces two kilowatts of electricity when winds are blowing at 20 miles per hour, enough for twenty 100-watt lightbulbs.

A. 1. This year 7000 people will die.
    2. They will drown.
    3. They will be adults and children.
    4. Forty percent of them know how to swim.

B. 1. The city of Hannibal, Missouri, was the boyhood home of Mark Twain.
    2. Hannibal holds a fence-painting contest each year.
    3. The contest is part of an annual celebration.
    4. The celebration is called "Tom Sawyer Days."

C. 1. The Senate learned something about the National Security Agency.
    2. The agency had monitored the mail of some 1200 American citizens and organizations.
    3. The agency had monitored the phone calls of some 1200 American citizens and organizations.

    4. Many of the citizens and organizations had been active in the civil rights movement.

    5. Many of the citizens and organizations had been active in the peace movement.

D. 1. Maria's world is a cluster of cardboard shacks.
    2. Maria's world is a cluster of crude huts.
    3. The shacks and huts are ringed by sanitation ditches.
    4. In the ditches, sewage flows openly next to the street.

E. 1. William Holden is a movie star.
    2. Holden admitted something.
    3. He had to shave his chest every day.
    4. This was during the filming of *Picnic*.
    5. The prevailing motion picture code said hairy chests were dirty.

F. 1. An article in *Newsweek* tells us something.
    2. An article in *Time* tells us something.
    3. An article in *The Chronicle of Higher Education* tells us something.
    4. We are in the midst of a crisis in the schools.
    5. It is yet another crisis.
    6. This time the crisis is in the teaching of language skills.

G. 1. At one table was a sailor.
    2. He was angular and slit-eyed.
    3. He had an outrageous pompadour.
    4. He joked hungrily with his companion.
    5. She was a puffy-faced girl.
    6. Her bouffant hairdo was overdone.
    7. Her eye shadow was overdone.

H. 1. Bill Bradley is a former basketball star of Princeton University.
    2. Bill Bradley is a former basketball star of the New York Knicks.
    3. Bill Bradley is most proud of something.
    4. He played the game the way it's supposed to be played.
    5. The way it's supposed to be played is together.
    6. The way it's supposed to be played is as a team.

I. 1. German armies occupied western Russia.

2. This was in 1941.
3. In doing so, they did what armies often do.
4. The armies are victorious.
5. They raped the civilian populations.
6. They looted the civilian populations.
7. The populations were in their path.
8. They burned their towns.
9. The burning was senseless.

J. 1. Japanese film directors are unlike their American counterparts.
2. Kurosawa is a Japanese film director.
3. Ozu is a Japanese film director.
4. Mizoguchi is a Japanese film director.
5. Oshima is a Japanese film director.
6. Japanese film directors tend to see themselves as prophets.
7. Japanese film directors tend to see themselves as saviors.
8. Japanese film directors tend to see themselves as those who will help restore the authentically Japanese style of life.
9. The restoration will be after decades of Western domination.

Sentence Combining Exercise

Combine the following sentences so as to develop the argument that babies delivered by Leboyer's methods are happier and healthier. Eliminate from your essay any facts or ideas in these sentences that do not directly support this thesis.

SMILING BABIES

1. "That's simply beautiful."
2. This was all the new orderly could say.

3. The baby girl lies in her mother's arms.
4. She lies quietly and contentedly.
5. She was born only two hours before.
6. Her eyes are bright and alert.
7. Her hands are relaxed and already groping around.

8. Her parents will probably name her Claudia.
9. They are both ecstatic over their first child.

10. This smiling baby seems almost too happy.
11. She is so new to the world.
12. She doesn't at all resemble most newborns.
13. Most newborns' faces are knotted in a frightened grimace.
14. Their bodies are tense and struggling.
15. They seem to be on guard.
16. They are like boxers.
17. The boxers defend themselves.

18. Lately, more and more of these happy babies have been born.
19. They have been born in Europe.
20. They have also been born in America.

21. Dr. Frederick Leboyer is responsible for this new phenomenon.
22. Dr. Leboyer is a French obstetrician.

23. Dr. Leboyer has revolutionized delivery room procedure.
24. He is author of *Birth Without Violence.*
25. It is a beautifully poetic book about childbirth.
26. He advocates a homey approach to childbirth.
27. His approach is simpler.
28. His approach is quieter.
29. His approach is better.

30. Many traditional physicians express doubts about the Leboyer system.
31. All results indicate that we can bear happier babies.
32. The babies stand a better chance of staying happy throughout their lives.
33. This is done by reducing much unnecessary trauma.

34. The Leboyer method is all about delivering happy babies.

35. Leboyer's mother spent 30 hours in childbirth with him.
36. Leboyer witnessed thousands of deliveries during his career.

37. He began to feel serious doubts about needless pain and trauma.
38. Modern medicine inflicts the pain and trauma upon the infant.

39. Traditional practice has always emphasized reducing the mother's pain.
40. It considers only the baby's immediate physical safety.

41. Lamaze is another French doctor.
42. He also has a new theory.
43. His theory reduces the mother's pain.

44. Leboyer claims that standard techniques hurt the baby.
45. The techniques hurt the baby with physical "birth marks."
46. The marks are left by the instruments.
47. They also hurt the baby with psychological scars.
48. These scars are not so obvious, at first.

49. Leboyer maintains that the delivery rooms foster aggression and violence in the baby.
50. The rooms have cold, glaring lights.
51. They have sounds.
52. The sounds may be shouts of instruction.
53. They may be shouts of encouragement.
54. The baby is still defenseless against such onslaughts.

55. Dr. Leboyer wants to deliver a smiling baby.
56. He doesn't want to deliver a crying baby.

57. Most people like smiles.
58. These babies start to please others as soon as they are born.

59. He turns traditional methods topsy-turvey.
60. He does that to deliver smiling babies.

61. His method is simple.
62. It is safe.

63. According to people, it is beautiful.
64. The people have witnessed a Leboyer birth.

65. The traditional delivery room is flooded with blazing lights.
66. The lights reflect off every possible surface.
67. The room is also flooded with grating noises.
68. The noises are from clinking instruments and squeaky carts.
69. They are also from noisy people.
70. Leboyer delivers in a darkened room.
71. There are soft moans.
72. There are soothing whispers.
73. There is gentle music.
74. These are the only sounds.

75. Standard deliveries subject the baby to spine-jerking dangling.
76. They subject the baby to upside-down dangling.
77. Immediate cutting of the umbilical cord follows the dangling.
78. A rush of oxygen follows the dangling.
79. A sharp slap triggers the rush of oxygen.

80. Leboyer gently lifts the baby.
81. He rests it on the mother's stomach.
82. On the mother's stomach the baby is gradually exposed to the new world.
83. It still feels warmth.
84. The warmth is from the mother's body.

85. After a few minutes the cord is cut.
86. The baby is lovingly massaged to induce breathing.
87. It is not spanked.
88. This is done unless some problem demands earlier care.
89. Leboyer always proceeds in a manner.
90. The manner is necessary for the baby's safety.

91. The baby is then treated to a bath.
92. The bath is in comforting lukewarm water.

93. Leboyer emphasizes the slow emergence of a new human being.
94. He emphasizes the delicate emergence of a new human being.
95. He emphasizes the loving emergence of a new human being.
96. The human being is usually smiling within minutes after birth.

97. It's all so simple.

98. Leboyer gears his method.
99. He reduces the jolt of being transferred from a womb to a world.
100. The womb is warm.
101. It is secure.
102. The world must frighten the newborn.
103. The world is intense.

104. In fact, Leboyer tries to re-create the womb environment.
105. He tries to minimize the shock of transition.
106. He does this with near darkness.
107. He does it with hushed sounds.
108. He does it with massages.
109. He does it with warm baths.

110. According to Leboyer, his approach results in a baby.
111. The baby is healthier physically.
112. The baby is healthier psychologically.

113. Traditional doctors have raised objections.
114. The objections are apparently more out of reaction to something new.
115. They are not from legitimate grounds.
116. The only real proof will come when Leboyer's babies grow up.

117. For right now, who can deny that a loving, careful entry into life is better.
118. It is better than one filled with bright lights.
119. It is better than one filled with harsh sounds.
120. It is better than one filled with a spanking to boot.

PART TWO

STRATEGIES

12. Rearrangement

By changing the order of words within sentences, you can adapt your writing to different situations. Just as the skilled orator sometimes speaks loudly and sometimes whispers, at one moment pounds the podium and at another stands motionless, you can make your writing more forceful by occasionally rearranging the normal word order of sentences.

There are two basic facts about sentence order. The first is that the sentence has naturally emphatic positions: the end of the sentence is the most emphatic position; the beginning of the sentence is next in emphasis; and the middle of the sentence is least emphatic. From this principle it follows that the most important words in a sentence should usually be positioned at its beginning or end, its least important words toward the middle. The second basic fact is that word order in English is relatively fixed. For this reason, most English sentences follow a pattern of subject-verb-object (or complement), and many sentence elements cannot be moved without either causing confusion or radically changing meaning. Given these conditions, even slight rearrangements of the normal word order are powerful ways of achieving sentence variety, of emphasizing important points, and of producing interesting effects.

In earlier units you worked with modifiers like participles and absolutes that can be moved from one position in a sentence to another. The sentence part that moves most freely is the adverb, a word or phrase that answers the question how, where, when, or how often. An adverb normally occurs just before or just after the word it modifies. An adverb shifted elsewhere in the sentence becomes more emphatic because, out of its normal position, it calls more attention to itself. Here is a sentence with the adverb in its normal position:

The rescue team **reluctantly** discontinued the operation.

If you choose to make **reluctantly** more important, move it to either the emphatic beginning or end position:

Reluctantly, the rescue team discontinued the operation.

OR

The rescue team discontinued the operation **reluctantly.**

Though adverbs can move with relative freedom, sometimes moving an adverb will produce awkwardness. Notice what happens if, to emphasize the phrase **too often,** in

American helicopters **too often** stray into North Korea.

you move it to the end of the sentence:

American helicopters stray into North Korea **too often.**

Whatever emphasis the adverb phrase might have gained from being in the final position is lost because of the resulting awkwardness of the sentence. The most emphatic position for **too often** is at the sentence beginning, where it gains power because the reader must stop at the comma:

Too often, American helicopters stray into North Korea.

Adverbs are rearranged not only to shift sentence emphasis but also to help connect one sentence to another. Consider the placement of the phrase **with military precision** in the following passage:

> The robbery was accomplished swiftly and neatly. The bank robbers divided into two squads **with military precision,** one standing guard over the tellers and patrons, the other moving into the vault.

Because the phrase **with military precision** in the second sentence makes more specific the adverbs **swiftly** and **neatly** in the first, moving the phrase next to those adverbs is an effective way of smoothly linking the two sentences:

> The robbery was accomplished swiftly and neatly. **With military precision,** the robbers divided into two squads, one standing guard over the tellers and patrons, the other moving into the vault.

Now see if you can improve the following sentence by moving the phrase **in the laboratories of the University of Chicago** to a different position:

> Research on the atomic bomb proceeded quietly **in the laboratories of the University of Chicago**—unknown to all but the highest level military and government officials.

You can shift the phrase to the beginning of the sentence:

> **In the laboratories of the University of Chicago,** research on the atomic bomb proceeded quietly—unknown to all but the highest level military and government officials.

This version improves upon the original because the phrase "unknown to all but the highest level military and government officials" now immediately follows the words it most closely modifies—"proceeded quietly."

It is sometimes useful to rearrange other sentence parts when you shift adverbs. Suppose you wanted to make the next sentence more forceful:

> The sound of shots came after midnight.

Moving **after midnight** to the beginning makes the sentence somewhat awkward because emphasis now falls on **came,** a relatively colorless word:

> After midnight the sound of shots came.

But if you move both **after midnight** and the verb **came** to the sentence beginning, the result is highly effective:

> After midnight came the sound of shots.

You have made the subject of the sentence, **the sound of shots,** more dramatic, both by placing it in the naturally emphatic end position and by reversing the normal subject-verb word order.

When reversing subject-verb order to achieve special emphasis, be sure that your sentence begins with an introductory phrase and that its subject is important enough to deserve such emphasis:

> From the wreckage **drifts the odor** of burned human flesh.

> Out of the lagoon and toward the village **crept the prehistoric creature** that for eons had slept undisturbed in ooze and slime.

> Following the sheriff's arrival **came the announcement** we all dreaded—little Sarah had not been found.

There are four special patterns of rearrangement that require adding words or phrases, not simply moving them. The first pattern makes use of **what** and a form of the verb **to be.** Imagine that you're writing an essay on the Soviet press, more specifically on what items are characteristically excluded from Soviet newspapers. Remembering that the end of a sentence normally gets the greatest emphasis, you carefully construct your thesis statement:

> Soviet newspapers never report Russian military production.

If you decide that the phrase **Russian military production** demands even more emphasis, you have the option of adding **what** and **is** to your sentence:

> **What** Soviet newspapers never report **is** Russian military production.

The use of **what** along with **is, are, was,** or **were** is especially effective for establishing contrasts between one sentence and the next. The contrast between the following two sentences is not particularly forceful:

> After the last guest left the party, the house seemed unnaturally quiet. The argument when our parents came home was not so quiet.

But the contrast can be made more striking with the addition of **what was:**

> After the last guest left the party, the house seemed unnaturally quiet. **What was** not so quiet was the argument when our parents came home.

The second special pattern of rearrangement, equally appropriate for emphasizing important points, involves the addition **it is** or **it was** along with **who** or **that.** If you were writing a press release for a congresswoman who had received more applause than any other convention speaker, the following sentence might not sound strong enough:

> Congresswoman Jordan received the largest ovation.

But the insertion of **it was** . . . **who** makes it more powerful:

> **It was** Congresswoman Jordan **who** received the largest ovation.

In the same way, inserting **it is** . . . **that** into the next sentence turns a simple comment into an assertion:

The full-size grand piano gives the room its charm.

↓

It is the full-size grand piano **that** gives the room its charm.

The third special rearrangement pattern makes use of the addition **there is** or **there are** along with **who** or **that,** again for the purpose of emphasis:

Few lawyers or physicians will testify against a colleague.

↓

There are few lawyers or physicians **who** will testify against a colleague.

This pattern is particularly helpful for strengthening a contrast:

The oil deposits in the Persian Gulf are vast, but a more extensive energy source lies beneath the grasslands of the American Great Plains.

↓

The oil deposits in the Persian Gulf are vast, but **there is** a more extensive energy source **that** lies beneath the grasslands of the American Great Plains.

The last special rearrangement pattern, called the PASSIVE, is probably the most common, most useful, and most misused of all rearrangements. To construct a passive, move the subject noun to the end of the sentence, add a word like **is, are, was, were,** or **been** before the verb, and insert the word **by** after the verb. Here are some examples of active sentences rearranged into passives:

Seventeen varieties of penguins inhabit the Antarctic.

↓

The Antarctic **is** inhabited **by** 17 varieties of penguins.

Since 1973 a regime which jails and tortures its opponents has governed Chile.

↓

Since 1973 Chile has **been** governed **by** a regime which jails and tortures its opponents.

AT&T, the American Telephone and Telegraph Company, dominates the telephone industry in the United States.

↓

The telephone industry in the United States **is** dominated **by** AT&T, the American Telephone and Telegraph Company.

Like all rearrangements, the passive should be used sparingly, in part because it is usually longer, more impersonal, and less forceful than the active version. But don't be afraid to construct a passive whenever it achieves the emphasis you want, allows a smooth transition from the previous sentence, or makes your writing less awkward. In the next sentence the passive eliminates the awkwardness caused by a long subject before a relatively short predicate:

Despair over the war in Vietnam, a growing concern for civil rights, distrust of the Nixon administration, and a general disillusionment with the government's ability to cope with · problems caused the unrest in the late sixties.

↓

The unrest in the late sixties **was** caused **by** despair over the war in Vietnam, growing concern for civil rights, distrust of the Nixon administration, and general disillusionment with the government's ability to cope with problems.

The **by**-phrase of the passive construction can sometimes be shifted within the sentence to produce interesting results:

Albert Einstein **is** called the greatest mind of the twentieth century **by those who know his work best.**

By those who know his work best, Albert Einstein **is** called the greatest mind of the twentieth century.

The **by**-phrase can be eliminated when it merely repeats information contained elsewhere in the paragraph or when its information is unimportant. If the sentence about Einstein were in a paragraph which made it clear that the comment was made by those who know his work best, the **by**-phrase would be unnecessary:

> Albert Einstein is called the greatest mind of the twentieth century.

In the next example, the phrase **by astronomers** can be dropped because it states an obvious fact:

> Quasars, sources of energy in space, **were** first discovered **by astronomers** in 1960.

$$\downarrow$$

> Quasars, sources of energy in space, **were** first discovered in 1960.

Since rearrangements always violate normal sentence order, make sure your own rearrangements are justified by a need for variety, for smooth transition, for removing awkwardness, or for emphasis.

Basic Pattern Exercise

Rearrange each sentence below as indicated by the example introducing each series.

Example I

International economics has become too complex for any single theory to explain or for any single government to control since World War II. (Adverb movement)

↓

Since World War II, international economics has become too complex for any single theory to explain or for any single government to control.

OR

International economics **since World War II** has become too complex for any single theory to explain or for any single government to control.

A. The Senate took a final vote on the measure to eliminate discrimination in mortgage lending yesterday.

B. Police kept their bargain in the aftermath of the raid to release the terrorist leader without bail, a move that prompted some criticism.

C. A dancer leaps out of the blackness into the stark, bright circle of light, a storm of energy caught in black tights and greasepaint.

Example II

Queen Elizabeth, the daughter of Henry VIII, finally brought England into the Renaissance and led it to greatness as a merchant power. (It was . . . who)

↓

It was Queen Elizabeth, the daughter of Henry VIII, **who** finally brought England into the Renaissance and led it to greatness as a merchant power.

D. The passion of Haley's narrative and its wealth of new material make *Roots* an event of social importance.

E. President Kennedy's 1961 White House Conference on Aging first focused the nation's attention on the concerns of old people.

F. Jerry Kapstein negotiated the athlete's eye-popping movie deal that pays $3,000,000 for a six-picture contract.

Example III

She wanted more than anything to leave the Midwest and go to New York, the Big Apple.
(What . . . was)

↓

What she wanted more than anything **was** to leave the Midwest and go to New York, the Big Apple.

G. Alfred Nobel hoped to be remembered for his peace prize, not for his invention of dynamite.

H. The scientists were trying to say that limiting possession of the atomic bomb to a few countries was impossible.

I. Olivier shows the audience that a great actor turns his body into a force to jolt the viewer into a higher consciousness.

Example IV

No book published in France sells more copies than the *Guide Michelin,* which rates restaurants according to the quality of their cuisine and service. (There is)

↓

There is no book published in France **that** sells more copies than the *Guide Michelin,* which rates restaurants according to the quality of their cuisine and service.

J. Little about Woody Allen's appearance connects him to the glamorous world of show business.

K. An important key to understanding Amin's erratic behavior is buried deep in his early personal relationships.

L. Millions of Americans retain strong religious ties in an age when religion is thought to be waning.

Example V

Men of sounder limb than Namath best play the game. (Passive)

The game **is** best played **by** men of sounder limb than Namath.

M. Sightings of a giant seal swimming near shore prompted the initial "sea monster" reports.

N. An administration and Congress unprecedented in their regard for the arts back up Carter.

O. Air travel doomed Europe's luxury sleeping car express trains, the victims of progress and of the lust for speed.

Sentence Combining Exercise

Combine the following sentences into an effective essay. Use several patterns of rearrangement.

TO TELL THE TRUTH

1. The middle-aged American couple was enjoying a vacation.
2. The vacation was in an ancient Mayan city.

3. They were tired of the sightseeing group.
4. They broke away to do some exploring.
5. They explored on their own.

6. They climbed a pyramid.
7. Its stepping stones were overgrown with weeds.
8. They wanted to reach one of the ledges.

9. The woman screamed suddenly.
10. And her husband fell over.
11. He was grasping his chest.

12. The two tumbled down to the horrified group below.
13. Their arms and legs were flailing.

14. What happened to the couple?
15. It is becoming more common.
16. At the same time the ruins develop into tourist attractions.

17. About 50 tourists a year fall from the ledges.
18. Or about 50 tourists a year panic.
19. And they have to be carried down.

20. This has led to fanciful conjecture.
21. The conjecture is about the origin of the ledges.
22. The conjecture is about this.
23. Why do people regularly fall from the pyramids?

24. Some Americans and Europeans claim this.
25. The ledges were built by ancient astronauts.
26. They used them to anchor their spaceships.
27. The pyramids continue to rock and sway.
28. They rock and sway as if they were still attached to interplanetary vessels.

29. The natives of the area blame the accidents on an ancient curse.
30. The curse was placed on the pyramids by the Mayans.
31. The curse protected the hoards of gold.
32. They had hidden the hoards of gold in the pyramids.

33. Mexican scholars have recently revealed the truth.
34. The truth is about the origin of the ledges.

35. It seems this.
36. The Mayans practiced human sacrifice.
37. It was part of their religion.

38. The practice developed.
39. The Mayan population outgrew the protein supply.
40. The protein supply was in the area.

41. The sacrifices became the means.
42. The means brought the population into harmony.
43. The harmony was with the natural resources.
44. The means added to the food supply.

45. The priests stood on the ledges.
46. The priests removed the hearts of their victims.
47. Then the priests threw the bodies down the steep sides of the pyramids.
48. The priests threw the bodies to the hungry masses below.
49. The hungry masses below practiced cannibalism.

50. The Mexican government explains the reason.
51. Why do the tourists fall with such regularity from those ledges?

52. It blames the tourists themselves.
53. The tourists are not used to heights.
54. The tourists develop vertigo or acrophobia on the steep-sided pyramids.
55. Vertigo is a dizzy sensation.
56. Acrophobia is a fear of heights.

57. The truth may be stranger than fiction.
58. But it is less romantic.
59. At least in this case it is less romantic.

60. Curses are nice fictions.
61. Hoards of gold are nice fictions.
62. Ancient astronauts are nice fictions.

Sentences in Context

In each of the following paragraphs, rearrange one of the sentences according to the instructions in order to emphasize an important point, to sharpen paragraph focus or to make a smooth transition.

Example

> At the beginning of the twentieth century, America yearned to be a global power, which in those days meant having a large navy. But the American Navy was divided into two fleets, one on the East Coast, one on the West. The completion of the Panama Canal in 1914 allowed the nation to fulfill its dream. By linking the two oceans, the canal made the separate fleets one great navy. (It was . . . that)

> At the beginning of the twentieth century, America yearned to be a global power, which in those days meant having a large navy. But the American Navy was divided into two fleets, one on the East Coast, one on the West. **It was** the completion of the Panama Canal in 1914 **that** allowed the nation to fulfill its dream. By linking the two oceans, the canal made the separate fleets one great navy.

A. Elias Howe is given credit for inventing the sewing machine. But Isaac Singer made it the most popular machine in history. With his partner, Edward Clark, Singer developed the marketing techniques of installment buying and trade-ins. He also overcame the nineteenth-century prejudice that allowing women to operate machines violated the laws of nature. (It was . . . who)

B. Sometimes changes in the meaning of words have produced interesting changes in the meanings of popular expressions. For instance, it is clearly not true that "the exception proves the rule." Exceptions disprove rules. The expression made sense because the word *prove* meant "test" originally. And exceptions do test rules. (Adverb movement)

C. To some, the number of people on welfare is shocking. They complain that welfare recipients are lazy and don't want to work. They don't know that only 3 percent of those on welfare are able to hold a job. The rest are young children, mothers trying to care for them, and those with severe health problems. (What . . . is)

D. The women's liberation movement has succeeded in eliminating barriers that once kept women out of the professions. But one barrier still keeps noncollege-educated women from equal status in the labor force—the "pink collar" barrier. Seven out of eight working women are employed at jobs that have little status and almost no chance for advancement, pink collar jobs like waitress, secretary, and salesclerk. (There is)

E. Several utopian communities thrived for short periods in nineteenth-century America. One was New Harmony, Indiana. A group of religious zealots who formed a commune to await the Second Coming founded it. They were hardworking farmers and craftsmen doomed to a brief existence as a community because of their celibate life style. (Passive)

Sentence Combining Exercise

Combine the following sentences into an effective essay. Use several patterns of rearrangement.

WORDS AND THINGS

1. A language is like a system.
2. The system is biological.
3. Its various parts are adapting to new situations.
4. They adapt constantly.

5. Words are the part of the system to study.
6. The part is the most interesting.

7. They are the amoeba of language.
8. They are forming.
9. They are dying.
10. They are splitting up into parts.

11. Some were the names of people originally.
12. Some are like *sandwich.*

13. The Earl of Sandwich didn't like to interrupt his gambling with meals.
14. So he had his servants slap some meat between two slices of bread.
15. It was a snack at the gaming table.
16. The snack was handy.

17. Thus the earl became immortal.

18. *Hamburger* took its name from the city.
19. The city made it famous originally.
20. The city was Hamburg, Germany.
21. Hamburger is the world's most famous sandwich.

22. It is never called a sandwich anymore.

23. In fact, the *burger* part of the word means any kind of meat.
24. The meat is ground.
25. The meat is in a bun.

26. So we are inundated with *beefburgers.*
27. We are inundated with *vealburgers.*
28. We are inundated with *steakburgers.*
29. We are inundated with *doubleburgers.*
30. We are inundated with *cheeseburgers.*
31. We are inundated with *pizzaburgers.*
32. The latter is not a ground-up pizza.
33. But it is a meat patty.
34. The meat patty has cheese and pizza sauce on it.

35. Ground beef isn't a *burger* anymore.
36. The ground beef is in tomato sauce.
37. But it is a *Manwich.*
38. A *Manwich* isn't a *sandwich.*
39. But it is a meal.
40. Or so one manufacturer of tomato sauce would have us believe.

41. Most words go further back into history than *hamburger*.
42. Most words go further back into history than *sandwich*.

43. The Indo Europeans are the ancestors of most of the European languages.
44. And the Indo Europeans are the ancestors of some languages in India and the Middle East.
45. The Indo Europeans were a group of people.
46. The Indo Europeans lived about six thousand years ago.
47. The Indo Europeans lived about where present-day Lithuania is.

48. Ultimately, most of the words come from Indo European.
49. The words are in our language.

50. These words have histories.
51. The words come from Indo European.
52. The histories are the longest.
53. And the histories are the most interesting.

54. For instance, the Indo-European *bhreu* became *brew* in Old English.
55. *Bhreu* meant to boil, bubble, or burn.
56. And *bhreu* became *bread*.
57. Possibly it became *bread* because the yeast in bread dough bubbles.

58. In French, it became *broth*.
59. *Broth* is a word the English borrowed for a warm *brew*.

60. And it took another turn to *brood*.
61. *Brood* means keeping offspring warm, as a chicken might.

62. The same Indo-European word also occurs in *fervent*.
63. *Fervent* is heated up over something.

64. The Indo-European word for salmon was *laks*.
65. Salmon is a fish.
66. The fish was abundant in northern European rivers.

67. The branch of the family had no more use for the word.
68. The branch of the family moved into India.
69. But they gave it to a resin.
70. The resin was salmon colored.
71. They found the resin in trees.

72. The English borrowed it back thousands of years later.
73. The English borrowed it back as *lacquer* and *shellac*.

74. Of course, you may live in a big city.
75. Then you're probably familiar with the salmon in delicatessens.
76. The salmon is smoked.
77. The salmon is *lox.*
78. *Lox* is the original *laks* borrowed from the northern European Jews.

79. It's hard to speak of *lox* without *bagel.*
80. *Bagel* comes from the Indo European *bheug.*
81. *Bheug* was a bent, curved, or swollen object.

82. *Bheug* also spawned the Old English *boga.*
83. *Boga* became *bow,* and *bow,* and *buxom.*
84. *Bow* is a curved arch.
85. *Bow* is to bend.
86. *Buxom* is swollen.

87. After all, the *bagel* is a round roll.
88. The *bagel* is a swollen roll.

89. That is, the *bagel* is a *bread.*
90. The *bread* is *buxom.*
91. The *bread* is eaten *fervently* as a *sandwich* with *lox.*

Judging Sentences

Choose from each set of four sentences below the one you find most effective in context. If you find two or more sentences equally acceptable, try to justify that judgment. If you don't like any of the four sentences, create a better version of your own.

A. Herbert Hoover, with his hands-off government policy, was unable to solve the problems of the Great Depression.
   1. It was Franklin Roosevelt who finally put the nation back on its feet with a series of government-sponsored projects.
   2. Franklin Roosevelt finally put the nation back on its feet with a series of government-sponsored projects.
   3. The nation was finally put back on its feet by Franklin Roosevelt with a series of government-sponsored projects.
   4. What Franklin Roosevelt finally did was put the nation back on its feet with a series of government-sponsored projects.
Roosevelt took men out of the soup kitchens and put them to work clearing forests and building bridges, schools, and hospitals.

B. One hundred years ago, you needed guts, determination, and some luck to get ahead in the world.
   1. A college education wasn't needed by you.
   2. You didn't need a college education.
   3. What you didn't need was a college education.
   4. It wasn't a college education that you needed.
It might even have gotten in the way, since there were few jobs for the highly trained and well educated.

C. In order to capture larger shares of the audience, many local TV stations have switched to the "Eyewitness News" format.
   1. On-the-scene reporting, informal atmosphere in the studio, expensive and elaborate sets, and good-looking young newsreaders characterize it.
   2. It is on-the-scene reporting, informal atmosphere in the studio, expensive and elaborate sets, and good-looking young newsreaders that characterize it.
   3. It is characterized by on-the-scene reporting, informal atmosphere in the studio, expensive and elaborate sets, and good-looking young newsreaders.
   4. What characterizes it is on-the-scene reporting, informal atmosphere in the studio, expensive and elaborate sets, and good-looking young newsreaders.

D. People can no longer take comfort in the knowledge that only they can communicate with language.

1. Linguists have also taught chimpanzees and gorillas to use sign language.
2. Chimpanzees and gorillas have also been taught to use sign language.
3. There are also chimpanzees and gorillas that have been taught to use sign language.
4. There have also been linguists who have taught chimpanzees and gorillas to use sign language.

One gorilla named Koko knows more than 300 words and has almost as much linguistic ability as a human child.

E. Paul McCartney abandoned art for commercialism. When he wrote for the Beatles, his work was powerful and innovative.
   1. It is harmless pap designed to sell records now.
   2. Now it is harmless pap designed to sell records.
   3. It is now harmless pap designed to sell records.
   4. It now is harmless pap designed to sell records.

Sentence Combining Exercise

Write an effective essay by (1) combining the following sentences into paragraphs and (2) concluding the essay with a final paragraph of your own. Emphasize the main point of your conclusion in a sentence that uses a special rearrangement pattern.

BUYING A STEREO SET

1. The faces of receivers, tuners, and amplifiers peer out of the shadowy recesses of the shelves.
2. The shelves line one wall of the stereo shop.
3. The dials and meters of the receivers, tuners, and amplifiers are shining mysteries.

4. Turntables fill more shelves.
5. And speakers stand in rows along the walls.
6. The speakers are shining monsters.
7. Their grills are a patchwork of colors.
8. And their grills are a patchwork of designs.

9. Stereo buyers are usually baffled.
10. And stereo buyers are sometimes frightened.
11. Stereo buyers are novices.
12. Stereo buyers are faced with such an array of equipment.
13. The equipment competes for their attention.
14. And stereo buyers are faced with terms.
15. The terms differentiate between the components.
16. The terms are like impedence, hertz, wow, flutter, and decibels.

17. But stereo shopping need not be an excursion through a wonderland.
18. The wonderland is mysterious.
19. The wonderland is electronic.

20. The average stereo enthusiast becomes familiar with a few simple principles.
21. The stereo enthusiast knows little about acoustics.
22. The stereo enthusiast knows little about electronics.
23. Then the stereo enthusiast can get good equipment for a small investment.

24. Choose your speakers first.
25. Whether you have a little money to spend.
26. Or whether you have a lot of money to spend.

27. A speaker system really determines the quality of your set.
28. And a speaker system really determines the cost of your set.

29. Choose your speakers according to your own listening preferences.

30. Some speaker systems reproduce jazz better than country.
31. Or some speaker systems reproduce classical better than hard rock.

32. So go down to the stereo shop with your favorite album.

33. And have the saleman play it through different speaker systems while you listen carefully.
34. You listen to this.
35. Do individual instruments come though crisp and sharp?

36. You can look for a power source once you've chosen a set of speakers.
37. The speakers suit your own listening requirements.
38. The power source is either a separate amplifier or a receiver.
39. The receiver is a combination of an amplifier and an FM tuner.

40. A receiver is fine for people.
41. The people enjoy radio listening.
42. But suppose you listen to records primarily.
43. Then an amplifier is a better buy.

44. You can add an FM tuner later.
45. You can add an FM tuner as your money allows.

46. Buy enough power to operate your speakers.
47. Operate your speakers at the level of loudness.
48. The loudness suits your taste.

49. The most common and costly mistake is to buy too much power.
50. The mistake is made by stereo novices.

51. Only you know how loud you like your music.
52. But remember this.
53. Most rooms require only low to medium power.
54. Low to medium power fills them with sound.

55. You've matched a power source to your speakers.
56. Then you can pick a turntable.
57. A turntable is the least crucial of the components.

58. Suppose you care for your records.
59. And suppose you like music more than scratches.

60. Then stay away from a record-changer turntable.
61. A record-changer turntable stacks several records at once.

62. A manual turntable may necessitate this.
63. You will get up to change records.
64. But complex turntables need repairs more frequently.
65. Complex turntables perform many functions.
66. Complex turntables cost more initially.

67. The best advice is this.
68. Keep it simple.

13. Repetition

Advertisers have long known that repetition helps to sell services and products. In advertising copy, words and sounds are often deliberately repeated to drive home a message to potential buyers. Eastern Airlines claims that "you don't have to take **charter** flights to get **charter** prices," and Delta promises that "every **nonstop** to Florida is a **nonstop** party." According to TWA, "being the best isn't the only **thing.** It's every**thing.**" *Mademoiselle* advertises its publication as "the magazine more **select** women **select,**" just as a manufacturer of peanut butter asserts that "**choosy** mothers **choose** Jif." Not to be outdone, Kahns bills its hot dog as "the **w**iener the **w**orld a**w**aited."

    Another form of repetition, equally popular with advertisers, does not involve single words or sounds but groups of words—phrases, clauses, even full sentences. What is repeated, in most cases, is the structure and rhythmic pattern of the entire word group. For example, a New York hotel tries to attract tourists with this slogan: "Long after you've forgotten the time, you'll remember the place." If you read the slogan aloud, you'll hear that the clause

you've forgotten the time corresponds in rhythm and structure to **you'll remember the place.** The correspondence is created by repeating some words (**you** and **the**) and by choosing others that are alike in rhythm and function: **forgotten** and **remember** are both three-syllable verbs; **time** and **place** are both one-syllable nouns. When a sentence or paragraph includes two or more elements similar in rhythmic pattern, and usually in grammatical function as well, the created effect is called BALANCE. Here are three short sentences with balanced elements:

> Don't let **a good ad** send you on **a bad trip.**
>
> Gospel music **is good news in bad times.**
>
> Othello is a board game that takes only **a minute to learn** but **a lifetime to master.**

A good ad and **a bad trip, is good news** and **in bad times, a minute to learn** and **a lifetime to master**—these balanced phrases function both to reinforce a contrast and to create distinctive rhythms.

Advertisers use balanced sentences because their repeated elements make the ads easy to remember. The travel agency that chose the balanced "Don't let a good ad send you on a bad trip" would surely have rejected the unbalanced "Don't let a good brochure send you on a vacation you won't enjoy." In the same way, "Gospel music is good news in bad times" loses its punch, along with its balance, when rephrased as "Gospel music is good news when you're feeling bad." Deprived of balanced phrases, the Othello slogan also loses much of its appeal: "Othello is a board game that takes only a minute to learn, but to master it requires a lifetime." Now listen to the balanced phrases of a Rolls Royce advertisement: "The Silver Shadow II is a new air of comfort, a new sense of quiet, and a new feeling of command." The repeated pattern **a new** . . . **of** . . . gives the sentence the same luxury, ease, and controlled power that the Rolls itself presumably offers.

Some advertisers make even more extensive use of repetition by repeating key words from one clause to the next and at the same time reversing word order to achieve an interesting rhythmic effect. For example, a tobacco company claims that "You can take Salem out of the country, but you can't take the country out of Salem." The makers of a chocolate liqueur tell us that "Vandermint isn't

good because it's imported; it's imported because it's good." And
the distributors of Teachers scotch whiskey use in their advertising
slogan both balanced phrases and key words repeated in reverse
order: "In life, experience is the best teacher. In scotch, Teachers is
the best experience."

The strategies of repetition appropriate to advertising copy
can work just as effectively in college writing to achieve emphasis,
to gain coherence, and to create rhythms which are forceful and
pleasing. Such strategies are useful on both the sentence and paragraph levels.

On the sentence level, repetition can help emphasize key
terms:

> The old man has **nothing** left, **nothing** except memories
> capable of filling volumes of books.

> Of the many **gray, faceless** bureaucracies in Washington,
> the Veterans Administration is probably the **grayest** and
> most **faceless** of them all.

> A director of the Central Intelligence Agency once said that
> his job in collecting information involved doing the in**de-
> cent** things as **decent**ly as possible.

As the sentence about the Central Intelligence Agency suggests,
repetition also works effectively to reinforce a contrast. Repeating
words and sound patterns is a way of inviting the reader's attention
to more important differences. In the following sentence, the contrast between the speaker's loafing and her friends' working is
strengthened by the repetition of **spent long, hot days** and by
the balanced phrases **on the job** and **in the sun:**

> While all my friends **spent long hot days** on the job, I
> **spent long, hot days** in the sun, soaking up a tan which
> made even the darkest-skinned girls envious.

Aside from achieving emphasis or reinforcing a contrast, repetition
can often turn two weak sentences into one that is more forceful:

> The struggle over energy policy will test the character of the
> American people. Whether the American nation is cohe-
> rent will also be tested by this struggle.

↓

> The struggle over energy policy will test the character of the American people and the coherence of the American nation.

The balanced phrases **the character of the American people** and **the coherence of the American nation** help make the second version more concise and more powerful than the first.

Strategies of repetition are equally useful and even more varied on the paragraph level. One such strategy involves beginning consecutive sentences with the same word or group of words. In the following paragraph, for example, the opening two sentences begin in the same way to reinforce a contrast between the children of the rich and the children of the poor:

> **If you are born into** an American family ranking in the top tenth of income, chances are one in three that you'll stay there. **If you are born into** a family in the bottom tenth, however, chances are less than one in 200 that you'll ever reach the top. So much for equality of opportunity.

In the next paragraph the middle three sentences all start with the same construction:

> If you don't vote, don't complain. **Never before** in history **have** American citizens held such power in their own hands. **Never before have** they had the opportunity to formulate such well-informed opinions. **Never before have** they been allowed such vigorous and unrestrained debate on the issues. Not to vote is to throw away your simplest and most effective means of political influence.

The repetition of **Never before have** lends both coherence and force to this brief paragraph. So does the repetition of **don't vote, don't complain** in the first sentence and of the infinitive phrases **Not to vote** and **to throw away** in the last. Obviously, there are choices of how much repetition to use. For instance, the third and fourth sentences of the paragraph about voting could have been constructed to repeat the longer phrase **Never before in history have American citizens:**

If you don't vote, don't complain. **Never before in history have American citizens** held such power in their own hands. **Never before in history have American citizens** had the opportunity to formulate such well-informed opinions. **Never before in history have American citizens** been allowed such vigorous and unrestrained debate on the issues. Not to vote is to throw away your simplest and most effective means of political influence.

Is this second version, with increased repetition, more effective than the first? Probably not, because its insistent repetition makes it seem overdone, even artificial and forced. Like any other writing strategy, repetition becomes ineffective when overused.

A second strategy of repetition within the paragraph involves repeating key elements of sentence structure from one sentence to the next. Read the next paragraph aloud to hear what is repeated:

There were many signs of summer that the gang and I looked for every year. The days and the mercury in our thermometer lengthened. Leaves and flowers appeared. Baseball season started, and school ended. All of these told us which season was approaching, but none was more dependable than Old Lady Murphy.

What is repeated here, and what makes the paragraph interesting, is the structure of the middle three sentences. Each of these short sentences, which include four clauses, not only follows the same subject-verb order but also consists of a one-word predicate— **lengthened, appeared, started,** and **ended.** Reread the paragraph aloud to hear how the repetition of similarly constructed sentences both contributes to paragraph coherence and creates a sense of cyclic movement that corresponds to the progress of the seasons.

Again, repetition can be overdone, as in this inferior version of the same paragraph:

There were many signs of summer that the gang and I looked for every year. The days lengthened. The mercury in our thermometer lengthened. Leaves appeared. Flowers appeared. Baseball season started. School ended. All of these

told us which season was approaching, but none was more
dependable than Old Lady Murphy.

Unfortunately, there are no infallible rules telling the writer when
some repetition becomes too much repetition. The best advice is to
trust your ears and to remember that good writing consists of repetition *and* variation.

Aside from repeating sentences that begin in the same way or
that follow similar structural patterns, you can repeat key words or
phrases at various places within the paragraph. Notice the different
kinds of repetition in the paragraph that follows:

> **Spinning, spinning,** the plastic plate twirls on the floor as
> the **beautiful** child sits mesmerized. Eyes crystal blue,
> hair braided to the waist, features clear and shapely, the
> little girl sits and watches—oblivious to the outside world.
> The plate continues to spin as a young woman enters the
> modern playroom and calls to her **beautiful** daughter.
> There is **no** reply, **no** eye contact, **no** body movement—
> this **beautiful** child is autistic.

This paragraph uses several kinds of repetition: the repeated
spinning of the first sentence to suggest the child's fascination
with the plate; the series of absolutes beginning the second
sentence; the repeated **no** of the last sentence to reinforce the
child's complete isolation; and, most importantly, the repeated
word **beautiful** to contrast the child's physical appearance with
her psychological condition.

A paragraph often gains impact when a key sentence, usually
its first or last, includes repeated elements. In the next paragraph,
the opening sentence—which is also the topic sentence—is
strengthened by the balanced phrases **your personal security**
and **your financial security:**

> In today's world, your personal security is largely your finan-
> cial security. A balanced checkbook and a savings account
> not only increase your future options but also protect your
> current life-style. Money makes it easier to live in a safe
> area, to have a nutritious diet, and to get a sound educa-
> tion. Although there is still no absolute protection from all

of life's hazards, wise financial planning can soften its harshest blows.

Aside from the balanced phrases of its opening sentence, this paragraph makes use of two additional strategies of repetition. First, it uses in its second sentence the paired coordinators **not only** . . . **but also** to call attention to a second set of balanced phrases— **increase your future options** and **protect your current life-style.** Paired coordinators like **both** . . . **and, either** . . . **or, neither** . . . **nor,** and **not** . . . **but** are especially suitable for introducing balanced constructions. Second, the paragraph includes a series, itself a form of repetition, with the preposition **to** repeated before each series item: **to** live in a safe area, **to** have a nutritious diet, and **to** get a sound education. Like paired coordinators and other strategies of repetition, repeated prepositions make your writing seem more tightly organized and more carefully constructed.

Look at the next paragraph to see if its weak concluding sentences can be improved through the use of repetition:

By the time American children reach adolescence, they have observed thousands of murders on television. Strangulations, decapitations, electrocutions, poisonings, stabbings, and simple shootings make up only part of the homicide catalog with which they become intimately familiar. Do you believe that children are immune to such constantly repeated violence? Then you are ignoring the most basic principles of developmental psychology.

One way of improving the paragraph conclusion is by combining the last two sentences with a repeated infinitive construction:

To believe that children are immune to such constantly repeated violence is **to ignore** the most basic principles of developmental psychology.

One of the more interesting—and risky—strategies of repetition involves rhyming words. Since rhyme is more appropriate to poetry than prose, it should be used sparingly and only to achieve effects not possible through the ordinary devices of prose. Despite these warnings, rhymed words can occasionally make good writing even better:

> After six years in Baltimore, my sister thought she had stumbled onto the ideal life when offered a job at a small university in Vermont. Vermont—the mere name evoked mystical and romantic thoughts. How wonderful to trade traffic jams for winding valley roads, skyscrapers for mountains, neon **lights** for star-filled **nights!**

The rhyming of **lights** and **nights** suggests something falsely romantic about the sister's hopes and tries to prepare the reader for her later disappointment. But the rhymes in the next paragraph do not suggest falseness so much as a rebellious spirit, an eagerness to violate the conventional standards of prose:

> Rock records are **made loud** to be **played loud.** The bass should make the floorboards **shake,** and the drums should make your bone marrow **quake.** The music means to taunt and seduce, to madden and liberate. It is a howling spirit, ill at ease in these spiritless times.

By rhyming **made loud** with **played loud** and **shake** with **quake,** the writer may be trying to communicate a sense of the taunting, maddening, and perhaps liberating spirit of rock music.

There are certain kinds of repetition that should generally be avoided. Except to create humor, it's sound practice not to repeat unimportant words, not to place words ending in -**ing** next to each other, and not to string together—except in a series—prepositional phrases beginning with the same preposition. Here are sentences that improve when their repeated elements are eliminated:

> Karen was a close friend of a girl I was dating and, unknown to **me,** she had a crush on **me.**
>
> ↓
>
> Karen was a close friend of a girl I was dating and, though I didn't know it, she had a crush on me.

> I swerved back and forth, send**ing** chill**ing** droplets fly**ing,** sting**ing** my arms and legs.
>
> ↓

As I swerved back and forth, chilling droplets stung my arms and legs.

The speaker was the chairperson **of** the Department **of** Physics **of** Tulane University.

↓

The speaker was the chairperson of Tulane University's Department of Physics.

I offered the tickets **to** the concert **to** the students **to** use on Saturday.

↓

I offered the students tickets to Saturday's concert.

One final strategy of repetition, called ELLIPSIS, uses and omits repeated elements within the same construction. For example, through ellipsis the sentence "Theodore Roosevelt was president from 1901 to 1909, and Franklin Roosevelt was president from 1933 to 1945" becomes the more concise statement "Theodore Roosevelt was president from 1901 to 1909, Franklin Roosevelt from 1933 to 1945." The words "was president" can be omitted because the structure of the second half of the sentence repeats that of the first. The following sentences lend themselves to ellipsis because, within a repeated structure, each includes words that can be omitted without loss of meaning:

Her hair is light brown, **and** her eyes **are** bluish-green.

↓

Her hair is light brown, her eyes bluish-green.

Some lawyers are arrogant, **and** some **lawyers are** simply reserved.

↓

Some lawyers are arrogant, some simply reserved.

One cold December morning Carter flew to Baghdad, Mondale **flew** to Tel Aviv, and Vance **flew** to Cairo.

↓

One cold December morning Carter flew to Baghdad, Mondale to Tel Aviv, and Vance to Cairo.

Like all strategies of repetition, ellipsis works particularly well in emphatic positions such as the end of a paragraph:

> One morning the valley's peace is interrupted by a rusty, grinding noise in the distance. Soon a yellow machine punctures the horizon to the east, then another, and another. The invasion continues for six months, and then the army retreats, leaving behind a deep, blackened gorge of mud and slime. Thanks to strip mining, the vegetation is gone, the soil ruined, the entire valley turned into waste.

Basic Pattern Exercise

Combine each of the groups of sentences below into a single sentence by using one or more of the strategies of repetition— ellipsis, repetition of key words, or balanced phrases.

Example
> **1.** For some students beer drinking has become a way of life.
> **2.** And other students drink beer in order to escape.

> Beer drinking has become a way of life for some students and a means of escape for others.

OR

> For some students beer drinking has become a way of life, for others a means of escape.

A. 1. Cincinnati is a city blessed with more than its share of good restaurants.
   2. Of smut, Cincinnati is blessed with less than its share.

B. 1. Women still don't get the recognition they deserve for their efforts.
   2. And for their crimes, the punishment they deserve is still not gotten by rapists.

C. 1. For some Catholics the injustice of celibacy is not just that priests cannot marry.
   2. But it is that married men can never become clergymen.

D. 1. The going gets tough.
   2. That's when people who are tough start moving.

E. 1. Oklahoma became a state in 1907.
   2. New Mexico became a state in 1912.

F. 1. The photographer does not create the beauty of a landscape.
   2. Even so, he controls how it will be remembered.

3. And, to some extent, how it will be interpreted later is controlled by him.

G. 1. To equalize economic opportunity, the Carnegie Council on Children recommends policies.
   2. The policies are fairly conventional in kind.
   3. But the policies are, in degree, fairly extreme.

H. 1. The 1976 presidential election forced voters to choose.
   2. One choice was an uncertain Democratic future.
   3. The other choice was a present with Republicans that was unsatisfactory.

I. 1. In historical terms, the 1976 election offered voters a choice.
   2. They could choose the possibility of another Franklin Roosevelt.
   3. Or they could choose a president who, certainly, would be like Calvin Coolidge.

J. 1. It is right, obviously right, that the Vietnam War should not be permitted to pass out of sight.
   2. It is correct to insist that its lessons are not yet learned.
   3. It is proper that its minutest details be recorded.

Sentence Combining Exercise

Combine the sentences below into a letter to the editor of a local newspaper. Argue persuasively for the abolition of capital punishment. Use at least one of the strategies of repetition in your letter.

CAPITAL PUNISHMENT: BARBARIC AND IRRATIONAL

To the Editor:

1. The death penalty is a barbarous punishment.
2. The death penalty is an archaic punishment.
3. The death penalty is inconsistent with modern justice.
4. Modern justice has complexities.

5. The death penalty reduces our laws to the tribal level of revenge.
6. Not only that, it rules out any chance for rehabilitation.

7. The death penalty forces the state.
8. The state must share the murderer's crime.
9. And the death penalty creates a legal mechanism.
10. If the mechanism is abused, it could put any citizen's life in jeopardy.

11. The death penalty is not a solution to the problem of homicide, finally.
12. A convicted murderer is executed.
13. It does not bring his victims back to life.

14. Proponents of capital punishment often argue.
15. They say we need a final penalty.
16. The final penalty will deter would-be murderers from killing.

17. There are studies, however.
18. One study was conducted by the University of Pennsylvania.
19. It was under the direction of Thorsten Sellin and Marvin Wolfgang.
20. These studies show that the fear of execution is not an actual deterrent to homicide.

21. States were compared with neighboring states.
22. This occurred in the University of Pennsylvania study.
23. States use the death penalty.
24. Neighboring states had outlawed the use of the death penalty.

25. Murder rates were compared.
26. The rates were in states with the death penalty.
27. The rates were in states without the death penalty.
28. No statistical difference in the frequency of murders could be found.

29. We are given such findings.
30. Why, then, is there still so heated a debate over capital punishment?

31. The answer may be this.
32. There is an urge for revenge.
33. It is deep within the human psyche.

34. People feel more and more helpless.
35. They are helpless in the face of rising crime rates.
36. Then they want to strike out.
37. They want to get even.
38. They want to find a simple solution.
39. They want to find a final solution.

40. It is unfortunate.
41. There are no simple answers.
42. There are complex problems.
43. And it is our duty.
44. We are rational human beings.
45. We must resist such appeals.
46. The appeals are irrational.

Sincerely,

Revising Exercise

Strengthen the last sentence of each of the five paragraphs below by using one or more of the strategies of repetition—ellipsis, repetition of key words, or balanced phrases.

Example

The central theme of the Frankenstein movies is that those who would attempt to create life will instead unleash the destructive forces of the universe. The films always open with the mad Dr. Frankenstein and his assistant in the unnatural act of robbing graves. Then, in a hidden laboratory, they fit together pieces of different corpses and create a monster not bound by the laws of nature. After terrorizing the populace, the monster is finally trapped and killed, and his master cap-

tured and punished. The story implicitly warns that to assume
the power of God is an invitation to nature's wrath.

↓

The story implicitly warns that any mortal who **assumes the
power of God invites the wrath of nature.**

OR

The story implicitly warns that **to assume the power of
God** is **to invite the wrath of nature.**

A. After political campaigns that last more than a year and that
   involve pie-eating and baby-kissing, speech-making and fund-
   raising, you might think that candidates could begin relaxing
   once the election results are in. Actually, the period between
   election and inauguration is difficult for winners and losers
   alike. The winners have more official problems than they can
   handle, and more regrets than they can bear have the losers.

B. We are so used to blaming modern industrial growth for the
   destruction of the natural environment that we sometimes over-
   look the damage done by less sophisticated means. Yet every
   year cattle and sheep farmers in nonindustrial societies turn
   nearly 17 million acres of land into desert by overgrazing. This
   process of "desertification" has destroyed three-fourths of the
   forestland in Argentina in 50 years and one-third of the arable
   land in western India in a single decade. Unchecked industrial
   growth may be polluting the air, but the land is being ravaged
   by herd management that is unscientific.

C. The microcomputer is the most recent addition to home electronic equipment. Resembling a typewriter with an attached TV
   screen, it can perform a wide range of tasks from providing
   children with electronic games to keeping up-to-date Christmas
   lists. With additional hardware, the microcomputer reports on
   water seepage, locks the doors at night, and lowers thermostats
   in unoccupied rooms. It may not be as helpful around the
   house as a maid, but manufacturers are betting that the microcomputer will become as fashionable as microwave ovens
   and, like pocket calculators, ubiquitous as well.

D. In 1948, South Carolina Senator Strom Thurmond ran for pres-
    ident on the ultraconservative States Rights' ticket, but in 1978,
    Senator Thurmond publicly identified himself with Edward
    Kennedy, an outspoken liberal. In 1968, Thurmond helped
    shape Richard Nixon's "Southern Strategy," which discounted
    black voters, but ten years later he helped get a South Carolina
    black appointed to the United States Court of Military Appeals.
    What apparently accounts for these changes is not that the
    Senator has abandoned his old political philosophy but that
    there is a new political reality he has recognized: fully 25 per-
    cent of South Carolina's registered voters are black.

E. Although scientists have long known of the close interrelation-
    ships in nature, they have only recently learned that the extinc-
    tion of an animal may cause the decline of a plant. On the
    island of Mauritius, best known as the last refuge of the bulky
    and flightless dodo bird, grow 13 beautiful and rare calvaria
    trees, each over 300 years old and dying. Not a single young
    calvaria has sprouted since the dodo became extinct three cen-
    turies ago, apparently because the thick-shelled calvaria seeds
    must be worn down in the digestive tract of the dodo before
    they can germinate. But help for the calvaria may be on its way.
    Since turkey gizzards contain stones for crushing food, much
    like those of the dodo, scientists are now experimenting to see
    whether the tree that declined with the loss of the dodo can,
    because of the help of the turkey, survive.

Sentence Combining Exercise

Combine the sentences below into a letter to the editor of a local
newspaper. Argue persuasively for the return of capital punishment. Use at least one of the strategies of repetition in your letter.

CAPITAL PUNISHMENT AND THE LIBERAL BREAST-BEATERS

To the Editor:

1. There is a current debate over capital punishment.
2. It has brought out the usual number of liberal
    breast-beaters.

3. It has brought out the usual number of teeth-gnashing liberals.
4. They are eager to whine about the poor little condemned criminal.

5. I agree with them in this.
6. The taking of human life is a serious matter.
7. At the same time I choose to reserve my tears for the innocent victim.
8. And for the victim's family my pity is reserved.

9. In fact, I feel that the taking of another person's life is serious.
10. Precisely because of this, I support the return of the death penalty.

11. The death penalty fits the crime.
12. The death penalty is the only punishment to do so.
13. And the death penalty is the only punishment strong enough to offer hope.
14. The hope is for the deterrence of future homicides.

15. Are you one of those people who have been impressed by the flurry of statistics?
16. The statistics are offered by the liberal camp.
17. If so, consider the following figures.

18. The murder rate increased 60 percent.
19. The increase occurred in New York City.
20. The increase occurred in the past six years.

21. Eighty percent of the murders in New York City were judged to be crimes of passion.
22. This was the case before the death penalty was abolished.
23. A crime of passion is one in which the killer and the victim know each other.
24. A crime of passion is one in which the murderer acts out of anger or some other strong emotion.

25. Only 50 percent of the murders in New York are crimes of passion.

26. This is the case now.

27. This is sadly ironic.
28. There are those who had an aim.
29. Their aim was in heightening the value of life.
30. The value of life would be heightened by abolishing the death penalty.
31. The very values they hold so dear have been cheapened, instead.

32. Any punk can murder.
33. This is the case now.
34. Punks who murder suffer only a minor inconvenience.
35. The minor inconvenience is a few years in prison.
36. At most it is a few years in prison.

37. There is a lack of risk.
38. It is this that lies at the bottom of our soaring homicide rates.

Sincerely,

Rewriting Exercise

In order to strengthen the following three paragraphs, rewrite them by using some of the strategies of repetition—repeated words, balanced phrases, and structures repeated from one sentence to the next.

Example

Chief Justice Warren E. Burger has become increasingly critical of the American lawyer. According to Burger, attorneys entangle the American populace in litigation and substitute legal manipulation for justice. Various federal agencies, commissions, and even Congress itself, where they hold more than 300 of the 535 seats, are dominated by barristers. Complex laws and obscure regulations are created by counselors-at-law who work in government and so business increases for attorneys whose work is outside of government. Above all, barristers flock to the big money of corporate law while 30 million poor Americans suffer from a counselor-at-law shortage. "The harsh truth," Burger told the American Bar Associa-

tion, "is that we may well be on our way to a society overrun
by hordes of lawyers, hungry as locusts."

↓

Chief Justice Warren E. Burger has become increasingly
critical of the American lawyer. According to Burger,
lawyers entangle the American populace in litigation and
substitute legal manipulation for justice. **Lawyers domi-
nate** various federal agencies, commissions, and even Congress itself, where they hold more than 300 of the 535 seats.
Lawyers who work in government **create** complex laws
and obscure regulations that increase business for lawyers
who work outside government. Above all, **lawyers flock** to
the big money of corporate law while 30 million poor Americans suffer from a lawyer shortage. "The harsh truth," Burger
told the American Bar Association, "is that we may well be on
our way to a society overrun by hordes of lawyers, hungry as
locusts."

A. According to comedian George Carlin, football is a ruthless,
warlike game, but baseball is a warm and pastoral game. Football, for example, is played on the gridiron, while baseball is a
game that takes place on a field. A defensive football player
tackles his opponent but, in baseball, an opponent is only tag-
ged by a defensive player. A violation in football draws a penalty, but a mistake is merely an error in baseball. A football
team can score on a bomb, but on a sacrifice a baseball team
can score. And, of course, the object of football is to reach the
end zone, while in baseball to run safely home is the idea.

B. Back in April of 1775, some 300 beaten British soldiers retreated 26 miles from Lexington and Concord to the safety of
their Boston barracks. As many as 3000 participants, every
April now for over 75 years, run from the Boston suburb of
Hopkinton to the city's fashionable Back Bay, a distance of 26
miles, to help commemorate the British defeat. The event is the
Boston Marathon. The winner's prize is a laurel wreath and a
bowl of beef stew.

C. He began planning it a year before he did it. First he started
saving his salary to pay for bail and lawyers' fees. Whatever he

could find about prison life he began reading next. His $25,000-a-year job with the United States Steel Corporation in Chicago he then quit, moving with all his belongings back to his family home in the San Francisco Bay Area. There, one by one, his three younger sisters were taken aside by him and told what he had done and what he was going to do. Then, after hiring a prominent criminal lawyer, Joseph Otto Egenberger surrendered himself to local police as the murderer, 14 years earlier, of a 20-year-old University of California sophomore.

Sentence Combining Exercise

Combine the sentences below into a persuasive essay. Make use of several strategies of repetition.

GRAVE RESERVATIONS

1. Imagine this.
2. People live in a tarpaper shack.
3. Or people live in a log cabin.
4. The shack or the cabin has only one small window.
5. A stovepipe is jutting out of the roof.
6. The roof is weighted down by old automobile tires.

7. Imagine this, too.
8. There is no electricity.
9. There is no running water.
10. Maybe there is not even an outhouse.
11. There are no less than six or seven people dwelling here.

12. This is a house on an Indian reservation in America to-day.
13. The house is typical.
14. The reservation is typical.
15. The reservation is impoverished.

16. Yet many Indians value their parcels of land.
17. Many Indians hold their parcels of land sacred.
18. The parcels are the last vestiges of a continent.
19. The Indians once freely roamed the continent.

20. It is for this reason.
21. Reservations should be preserved.
22. Reservations should be protected.
23. Any move should be suppressed.
24. The move would dissolve the reservations.
25. The move would force Indians into mainstream American culture.
26. Indians would be forced against their will.

27. The reservations' biggest problem is their poverty.
28. Many whites want to use poverty as an excuse.
29. The excuse is for abolishing the reservations.

30. This is true.
31. Indians are dependent on the federal government.
32. They depend on the government for housing.
33. They depend on the government for employment.
34. Sometimes they depend on the government for food.
35. Sometimes they depend on the government for clothing.

36. This is also true.
37. Infectious and communicable diseases are widespread among Indians.
38. In part, this is because of their flimsy shacks.
39. The flimsy shacks are often freezing in winter.
40. In summer, the flimsy shacks are often stifling.

41. This is equally true.
42. Large sums of money are spent on Indians by the Bureau of Indian Affairs.
43. In spite of this, the poverty never seems to go away.

44. Some people think the Indians should be driven off their reservations.
45. Some people think the Indians should be driven into white society.
46. Then the poverty would go away.
47. The people are mistaken.

48. The reservations themselves are not the major cause of Indian poverty.

49. This is a fact.
50. There are Indians who live in large cities.
51. The cities are far from the reservations.
52. Most of these Indians find themselves in urban slums.

53. But the reservations are a major source of Indian pride.

54. Reservations exist for a reason.
55. Reservations help preserve Indian heritage.
56. Reservations help preserve Indian culture.

57. Reservations exist for another reason.
58. Indian leaders do not want their people mixing with non-Indians.

59. Reservations exist for still another reason.
60. The federal government is under solemn treaty obligations.
61. The obligations are to keep the reservations intact.

62. One Indian leader said this.
63. An Indian is forced out of the tribe.
64. The Indian becomes "alienated, irritable, and lonely."
65. The Indian longs to return to the tribe.
66. The longing is desperate.
67. The return will restore the Indian's sanity.

68. The center of the Indians' universe is the tribe.
69. This is true today.
70. It was true in the past.
71. Without the tribe there is no culture.

72. But suppose there is no reservation.
73. Then there is no tribe.

74. So Indian poverty must be wiped out.
75. This is the way it should be done.
76. It should not endanger the existence of the reservation.
77. The reason is that the Indians have a primary goal.
78. Their primary goal is preserving their tribal life-style.

14. Emphasis

All ideas in a sentence and all sentences in a paragraph are not equally important. You normally emphasize a word or sentence because you attach more importance to it and want it to be noticed. In speaking, you can easily direct your audience's attention to a certain word simply by pronouncing it louder than the rest of the sentence. For example, if you want to stress the fact that it was Nickie, not someone else, who won the jackpot, you can pronounce the word "Nickie" the loudest of all the words in the sentence

Nickie won the jackpot.

Perhaps, to increase the emphasis, you will even nod or point in Nickie's direction if she happens to be nearby.

But if you want to convey this same information in writing, you must use some other strategy for emphasis—one that will enable your reader to know what you consider important. The written sentence "Nickie won the jackpot" is likely to be read with the word "jackpot" emphasized most, because in an English sentence the emphasis normally falls near the end. But how can you get the reader to emphasize "Nickie"? How can you communicate emphasis at all?

Perhaps the simplest way to call attention to an otherwise unemphatic word or phrase is with a device such as underlining:

Nickie won the jackpot.

Such visual devices, as well as various punctuation marks like colons, dashes, and exclamation marks, are often used to indicate emphasis. For example, underlining (or italics or boldface or capital letters) can emphasize a contrast that otherwise might be unclear, as in this passage:

> Although the terms are often used interchangeably, there's a difference between a comedian and a comic. A comedian, like Johnny Carson, says funny things. But a comic, like Peter Sellers, does funny things.

> Although the terms are often used interchangeably, there's a difference between a comedian and a comic. A comedian, like Johnny Carson, says funny things. But a comic, like Peter Sellers, does funny things.

On reading the second and third sentences of the first version, we are likely to stress the words "funny things" (where the emphasis naturally falls), because not until we get to the word "does" in the third sentence do we recognize the contrast between "says" and "does." We are almost forced to backtrack and read the passage again, now properly stressing "says" and "does." But the underlining of these words in the second version gives a clue to the contrast from the beginning and saves the reader from the momentary confusion.

Similarly, some punctuation marks prompt the reader to give a word or sentence more than usual emphasis. For example, a command with a period (Watch out.) does not evoke the same emphatic response as the same command with an exclamation mark (Watch out!). Nor does a comma, as in

The verdict was what he had expected, death.

normally have the same emphatic force as a dash or colon:

The verdict was what he had expected—death.
The verdict was what he had expected: death.

What creates much of the emphasis here is the pause preceding the word to be emphasized: the longer this pause, the greater the emphasis the word "death" receives.

Useful as such graphic methods are for directing the reader's attention to emphatic elements in a sentence, you also have a wide range of options for achieving emphasis through the choice and arrangement of words. The bluntest way to emphasize something is by openly telling the reader that it is important. For example, you can introduce a sentence with an expression like **especially, particularly, crucially, most importantly,** or **above all.** Furthermore, you can direct attention to an important word by repeating it. Emphasis by repetition can be especially effective in a series, such as

Washington was **first** in war, **first** in peace, and **first** in the hearts of his countrymen.

and it is commonly exploited in advertisements. For example, the next passage repeats three times the key word **pictures:**

See your good times come to color in minutes—**pictures** protected by an elegant finish . . . **pictures** you can take with an instant flash . . . **pictures** that can be made into beautiful copyprints and enlargements.

The purpose of advertisers is, of course, to hit you in the eye and, ultimately, to hit you in the pocket. Repeated words are effective attention-getters. But notice that in this ad, and in the slogan about Washington as well, it is not just the repetition of a word that creates the emphasis. Rather, the emphasis comes in part from repeating a word at a certain point in the sentence, as part of a recurring structural pattern: **first** in war, **first** in peace, **first** in the hearts . . .; and **pictures** protected . . ., **pictures** you can take . . ., **pictures** that can be made. . . . In each case the writer has controlled the sentence structure, as well as the choice of words, to achieve the emphasis.

In emphasizing some elements over others by controlling the sentence structure, you are likely to use one or both of two basic strategies of emphasis: (1) breaking established patterns or expectations and (2) exploiting emphatic sentence positions.

The first strategy involves a deliberate departure from the usual or the expected. The pattern or expectation which is to be broken for emphasis may be set up by the context, or it may be provided by the structural patterns of the language. To take the first case, the kind of context you create—the way you construct your sentences and put them together to build paragraphs—tends to condition your reader to expect more of the same. When suddenly what comes next is *not* the same, that is, when the established pattern is abruptly broken, the disruption is likely to be noticed by the reader and therefore becomes a source of emphasis. For this reason, an abrupt short sentence following a long sentence (or a sequence of long sentences) is often emphatic, as in the second version below; compare the unemphatic ending of the first version, which consists of one sentence instead of two:

> When two of the world's most famous and literate scientists collaborate to produce a book aimed at expanding contemporary ideas about the nature of living things, the book should be well worth reading, but this one isn't.

> When two of the world's most famous and literate scientists collaborate to produce a book aimed at expanding contemporary ideas about the nature of living things, the book should be well worth reading. **But this one isn't.**

Here the short sentence **But this one isn't** in the second version, unlike the clause **but this one isn't** in the first, attracts notice in part because it breaks the monotony of the preceding long sentence. The longer pause before the new sentence beginning with **But** encourages greater emphasis on the key word **isn't** at the end of the sentence, and thus helps sharpen the contrast between the anticipated and the actual worth of the book.

In the following example the final short sentence is a question, a sentence type frequently suggesting emphasis. Here the question achieves impact by making readers wonder whether strenuous exercise is really as healthy as they thought:

> The increased number of joggers, the booming sales of exercise bicycles and other physical training devices, the record number of entrants in marathon races—all clearly indicate the growing belief among Americans that strenuous, prolonged exercise is good for their health. **But is it?**

The abrupt, short element used for emphasis need not be a complete sentence. Exclamations and other deliberate fragments are often even more effective as attention-getters than grammatically full sentences. Here are a couple of examples:

> Except for its most severe forms, society laughs at wife-beating. Such abuse is considered a man's right when he "owns" a wife. **What rubbish!** But what tops it all is that some wives accept their lot by saying they deserve it or take violence as a proof of tender loving care.

> Gales of laughter followed when the Ouija board told Jane she would never marry. Pressed further as to why, the board spelled out laboriously, letter by letter, "Because you will die." **Nonsense. Black magic.** We laughed some more. Imagine my shock when, three years later almost to the day, I read in the alumni journal that Jane had died of an incurable disease.

Sometimes the pattern or expectation set up by the context is more tightly structured. When such a pattern is broken for emphasis, the effect can be even sharper. In the saying popular when the Senators were a Washington baseball team,

> Washington is **first** in war, **first** in peace, and **last** in the American league.

the word **last** gains emphasis because it disrupts the pattern established by the two earlier occurrences of **first.** And, of course, the phrase beginning with **last** fails to satisfy the reader's anticipation of an ending that will correspond to the original form "**first** in the hearts of his countrymen."

Besides disrupting an expectation set up by the context, you can also work emphasis into a sentence by departing from the basic structural patterns of the language. The most basic structural pattern of English involves the word order *subject-verb-object.* This basic pattern is psychologically so strong that the reader tends to look for it in *every* sentence and notice any departure from it. Changing the pattern often creates emphasis. For example, questions and especially commands are more emphatic than statements, in part because they ordinarily lack the expected *subject-verb-object* sequence. Some special "emphatic" sentence constructions, which slightly alter the basic word order, enable you to vary the emphasis even in statements. Thus in the sentence **The merchants protested the new taxes,** the word **merchants** is not emphatic, but in each of the following versions the special emphatic pattern forces the reader to stress **merchants:**

> The **merchants** were the ones who protested the new taxes.
> It was the **merchants** who protested the new taxes.
> The ones who protested the new taxes were the **merchants.**

Of course, you can emphasize any of the other elements in the sentence by using an emphatic pattern. To emphasize **protest,** you can say

> What the merchants did was **protest** the new taxes.

To emphasize **the new taxes,** you can use one of several patterns:

> What the merchants protested were **the new taxes.**
> **The new taxes** were what the merchants protested.
> It was **the new taxes** that the merchants protested.

Certain words, such as the word **only,** often come before an emphatic element:

> Although the belief in ghosts and goblins has been with us since the Old Stone Age, scientists have turned their attention only recently to these enduring examples of occult phenomena.

↓

> Although the belief in ghosts and goblins has been with us since the Old Stone Age, **only recently have** scientists turned their attention to these enduring examples of occult phenomena.

Here the phrase **only recently** gains emphasis partly from upsetting the expected subject-verb order **scientists have turned** and partly from directly following the phrase with which it contrasts, **since the Old Stone Age.** Such inversions of word order can be especially effective when they come at the climax of a buildup in a longer passage. Note the strong emphasis on the inverted word **then** in the last sentence below:

> A good base stealer relies as much on intelligence as on speed. He must study pitchers and learn their motions, so that he will know when they intend to pitch to the plate. He must know how far he can stray off first base without being picked off by the pitcher, so that he can gauge his headstart to second base. And he must know that the next batter will pass up a good pitch, so that he can take off and run. Only **then** does speed become important.

The expected *subject-verb* sequence can also be broken up by an interrupting phrase, as in the second version below:

> Freud would have remained in Vienna, had not the Nazis forced him to leave, much against his desires.

> Freud would have remained in Vienna, had not the Nazis— **much against his desires**—forced him to leave.

Interrupting elements are normally emphatic when they appear either at an unusual point in the sentence, as in the above example, or just before the last and the most emphatic element, as in the next:

> A good-looking cop stopped her, lectured her for a while, gave her a speeding ticket, and then—**listen to this**— invited her out to dinner!

Without the interrupting element **listen to this,** the last clause is still emphatic, but it no longer has the same dramatic effect:

> A good-looking cop stopped her, lectured her for a while, gave her a speeding ticket, and then invited her out to dinner!

Or, finally, for another way to alter the basic structural pattern to achieve emphasis, begin a sentence with a series and then start your main clause with **this** or **that:**

> Interesting work, enough money, plenty of exercise—**that**'s my idea of a good life.

Compare a possible unemphatic alternative:

> My idea of a good life is interesting work, enough money, and plenty of exercise.

The alteration of the basic sentence pattern for emphasis is often most effective when combined with the second major strategy of emphasis—exploiting the naturally most emphatic sentence positions. These two strategies are so closely related that both have been illustrated by many of the examples given so far. In these examples the emphasis normally occurs at the end of a sentence. But when the basic word order places in the end position an element you don't want to emphasize, you can move it out to make room for the word or phrase that *is* important. A prepositional phrase, for example, is easily shifted from the end position to the beginning of the sentence. In the next case, such a shift enables the key word **biorhythms** to be in the most emphatic spot:

> Biorhythms, the great foreteller of all things, come in the wake of astrology and palm reading.

> ↓

> In the wake of astrology and palm reading come **biorhythms,** the great foreteller of all things.

It is especially important to organize your sentence so that its "punch line" will occur in a stressed position:

> The United States Travel Service, the national tourism office
> which promotes travel by providing free advice on where to
> go and what to see, now offers a guide to haunted houses in
> the United States—**the "Who's Whoooooo."**

Of course, there are other effective versions of this sentence, but
notice how misplaced emphasis can deprive the sentence of much
of its humor:

> A guide to haunted houses in the United States, called
> "Who's Whoooooo," is now offered by the United States
> Travel Service, the national tourism office which promotes
> travel by providing free advice on where to go and what to
> see.

How emphasis is distributed over a longer paragraph is
closely related to the development of the central idea. In a skillfully
built paragraph those words and sentences that support the central
idea tend to occur in more emphatic positions than those that do
not support it. Both passages below contain the same
information—that skateboarding is exhilarating and dangerous.
But they do not make the same points. How do they differ?

> 1. Skateboarding—its enthusiasts tell us—is the most
> exhilarating of all sports. Hospitals tell us that it is also the
> most dangerous. Apparently the thrill comes from the
> speed—some champs do 65 mph now—and from the chal-
> lenge posed by the unlimited possibilities for new stunts. Al-
> though few have tried "pipe riding" or the "gorilla grip," in
> one recent year skateboarders still suffered over 130,000 in-
> juries, 20 of them fatal. Devotees insist that what you can do
> with skateboards has no limit. At least 20 of them learned
> otherwise.

> 2. Although it may be the most dangerous sport,
> skateboarding—its enthusiasts tell us—is also the most
> exhilarating. Injuries do occur—over 130,000 in one recent
> year, 20 of them fatal. But consider the thrill that comes from
> the speed—some champs do 65 mph now—and from the
> challenge posed by the unlimited possibilities for new stunts,
> like "pipe riding" and the "gorilla grip." While some prac-

titioners will inevitably perish in trying new tricks, devotees insist that what skateboards can do has no limit.

These two paragraphs obviously convey two opposite messages. According to (1), the dangers involved in skateboarding overshadow the thrills you might get out of it. But paragraph (2) makes just the opposite point—that, although admittedly dangerous, skateboarding is full of limitless potential for thrills. How are these contrasting effects accomplished? In (1), the second sentence ends in the key word **dangerous,** placed at the emphatic tail end of the parallel structure **the most exhilarating . . . the most dangerous.** The danger is echoed in the short last sentence, where the last word, **otherwise,** suggests that death indeed does set a limit to skateboarding. But in paragraph (2), the phrase **the most dangerous sport** appears in an unemphatic subordinate clause, which downplays the dangers, while the emphasis falls on the word **exhilarating.** The second sentence admits that injuries do occur, but the connective **But** at the beginning of the next sentence emphasizes the **thrill** of skateboarding in contrast to the dangers that the statistics on injuries suggest. And the last sentence, again, contrasts **perish** in the unemphatic subordinate clause to the key words **no limit** in the most emphatic final position. Just by controlling the emphasis, we have conveyed two opposite views of skateboarding.

For a last illustration of how emphasis can be skillfully handled in a longer passage, read the two versions below and decide which one you like better:

In September of 1969, with winds gusting up to 200 miles an hour, Hurricane Camille came roaring into the Eastern Gulf of Mexico. The warnings to evacuate endangered areas were urgent—the Director of the National Hurricane Center simply told residents to "run for their lives"—and almost 75,000 responded by fleeing inland to higher ground.

1. But others chose to stay. At the Richelieu Hotel, a solid-looking, brick-and-concrete structure located 100 yards from the gulf, 25 guests planned a hurricane party. They decorated their rooms with crepe paper, balloons, and streamers. They set up tables for refreshments and poker. Before the party began, 23 of them were dead.

OR

2. But others chose to stay, among them 25 guests at the Richelieu Hotel, a solid-looking, brick-and-concrete structure located 100 yards from the gulf. They planned a hurricane party. But the hurricane struck even before the party began, and only two of the guests managed to survive.

Perhaps you will agree that version (1) is superior. It succeeds in part because it places emphasis on the key words that describe this foolish and unnecessary tragedy: **dead** at the end of the last sentence and, in contrast, **stay** at the end of the first. With the word **stay** stressed more and followed by a longer pause than in (2), allowing the reader to ponder the possible consequences of "staying," the first sentence in (1) already sets a somewhat ominous tone. This effect is heightened, and suspense created, by the concrete details about the preparations for the party given in separate, simple sentences (**They decorated** . . . , **they set up** . . .). Then the last sentence in (1) hits with the quickness of the hurricane itself—abruptly, without a connective (compare **But** in 2), and concisely, enabling the final word **dead** to receive maximum emphasis.

Patterns of Emphasis

Make the changes indicated in parentheses to create emphasis.

Example
> Archeologists might presume Ronald McDonald was a god if they were to dig out the ruins of America 1000 years from now and discover all those M-shaped golden arches spread across the continent. (Reorder the clauses to emphasize "god.")

$$\downarrow$$

> If archeologists were to dig out the ruins of America 1000 years from now and discover all those M-shaped golden arches spread across the continent, they might presume Ronald McDonald was a god.

A. Thirteen-year-old Cynthia Blake of Argo, Illinois, refused to take coeducational swim classes because her religion said it would be immodest to show her body in the presence of the opposite sex. The school principal said that Cynthia was not going to graduate without four years of physical education, because the state law requires it. (Rearrange the last sentence to emphasize "graduate.")

B. Dozens of students at a New York university were recently coerced into taking part in psychology department experiments that involved electric shock machines. The coercion consisted of giving students a choice between writing a term paper and participating in the experiments. This was some choice they were given. (Change the last sentence to an emphatic fragment.)

C. While the rest of the world played soccer, Americans played football, basketball, and baseball. But now soccer is rapidly escalating into a major sport in the United States for reasons as simple as the game itself—school officials like it and kids like it. High school athletic departments, strapped for operating funds, can fully outfit a soccer player for less than the price of a football helmet. And kids don't need to be big to play soccer.

They need the desire to run. (Change the last sentence into an emphatic construction.)

D. Carl Sandburg was a sensitive poet, yet a brilliant scholar. He wrote of democracy, yet lived like a king. He was a socialist, yet hobnobbed with the rich and powerful. He wrote lively stories for children, yet didn't like children. He wrote of love for humanity, yet carried grudges all his life. Sandburg was a man of contradictions. (Introduce the last sentence with a connective phrase indicating importance.)

E. Women are not new to terrorism. Charlotte Corday stabbed Marat to death in his bath during the French Revolution. Maude Gonne took part in the Irish Rebellion of 1916. But now more and more women become members of terrorist groups. One psychologist studying the phenomenon of increasing female terrorism links it to the determination of women to prove they are as good as men, even at crime. (Change the punctuation to emphasize "even at crime.")

Sentence Combining Exercise

Combine the following sentences into a short essay. Use several strategies of emphasis.

IT'S ALL IN THE MIND

1. You don't always need medication.
2. You want to recover from an illness.

3. You need confidence in this.
4. You will recover.

5. It turns out to be the case.
6. For many types of diagnosis a placebo can be potent.
7. A placebo can be as potent as the medication it replaces.
8. A placebo is a "nothing" drug.
9. A sugar pill is an example of a nothing drug.
10. A shot of sterile fluid is an example of a nothing drug.
11. An empty capsule is an example of a nothing drug.

12. Is this another old wives' tale?

13. Yes, in a way, this is another old wives' tale.

14. Doctors and medicine men have managed to treat diseases.
15. They have done this over the centuries.
16. They have done this with an array of cures.
17. The cures ranged from sawdust and powdered mummies.
18. The cures ranged to animal dung and frog sperm.

19. Medical experts now suspect this.
20. Patients survived such treatments because of this.
21. Patients survived the diseases because of this.
22. Doctors gave patients something more valuable than medicine.
23. Doctors gave patients the belief.
24. The patients believed they got something that was good for them.

25. This is in fact the case.
26. The recognition is now revolutionizing medical science.
27. It is recognized that the mind can trigger biochemical changes.
28. The changes are essential to combating disease.

29. The old snake oil salesmen weren't so far wrong, after all.

Controlling Paragraph Emphasis

Rewrite each paragraph to change the emphasis as suggested in parentheses.

Example

Fresh air—there doesn't seem to be enough of it around any more. At least that's what nonsmokers are claiming as they carry on their fight to breathe freely. Now they can cite you in a court of law if you violate the nonsmoking territories set aside for them in "places of public assembly." But there's one thing they can't make you do. They can't make you quit. (Emphasize nonsmokers' rights.)

↓

Fresh air—there doesn't seem to be enough of it around any more. So nonsmokers carry on their fight to breathe freely. To be sure, they can't make you quit. But now they can do something about it if you violate the nonsmoking areas set aside for them in "places of public assembly." They can cite you in a court of law.

A. Any kid will tell you that Robin Hood was a hero—a noble bandit who robbed the rich in order to give to the poor. How romantic! In reality, the original Robin Hood was a small-time mugger, and his Merrie Men a band of crooks and drunks. Once, sticky-fingered Little John ripped off $900 worth of household silver while his boss was out hunting. And Robin even conned the 18-year-old Maid Marion into living with him for seven years without benefit of clergy. Some noble bandit! (Emphasize that Robin Hood was a hero.)

B. To get a nose job done, you need to stay in the hospital only a couple of days. You are understandably not comfortable, but there is no pain. Your face, particularly your nose, is bandaged up, requiring you to breathe through the mouth, which in turn results in swollen tonsils. In fact, your whole face may be swollen. Since your nose was broken, two black eyes will be inevitable, but they will disappear within two weeks. Some vomiting may result from the seepage of blood into the stomach, or the nose itself may bleed. All right. But look what you gain. When you look good, you feel good. With a nose that looks the way *you* want it to look, you gain more self-confidence and self-respect. Believe me, people will notice the difference, and they won't laugh at you any more. (Emphasize the discomfort.)

C. As we toured the city, we stopped to watch a blind native sitting in a court yard, clad in rags that left parts of his body uncovered. His profile was turned to us. He sat there in the sun in an attitude of reflection with his knees crossed and his head resting on his hand. He was covered with swarms of flies but seemed impervious to them, making no attempt to brush them off. We walked around to look at his face, and realized his condition. (Emphasize that the man was blind.)

Sentence Combining Exercise

Combine the following sentences into a short essay using several strategies of emphasis.

SUPERMOM

1. Television commercials portray a picture of the American home.
2. The picture is far from realistic.

3. Houses are always tidy.
4. They are never in need of more than a dusting.
5. The dusting is with the proper lemon oil spray.

6. Fathers are always handsome.
7. And they are always well dressed.
8. They have no worse problems than dirty collars.

9. Children are cute.
10. But they are always in need of sugary goodies.

11. And mothers are the least realistic of all.

12. Mothers are svelte.
13. Mothers are sexy.
14. Mothers are maternal.
15. They are these things at once.

16. They are mothers.
17. They are mistresses.
18. They are homemakers.

19. They mop kitchen floors happily.

20. Why shouldn't they?

21. They always use the correct acrylic wax.

22. The children come home from school.

23. Then TV mothers are prepared.
24. They have enough Hostess cupcakes to supply an army.

25. They are smart enough to do this.
26. They guzzle Geritol.
27. Then husbands arrive.

28. Their iron needs are sated.
29. They meet the provider.
30. They are clad in lingerie.
31. They are smiling.
32. They are lip-glossed.

33. TV mothers are Supermoms.
34. They are docile.
35. They are patient.
36. They are understanding.
37. They are unmarked by the trauma of childbirth.

38. Their bras cross their hearts upliftingly.

39. Their pantyhose flatter their tummies.

40. Their worst problems are in this.
41. They convince their neighbors of this.
42. Certain vegetable oils fry grease-free.

43. So they keep spare loaves of bread.
44. They fry them for proof.

45. TV moms are hardly more than overgrown Barbie dolls.
46. They have all of Barbie's intelligence.
47. They are this, in short.

48. They are not like real mothers.
49. Real mothers kick.
50. Real mothers scream.
51. Real mothers cry.
52. Real mothers love.
53. And real mothers grow old.
54. Real mothers are just like other human beings.

55. TV Supermoms may look like Wonder Woman.
56. TV Supermoms may act like Wonder Woman.
57. But they are no more useful than the sugared goodies they dispense.
58. They are unlike real mothers.

Judging Paragraphs

A part of each passage below is given in three different versions. In each case, select the version in which the boldface portion is the most emphatic. If you think that two versions are equally emphatic, explain your judgment. If you don't like any of the versions given, create one of your own.

A. 1. It wasn't supposed to happen. Yet, while everyone turned the other way, thousands of tiny places across the country quietly reversed what was supposed to be an "irreversible" population trend. **They stopped dying.**
  2. It wasn't supposed to happen. Yet, while everyone turned the other way, thousands of tiny places across the country **stopped dying,** and thus quietly reversed what was supposed to be an "irreversible" population trend.
  3. It wasn't supposed to happen. Yet, while everyone turned the other way, thousands of tiny places across the country quietly reversed what was supposed to be an "irreversible" population trend **because they stopped dying.**
  What's more, the "boondocks" are burgeoning, growing twice as fast as metropolitan areas and, for the first time since frontier days, beginning to wield political and economic influence.

B. 1. For a long time, **but not any more,** Japanese corporations used Southeast Asia merely as a cheap source of raw materials, as a place to dump outdated equipment and overstocked merchandise, and as a training ground for junior executives who needed minor league experience.
  2. **Though they don't do this any more,** for a long time Japanese corporations used Southeast Asia as a cheap source of raw materials, as a place to dump outdated equipment and overstocked merchandise, and as a training ground for junior executives who needed minor league experience.

3. For a long time Japanese corporations used Southeast Asia merely as a cheap source of raw materials, as a place to dump outdated equipment and overstocked merchandise, and as a training ground for junior executives who needed minor league experience. **But not any more.**

Japan has learned that Western countries which have closed their doors on merchandise labeled "Made in Japan" willingly accept goods from an underdeveloped country like Thailand or Malaysia.

C. On a September night in 1962 when I arrived at Lydia Pinkham College and changed from short shorts into my bleached blue jeans, the phone rang. My mother was on the line, crying. She had heard at a cocktail party from a well-informed gentleman that there were no virgins on the Lydia Pinkham campus.
1. **Times have changed since then.**
2. **How we have changed!**
3. **But the situation is different now.**

Recently, the development office got a call from an alumna in Palm Beach who was upset by the rumor that the campus is now 50 percent gay.

D. 1. **The kiwi fruit** is now replacing the orange, fruit of the Florida Sunshine tree. The kiwi is a fuzzy, dark newcomer from New Zealand.
2. The fruit of the Florida Sunshine tree must now make room for **the kiwi fruit,** a fuzzy, dark newcomer from New Zealand.
3. Fruit of the Florida Sunshine tree, move over to make room for a fuzzy, dark newcomer from New Zealand—**the kiwi fruit.**

Dieters are discovering that the kiwi offers twice the orange's vitamin C with one-third the calories. And since the sweet, delicious kiwi satisfies even a weight-watcher's longing for dessert, dinner may soon replace breakfast as the meal that supplies the family's daily requirement of vitamin C.

E. Shakespeare asks "What's in a name?" and concludes that a rose by any other name would smell as sweet. But Hollywood seems to think otherwise, if the number of stars who change their names is any indication. After all, would Doris von Kap-

pelhoff have become as famous as Doris Day? Would William
Pratt have scared us as much as Boris Karloff? Or would Marion
Morrison have made it as big as John Wayne?

1. **So what's in a name? A lot.** Perhaps an entire career.
2. **So there's a lot in a name,** isn't there?
3. One can therefore conclude, contrary to Shakespeare, **that
   there is a lot in a name.**

Sentence Combining Exercise

Reorder the 13 groups of sentences below into a humorous essay
that explains and illustrates why Americans are increasingly living
together outside of marriage. Construct your sentences, paragraphs, and essay as a whole so that its humor falls in the most
emphatic positions.

SHACKING UP

A. 1. The most recent census figures say this.
    2. More Americans are living together than ever before.
    3. They do not bother to get married.

B. 4. Sociologists are always eager to offer an opinion.
    5. Sociologists cite a number of reasons.
    6. The reasons are for the expanding popularity of living
       together.

C. 7. Janet and Dave are in the midst of this.
    8. Their parents call it an unholy alliance.
    9. Janet and Dave consider it a meaningful relationship.

D. 10. Even senior citizens have begun shacking up.
   11. The senior citizens are scandalizing their children in the
       process.
   12. The senior citizens are scandalizing their children's chil-
       dren in the process.
   13. The aim of the senior citizens is pooling their fixed in-
       comes.
   14. The aim of the senior citizens is fending off loneliness.

E. 15. Sociologists point to the emancipation of women.
   16. Sociologists point to the Beatles.
   17. Sociologists point to the pressures of modern life.
   18. Sociologists point to soap operas.
   19. Sociologists point to the Pill.
   20. These are all partial explanations.
   21. The explanations are of the expanding popularity of living together.

F. 22. Janet and Dave have tried to explain this.
   23. The explanation is to their parents.
   24. Why are they living together?
   25. They have explained in terms of shared growth.
   26. They have explained in terms of mutual independence.
   27. They have explained in terms of freedom.
   28. The freedom is to be themselves.
   29. The freedom is to be without any of society's hang-ups.

G. 30. Of course, Janet's dad may be right.

H. 31. Janet's dad thinks this.
   32. It's all a conspiracy.
   33. The conspiracy is godless.
   34. The conspiracy is Communist.

I. 35. Small communal groups have sprung up across the nation.
   36. They dedicate their energies to plump Korean prophets.
   37. Or they dedicate their energies to Buddha.
   38. Or they dedicate their energies to Marx.

J. 39. Dave's mom isn't speaking to Dave.
   40. Dave's mom isn't speaking to Janet.
   41. Janet isn't speaking to her dad.
   42. Dave isn't speaking to Janet's dad.
   43. Janet's dad broke Dave's nose.

K. 44. The course of true love never seems to run smooth.
   45. This is the case even when love is freed from marriage vows.

L. 46. Most unmarried households are composed of young lov-
       ers.
   47. Janet and Dave are young lovers.
   48. Many others are getting into this new way of life.

M. 49. Janet prefers to believe this.
   50. Dave prefers to believe this.
   51. Practicality has at last triumphed.
   52. The practicality is American.
   53. The practicality is native.
   54. The triumph is over hypocrisy.
   55. The hypocrisy is Victorian.
   56. The hypocrisy is imported.

15. Coherence

Consider this short passage:

> Many people exercise every day and never lose weight. Exercising is important. The only sure way to lose weight is to stop eating.

This passage has some merit. It has unity and order, and—however vaguely—it makes a point. It also gains continuity from the repetition of the phrase **lose weight** and from the similarity between **exercise** and **exercising.** Yet something, we feel, is missing—a transition that would make the logical relationship clear. Both of the sentences below provide such a transition:

> Many people exercise every day and never lose weight. **While** exercising is important, the only sure way to lose weight is to stop eating.

OR

> Many people exercise every day and never lose weight. Exercising is important. **Still,** the only sure way to lose weight is to stop eating.

Although the meaning of the passage hasn't changed, both of the revised versions are more COHERENT than the original one, for in the revisions the connectives **while** and **still** clarify the contrast between the two approaches to losing weight. A paragraph is coherent when its ideas flow smoothly from sentence to sentence and when the reader is able to follow the train of thought without disruption. There are several STRATEGIES OF COHERENCE for linking sentences to one another and for introducing new paragraphs: the use of connectives, reference to earlier words and phrases, and the patterning of sentences.

Before using a CONNECTIVE, perhaps the most common linking strategy, you need to make two decisions. First, do you need a transition at all? The continuity between two adjacent sentences may be so obvious that their relationship need not be signaled. In such a case the use of a connective is optional:

> Most people can learn the basics of a craft quickly. They can learn to carve, weave, or solder in weeks.

OR

> Most people can learn the basics of a craft quickly. **For example,** they can learn to carve, weave, or solder in weeks.

> The royal crown has been returned to the country that owns it. The case is closed.

OR

> The royal crown has been returned to the country that owns it. **So** the case is closed.

But whenever the connection between two sentences is not adequately established by the relationship in meaning alone, a formal transition can provide a link between them. Your second decision, then, is what connective to use. The choice of a connective is determined by the relationship between the two sentences.

Here are some common connectives for indicating specific types of relationships:

    1. the second sentence gives an illustration or example: **first, thus, for example, for instance, for one thing, to illustrate;**

    2. the second sentence adds another point: **and, also, too, then, second, equally, for another thing, furthermore, moreover, in addition, similarly, next, again, above all, finally;**

    3. the second sentence restates, summarizes, or shows a result: **in fact, so, therefore, as a result, accordingly, of course, indeed, to sum up, consequently, in other words;**

    4. the second sentence expresses a contrast: **but, still, yet, however, by contrast, on the contrary, nevertheless, on the other hand.**

As you read the next paragraphs, try to insert an appropriate connective from the preceding list in each of the blanks:

A prison should serve as a correctional institution where a criminal is taught to deal with the outside world. _____, our prisons often harbor more crime within their walls than criminals find on the street.

What explains the growing trend toward delayed childbearing? _____ (a), the high divorce rate is making newlyweds think twice about starting a family right away. _____ (b), many young couples want to be more financially secure before having children. _____ (c), more married women prefer to devote time to their careers before having a baby.

In the first example the contrast between what a prison should be and what prisons often are, can be signaled by a contrastive connective such as **yet, however,** or **nevertheless.** To help the second paragraph read more smoothly, you might have used **first** or **for one thing** in (a), **furthermore** or **for another thing** in (b), and **above all** or **finally** in (c).

In revising a paragraph, you may find that in order to fill a gap between two sentences you need a more substantial transition than any of the usual connectives can provide. Longer prepositional and infinitive phrases, for example, are often used as connectives when additional clarification is needed. The next paragraph calls for a more extensive transition before the last sentence in order to clarify the connection between the restrictions imposed on the use of marijuana and the federal order to reexamine its use:

> Since the passage of the Controlled Substances Act in 1970, marijuana has been classified as a "dangerous drug," its possession subject to federal felony charges. This act has prevented the use of the drug even for medical purposes. A federal court in Washington has ordered a thorough reexamination of marijuana, including its potential for medical use.

↓

> Since the passage of the Controlled Substances Act in 1970, marijuana has been classified as a "dangerous drug," its possession subject to federal felony charges. This act has prevented the use of the drug even for medical purposes. **But now, in an attempt to clarify its status on the basis of available scientific evidence,** a federal court in Washington has ordered a thorough reexamination of marijuana, including its potential for medical use.

A second major strategy of coherence is making REFERENCE to an earlier word or phrase. The simplest way to use this strategy is by repeating an important word (or several important words) within the paragraph. If your paragraph is unified and deals with a single topic, you are likely to repeat some key words automatically; but repetition is especially effective when it occurs at points easily noticed by the reader. The point of the next paragraph, Agatha Christie's **mysterious disappearance,** is established in the first two sentences; but this point is further reinforced by the recurrence of these crucial words in the last sentence. The repetition contributes to the paragraph's coherence by forming a bridge between its beginning and end:

Agatha Christie earned world renown as the author of numerous **mystery** tales. But none of these tales are more **mysterious** that that of her own **disappearance.** Waves of shock rumbled through the British public when, in December of 1926, the newspapers proclaimed that she had vanished. Not until several months later was she discovered, supposedly afflicted with amnesia and working as a nanny in a Yorkshire manor house. To this day, her fans are intrigued by the **mystery** of her **disappearance.**

But like any potentially effective strategy, direct repetition can be overused and become tedious. To avoid this effect, you can choose among some alternative modes of reference. One such alternative strategy is using a SYNONYM for reference, that is, another word with the same or a similar meaning. In the next example the excessive repetition of the word **bicycle** becomes awkward and cumbersome. With synonyms substituted, the passage retains its coherence but is no longer repetitious:

Bicycling in America has grown at an explosive rate. **Bicycles** used to be sold to parents for their children. Now those same parents are buying **bicycles** for themselves, as well as for their children. Young executives ride **bicycles** to work to stay out of traffic jams. Young mothers are using **bicycles** to do their shopping without competing for a parking place at the shopping center. College and high school students find **bicycles** an economical alternative to cars and buses. And even grandma and grandpa enjoy riding **bicycles** to picnics and barbecues.

↓

Bicycling in America has grown at an explosive rate. **Bicycles** used to be sold to parents for their children. Now those same parents are buying **them** for each other, as well as for their children. Young executives ride **bikes** to work to stay out of traffic jams. Young mothers are finding **a way** to do their shopping without competing for a parking place at the shopping center. College and high school students find **biking** an economical alternative to cars and buses. And even grandma and grandpa enjoy **bicycling** to picnics and barbecues.

Synonyms can also cover a wider range of meanings. Throughout the next passage, for example, the various synonyms for **endanger** restate and reinforce the topic sentence, that the red wolf is an endangered species. They also remind the reader of the relationship of each sentence to the preceding one, as well as to the point of the paragraph:

> The red wolf is an **endangered** species. Its numbers have **perilously declined** both because of willful **slaughter** subsidized by government bounty and because of the wolf's **susceptibility** to the **deadly destructiveness** of intestinal parasites. And now the species may face total **extinction** because of its ability to interbreed with a closely related but far more numerous cousin, the coyote. Thus, having survived the worst that man and worms can do, the red wolf now faces what may be its final **extermination** in the **threat** of the **loss** of its own distinguishing genes.

Sometimes a synonym with a broader meaning refers to and summarizes one or more preceding statements. In the following passage, **such migrations** is used as a summarizing synonym:

> Eels, whales, salmon, turtles, and birds—and even bees and butterflies—annually travel long distances, sometimes thousands of miles. While **such migrations** have been known since the beginnings of recorded history, there is still no clear answer to the question, How do animals navigate?

Here **such migrations** establishes coherence by linking the second sentence to the first. Summarizing synonyms are commonly accompanied by words like **such, this, these,** and **of this sort.**
A second alternative mode of reference is the use of PRO-NOUNS, such as **she, he, it, they, this, that, some,** or **another.** A pronoun, too, is a kind of synonym, but it gets its meaning by referring to an earlier word or group of words. Since a pronoun can replace any noun, it can replace a summarizing synonym as well. In the last example the phrase **such migrations** could be replaced, with some loss of precision, by the pronoun **this:**

Eels, whales, salmon, turtles, and birds—and even bees and butterflies—annually travel long distances, sometimes thousands of miles. While **this** has been known since the beginnings of recorded history, there is still no clear answer to the question, How do animal navigate?

But pronouns are the most effective when their reference is clear, such as **they** and **their** in the following:

Virgos are simple and gentle people, with a need to serve humanity. Careful and precise by nature, **they** make excellent secretaries and nurses. The warm, shining eyes and the bright appearance of Virgos conceal **their** deeply burning desire for love.

In the next passage, not only is the reference of the pronoun clear—**the Apostle Paul**—but the recurrence of the subject **he** links the successive sentences into a forceful and effective pattern. So you don't forget that **he** refers to **the Apostle Paul,** the last sentence repeats his name and neatly winds up the passage—perhaps with a touch of sarcasm:

The Apostle Paul may have been an early example of a male chauvinist. **He** considers women the "weaker vessel," inferior to men. **He** advises wives to obey their husbands, because men are masters over their women just as Christ is master over the Church. **He** advises men not to marry, although **he** admits that marriage may be necessary for those who lust after women; for it is better to be married and sexually gratified than to be single and sex-crazed. But to be single and rid of women, says **the Apostle Paul,** is best of all.

The third major strategy of coherence is the ARRANGEMENT of sentences into structural patterns, including the proper ordering of old and new information.

Look for the possibility of patterning whenever you are discussing parallel points. Suppose, for instance, you have collected some notes on the thesis that in the early 1960s pop music was shaped by radically different geographical and cultural influences, and you try a paragraph like this:

The late 1960s brought to pop music a fusion of radically different geographical and cultural influences. The influence of religion and mysticism, which came from the East, made popular such instruments as the tabla and the sitar. A Latin influence was southern in origin, branching into such forms as reggae and calypso, with its steel drums and marimbas. But folk music, perhaps the most important influence on pop music at the time, with its simple melodies and melodramatic lyrics, came from the West, particularly from Britain and the American Midwest.

Although this paragraph has a clear topic sentence and contains interesting details, the relationship of these details to the topic sentence could be more sharply focused. Since the topic sentence deals with "different influences," you can revise the paragraph by asking where those influences came from. Clearly, some came from the East, some came from the South, and some came from the West. Equipped with this new organizing principle, you might revise the passage as follows:

The late 1960s brought to pop music a fusion of radically different geographical and cultural influences. **From the East came** the influences of religion and mysticism, which made popular such instruments as the tabla and the sitar. **From the South came** a Latin influence, with its steel drums and marimbas, branching into such forms as reggae and calypso. **And from the West,** particularly from Britain and the American Midwest, **came** folk music with its simple melodies and melodramatic lyrics, to become perhaps the most important influence on pop music at the time.

Note that patterning does not mean mechanical repetition. The last item in this series is introduced by **and,** and it is separated from the verb **came** by the prepositional phrase **particularly from Britain and the American Midwest.** Here repetition of the pattern contributes to clear organization and a smooth flow of sentences; interruption of the pattern helps to add interest and variety.

By becoming pattern-conscious, you are in a better position to recognize the lack of coherence in your first drafts and to make the necessary revision. Consider the next paragraph:

But what of the personal side of the story? What of retired mail clerks or janitors who have to contend with the continuous rise in the cost of living? They are no longer secure with a company's pension or with society's "gift" of social security. Government figures show that five million persons 63 years and older are living on an income under $5000.

The reader senses vaguely that the last sentence has something to do with what comes before, but the connection is obscure because this sentence breaks the pattern established by the second and third sentences: **mail clerks or janitors** and **they.** A transition such as **in fact** or **to illustrate** would help little; but if we revise the last sentence so that it continues the structural pattern with **they** as subject, the paragraph becomes more coherent:

But what of the personal side of the story? What of the retired **mail clerks or janitors** who have to contend with the continuous rise in the cost of living? **They** are no longer secure with a company's pension or with society's "gift" of social security. If **they** are among the five million persons 63 years and older who, according to government figures, live on an income under $5000, **they** can do no more than survive on or below subsistence level.

A second way to create coherence through arrangement is by placing old and new information in proper sequence. A sentence tends to contain both types of information. The repetition of old information, that is, some reference to what has already been said before, assures the continuity of thought. New information, on the other hand, carries the thought further. Ordinarily, the old information appears near the beginning of a sentence, and the new information comes toward the end, where the emphasis naturally falls. The next paragraph sounds odd partly because the second sentence violates this principle.

Perhaps *Naked Came the Stranger* was the greatest literary hoax of the century. *Newsday* staff members wrote its chapters, each writing independently and not knowing of the others' work. It was intended as an incoherent pornographic novel, to be published under the name Penelope Ashe.

The phrase **Newsday staff members** in the second sentence does not link up with anything in the first. By moving **its chapters** to the beginning of the second sentence, we not only order old and new information properly, but at the same time create a pattern of structurally parallel sentences: **Naked Came the Stranger was. . . . Its chapters were. . . . It was. . . .:**

> Perhaps *Naked Came the Stranger* was the greatest literary hoax of the century. **Its** chapters were written by *Newsday* staff members, each writing independently and not knowing of the others' work. **It** was intended as an incoherent pornographic novel, to be published under the name Penelope Ashe.

Finally, many of the same strategies of coherence that work within the paragraph can also be used to link one paragraph to another. Often a simple connective will provide sufficient transition between two paragraphs, but sometimes a more extensive transition is needed.

For example, the second paragraph in the next passage lacks a transition. Since it appears to cite an additional argument against capital punishment, this paragraph could begin with a connective such as **furthermore:**

> Capital punishment complicates the administration of justice; it leads to lengthy trials and unjustified verdicts, and it places a burden on appelate courts. It also forces taxpayers to support all those waiting their turn for execution on death row.
> "Cruel and unusual" punishment is explicitly barred by the Eighth Amendment to the Constitution.

$$\downarrow$$

> **Furthermore,** "cruel and unusual" punishment is explicitly barred by the Eighth Amendment to the Constitution.

But notice that the second paragraph introduces a much more fundamental argument against capital punishment than those cited in the first. When a person's life is at stake, lengthy trials and higher taxes seem trivial in comparison to constitutional questions. To focus on this difference between the trivial and the crucial, you might try a more elaborate transition:

> Capital punishment complicates the administration of justice; it leads to lengthy trials and unjustified verdicts, and places a burden on appelate courts. It also forces taxpayers to support those waiting their turn for execution on death row.
> **But when a person's life is at stake, such inconveniences seem trivial. A far more fundamental objection to capital punishment is a constitutional one:** the Eighth Amendment explicitly bars "cruel and unusual" punishment, **and execution is surely a cruel and unusual punishment.**

Using Strategies of Coherence I

Improve the coherence of each paragraph below by inserting connectives, as in Example I, or connective phrases, as in Example II. Make any other change that will further improve paragraph coherence.

Example I

Over half the states accept simple incompatibility as legitimate grounds for divorce. Like some other well-meant reforms, no-fault divorce is proving to have unexpected disadvantages. It may be doing as much harm as good.

Over half the states accept simple incompatibility as legitimate grounds for divorce.
Nevertheless,
But, } like some other well-meant
Yet,
reforms, no-fault divorce is proving to have unexpected disadvantages. **In fact,** it may be doing as much harm as good.

A. Rape clinics discuss various methods of self-defense for women. Panic stricken women cannot always use this training in a real situation.

B. Walking is a skill people learn as babies. There must be more to it than putting one foot ahead of the other. In any given year, some 15 thousand American pedestrians are killed by motor vehicles.

C. The International Olympic Committee tries to enforce the amateur status of Olympic athletes. Many people charge that government-sponsored athletes from Communist countries compete on the professional level.

D. All mushrooms are fungi. Not all fungi are mushrooms in the popular sense. There are an estimated 100 thousand species of fungi. Mushrooms are two types, poisonous and nonpoisonous. It is these poisonous mushrooms that we commonly call toadstools.

E. The porpoise is an especially appealing animal—intelligent, playful, and altogether winsome. No one but a brute would desire its extinction. Every time a large tuna boat makes its catch, hundreds of porpoises are killed. The U.S. government enforces strict regulations against the tuna fishermen. Many fishermen threaten to join the fishing fleets of other nations less concerned about the well-being of porpoises. Many have already gone. With every fisherman's departure, the plight of the porpoise becomes more desperate. If the American fleet is disbanded, the American regulations will have no protective force, and the porpoise is doomed.

Example II

Some arid regions of the world receive an average of only two- or three-hundredths of an inch of rain annually and may go on for years without getting a drop. Rain usually comes in torrential downpours.

Some arid regions of the world receive an average of only two- or three-hundredths of an inch of rain annually and may go on for years without getting a drop. **But when the rain does come,** it usually comes in torrential downpours.

F. In the 1970s the Supreme Court gave states and municipalities the power of discretion in establishing penalties for certain crimes. For example, it has given localities the right to establish their own obscenity laws, with the result that books and movies prohibited in one county may be available only a few miles away. The Court has allowed state and local powers to supersede federal powers.

G. Travelers are surprised to find almost no eyeglasses on Chinese children. All children perform a series of eye exercises for 20 minutes each day in school to strengthen their vision.

H. With the president's decision not to build the new supersonic B1 bomber, the aging, subsonic B52 may well remain the backbone of our nuclear deterrent force into the 1990s. Many

B52s would be pushing 40 years of age—older than the Wright Brothers' plane would have been on Pearl Harbor Day.

I. Applying to graduate school is a time-consuming, expensive, and unpredictable venture. Undergraduates must take the required graduate examination and, after deciding where they would like to apply, write to the schools for application forms. They must ask three or four professors to write letters of recommendation and request the registrar to send off transcripts of their undergraduate records. The cost can be from as little as two dollars to forward the transcripts to as much as 25 dollars for application fees. There is no guarantee of acceptance.

Sentence Combining Exercise

Combine the following sentences into an effective essay. Use several strategies of coherence—connectives, structural patterns, and references to earlier words of phrases.

TOMBSTONES

1. Tombstones would seem to record only remembrances.
2. The dead are remembered.
3. Tombstones are actually highly eloquent interpreters.
4. They interpret the culture of the living.

5. Tombstones change over the centuries.
6. These changes clearly reflect changes in values.
7. The values belong to the civilizations.
8. The civilizations created the tombstones.

9. The stones of colonial America are an instance.
10. The stones are frequently adorned with a head.
11. The head has wings.
12. The head depicts death.
13. Biographical facts are engraved.
14. These facts are often augmented by a warning.
15. They warn the passerby.
16. They warn of the inevitability of death.

17. These stones give mute witness.
18. The witness is to the solemn piety.
19. Our Puritan forefathers had solemn piety.

20. The willow and urn motif testifies.
21. The motif came a few generations later.
22. The motif showed a rendering of life out of death.
23. The rendering was symbolic.
24. The motif testified to the romanticism.
25. The romanticism was more hopeful.
26. The romanticism was of the early nineteenth century.

27. The Victorian preoccupation is demonstrated.
28. The early twentieth-century preoccupation is demonstrated.
29. The preoccupation was with status.
30. The preoccupation was with material goods of the world.
31. It is demonstrated by tombstones and mausoleums.
32. The tombstones and mausoleums are massive and ornate.
33. The tombstones and mausoleums are of that period.

34. One wonders.
35. How will future generations read this?
36. They will read our present civilization.
37. They will read when they consider the anonymity.
38. The anonymity is flat and uniform.
39. Gravemarkers are anonymous.
40. The gravemarkers are row upon row.
41. The gravemarkers are mechanically perfect.
42. The gravemarkers grace our modern "Memorial Parks."

Using Strategies of Coherence II

Improve the coherence of each passage below by (1) using pronouns or synonyms for reference, as in Example I, or by (2) arranging sentences into structural patterns, as in Example II. Make any other change that you feel is necessary.

Example I

Dancing is a cultural universal. In many cultures dancing serves as an integrating force to group identity and morale.

Dancing often has a central place in festive or religious events, and dancing may be an important factor in courtship.

↓

Dancing is a cultural universal. In many cultures **it** serves as an integrating force to group identity and morale. **It** also often has a central place in festive or religious events and may be an important factor in courtship.

A. Chicago, at the southern tip of Lake Michigan, has spent a half-century and billions of dollars developing a good water system. Chicago draws a billion gallons a day from the lake, to serve over 5 million people. But now that Chicago's lake water has become almost too dirty for treatment, Chicago may be forced to get water elsewhere—and pay more for it.

B. Books and films have given motorcycle gangs a bad reputation, showing the gangs constantly at war with each other, with gang members brandishing guns, switchblades, and clubs. In fact, motorcycle gangs are rebellious young men, defiant, reckless, and independent; but the gangs are not always tough and ruthless. Often money is contributed to charity organizations, and sometimes the gangs volunteer their services to youth organizations. Still, motorcycle gangs have far to go if their image is to change.

C. Patchwork quilts today are among the antiques increasing steadily in worth. Once common in every household, the quilts were treasured, too, by the pioneers who made the quilts. The quilts provided color and gaiety for the crude, drab pioneer cabins. The quilt's combination of small, various shaped pieces in geometric designs made use of otherwise useless scraps of fabric. And, since many patchwork pieces were cut from old clothing, the quilts even provided a sense of continuity with the past.

Example II
To become finalists in the competition for scholarships, the semifinalists must supply biographic information, maintain

high academic standing, and perform well on a second examination. In addition, their high school principal must endorse them.

↓

To become finalists in the competition for scholarships, the semifinalists must supply biographic information, maintain high academic standing, perform well on a second examination, **and be endorsed by their high school principal.**

D. For the Northerners, Lincoln was a hero because he ended slavery and saved the Union. But because he threatened to destroy one of the staples of the economy, Lincoln was regarded as a villain by Southerners.

E. In the wake of the Watergate scandal, the government has tried to demonstrate to the public that it can be its own watchdog. Consequently, the amount of money an individual or special interest group may contribute to a candidate's political campaign has been restricted.

F. Because they are produced when conscious controls are lowered, doodles reveal personality in much the same way dreams do. Psychologists at Michigan State University found that students who draw houses on their lecture notes yearn for security, while aggressive personalities draw sharp objects. Spiders, bugs, and mice are drawn by deeply troubled people. And if you have a normal personality, you are likely to draw pictures of domestic animals—dogs, cats, and horses.

G. The weatherperson on the evening news may have all the latest information from radar and satellites to give an accurate forecast. Oldtimers claim you can be accurate just by watching natural signs. For an indication of fair skies ahead, look for gnats swarming in the setting sun. Noisy woodpeckers signal rain on the way. When bubbles collect in the middle of your morning coffee, fair weather is coming. But it's time to look for an umbrella when the bubbles ring around the edge.

Sentence Combining Exercise

Combine the following sentences into an effective essay that uses several strategies of coherence.

DREAMS

1. Many people have dreams.
2. The dreams are too confusing to figure out.
3. The dreams seem to be telling them something.

4. You may have been puzzled by such dreams.
5. If so, you may still wonder about this.
6. What, if anything, are those midnight messages saying?

7. There are no infallible formulas.
8. Formulas are for interpreting dreams.
9. One thing is certain.
10. Dreaming is a meaningful experience.
11. The experience should not be ignored as nonsense.

12. Perhaps the most frequent type of meaning is knowledge.
13. The dreams communicate the meaning.
14. The knowledge is about ourselves.

15. Things often get repressed.
16. Things often get pushed out of our consciousness.
17. We have done things in the past.
18. For some reason, we don't want to remember the things.

19. But a memory recurs in a dream.
20. The memory recurs often with exaggerated clarity.
21. Then we are forced to confront the memory again.
22. The memory is of the time we stole our little sister's ice cream cone.
23. The memory is of the time we cheated on the chemistry exam.
24. The memory is of the time we lied.
25. Where had we been the night before?

26. Dreams won't let us forget.

27. Dreams force us to recognize that part of ourselves.
28. Our walking consciousness tries to ignore that part of ourselves.

29. The second type of meaning is an insight.
30. Dreams often reveal meaning.
31. The insight is into a problem.

32. We puzzle for hours over an English term paper.
33. This won't help us figure out Huck Finn's reasons.
34. Huck Finn went down the river.

35. Problems with lovers are even more difficult.
36. We untangle problems with lovers.
37. Emotional knots are never easy to untie.

38. We drift into dreamland.
39. This often helps take care of such questions.
40. Our minds continue working as we sleep.
41. The answers can appear to us in a dream vision.

42. Dreams often anticipate future events.

43. Some prophetic dreams concern our personal lives.
44. Perhaps we foresee an unannounced visit by a close friend.
45. Perhaps we make an unplanned trip to a city.
46. We always wanted to see that city.

47. Prophecies may concern others.
48. We might dream about the birth of a friend's baby.
49. Somehow we might know the sex of the baby.
50. Somehow we might know the exact time it was born.

51. There are also ominous dreams.

52. Jeanne Dixon tried in vain to warn John Kennedy not to go.
53. Kennedy went to Dallas.
54. Jeanne Dixon had dreamed of Kennedy's assassination.
55. And it is common for a mother to dream.

56. The mother dreams of her son or daughter crying for help.
57. The mother dreams the very minute this happens.
58. The son or daughter meets unexpected death.

59. It is difficult to see.
60. How can a person laugh off a prophetic dream as nonsense?
61. The person has experienced a prophetic dream.

62. Dreams may be obscure and confusing.
63. Yet dreams usually carry meanings.
64. We shouldn't ignore the meanings.

65. Many people still regard dreams as superstitious hogwash.
66. Many people are forever puzzled by those nocturnal fantasies.
67. But understanding dreams can help us understand ourselves.
68. Understanding dreams can help us understand the rest of the world.
69. This is true, provided we just give dreams a chance.

Judging Paragraph Coherence

In each example below, complete the paragraph by choosing the one option among (1), (2), or (3) that makes the paragraph most coherent. The rest of the paragraph need not be changed.

A. In the early 1960s, President Kennedy gave the United States two goals—to send a man to the moon by the end of the decade and to eliminate hunger "within our lifetime." The first goal was achieved when two Americans landed on the moon in July 1969.

   1. But with the world's population increasing faster than its capacity to feed itself, the chances of reaching the second goal are growing more remote.

2. But the chances of reaching the second goal are growing more remote, because the world's population is increasing faster than its capacity to feed itself.

3. The world's population is increasing faster than its capacity to feed itself, so the chances of reaching the second goal are growing more remote.

B. Do you believe that you are paying too much for your apartment? Could you find another at an affordable price without sacrificing clean and well-maintained surroundings?

1. Rent control could possibly give you welcome relief, if your answer is yes to either or both of these questions.

2. If your answer is yes to either or both of these questions, then rent control could possibly give you welcome relief.

3. You might find welcome relief in rent control, if your answer to either or both of these questions is yes.

C. Publishers have given us a new word: "novelization." It refers to the practice of converting successful film scripts, like *Star Wars*,

1. into novels. Reversing the long-established practice of turning novels into films.

2. into novels. The long-established practice of turning novels into films is thus reversed.

3. into novels, and thus suggests a reversal of the long-established practice of turning novels into films.

D. The clang, clang, clang of the trolley could be heard in every major city of the nation before World War II.

1. But as people moved to the suburbs and built superhighways after the war, cars and buses replaced the electrically powered vehicles.

2. But as people moved to the suburbs and built superhighways after the war, the electrically powered vehicles were replaced by cars and buses.

3. But cars and buses replaced the electrically powered vehicles after the war, as people moved to the suburbs and built superhighways.

Now, once again, city planners are looking into the possibility of building new trolley systems, because they are cheaper and cleaner than other forms of mass transportation.

E. An American company under government contract is often faced with the choice of buying American-made goods, which are expensive, and foreign-made goods, which are cheap. If the company buys American goods, it may anger taxpayers by failing to keep prices low.

1. But if foreign goods are bought, the jobs of American workers may be endangered.

2. But if it buys foreign goods, it may endanger the jobs of American workers.

3. But the jobs of American workers may be endangered if foreign goods are bought.

Confronting the issue, Congress has passed a law compelling American companies with government contracts to give preference to domestic goods and services.

Sentence Combining Exercise

Turn the following sentences into an effective essay by (1) rearranging the sentences within each of the four paragraphs (A–D) into a coherent order and by (2) rearranging the four paragraphs into a coherent order.

GENE BLUES

A. 1. Because the transplanted genes are accepted readily by the bacteria and are able to reproduce themselves in succeeding generations, the result of the transplant is a permanent new life form.

2. No one knows how it would react to the environment outside the laboratory or to humans and animals.

3. These creations are a part of recombinant DNA research, which involves transplanting one or more foreign genes into loops of DNA in a bacteria.

4. All that is known about this new life are its observable physical characteristics.

B. 5. Perhaps scientists, who usually oppose public control of their research, have agreed so readily to these guidelines because they, too, fear the consequences of a mistake.

6. But since so little is known about the newly created organisms, how can scientists know that the safeguards are adequate?

7. And the safeguards do not apply to commercial companies, like Eli Lilly and General Electric, which are also conducting research in the field.

8. In response to these fears, the National Institute of Health offered a set of guidelines to ensure the safety of recombinant research.

9. They cannot.

10. One safeguard was a complete ban on the transplantation of cancer viruses.

11. No such mistakes have been made yet, though perhaps one is the limit.

12. Another safeguard required that only weakened *E. coli* bacteria be used, so that they could not survive for long away from the lab.

C. 13. Perhaps these creations could wreck the environment, eating up chemicals or destroying the soil.

14. Some people are afraid that cancer viruses transplanted into bacteria could spread cancer.

15. And, since most of the experiments use the bacteria *E. coli,* which live in humans, a new combination could turn out to be highly infectious to people.

16. They are afraid that a transplant between two completely different species, such as frogs and bacteria, could create new diseases to which humans would be susceptible.

17. Because of this uncertainty, fears have flared up.

D. 18. No one knows what would happen if some of these organisms were to escape from the laboratory, but doubtless there is a risk of disease or death in humans.

19. Scientists are creating new forms of life, and these new creatures do not have spikes through their necks, like Frankenstein monsters.

20. These forms of life involve gene transplants and are locked away in research laboratories, hopefully in safekeeping.

21. Yet they may be more dangerous than any Frankenstein monster could ever be.

16. Tone

The tone of your writing indicates your feelings toward your material and your readers. Because tone reflects your frame of mind, it reveals whether you are being humorous or somber, playful or serious, whether you are angry or tranquil, bitter or confident. Through tone, your attitude toward what you are writing about and your relationship to your audience become clear.

Controlling tone is largely a matter of selecting words, structuring sentences, and choosing details so as to make them consistent with each other and with the purpose of your writing. Suppose, for example, you are writing a paragraph or brief essay on the increased sales of vitamin E. In your opening sentence you intend to include these two facts:

> The sales of vitamin E have doubled in the past five years.
> The increase in sales has been helped by statements from health food enthusiasts and doctors.

You might put these facts together into a sentence like this:

> The sales of vitamin E, helped by statements from health food
> enthusiasts and doctors, have doubled in the past five
> years.

This sentence is impartial in tone because it doesn't reveal your
attitude toward the increased sales of vitamin E. If you began with
such a sentence, your reader would not know, at least at first,
whether you thought the American public was wise or foolish in
doubling its consumption of the vitamin. Of course, there's nothing
wrong with being impartial. If you either have no opinion or want
to seem factual and objective, rather than personal and subjective,
impartial sentences are precisely what you want to write.

But let's suppose that you want a sentence reflecting your
belief that vitamin E sales have surged because of a deceptive and
misleading advertising campaign. One option is to state your position openly and explicitly:

> The sales of vitamin E, helped by the **deceptions and lies**
> of health food enthusiasts and doctors, have doubled in the
> past five years.

Strong in tone and clear in attitude, this hard-hitting sentence may
be exactly the way you want to begin your paragraph. Its tone
would be especially appropriate for readers who share your negative attitudes toward vitamin E. But for readers who don't begin on
your side, the sentence may sound too strong, too opinionated,
perhaps even biased. If so, you may try to suggest your feelings
instead of stating them:

> The sales of vitamin E, helped by the statements of health
> food **freaks** and **quack** doctors, have doubled in the
> past five years.

In this version you have not openly labeled the statements as de-
ceptions and lies, but through your choice of words—**freaks** and
quacks—you have given the sentence a definite tone. The reader
senses not simply your reservation about the worth of the vitamin
but also your contempt of those who promote it. Indeed, this sentence is almost as strong in tone as the explicit statement above, so
strong that your reader may consider it exaggerated and may even
begin to question its truth and your credibility. One way to guard

against your reader's suspicions is to tone down the sentence by making it more suggestive and less explicit:

> The sales of vitamin E, helped by the **claims** of health food **faddists** and doctors, have doubled in the past five years.

This sentence has a more clearly defined tone than your original version, but it is not as openly negative as your second or third. Its tone is negative because **faddists,** unlike **enthusiasts,** is a word with unfavorable associations and because **claims,** unlike **statements,** encourage the reader to doubt their truth. The sentence can be made still stronger in tone without making it seem biased by inserting the detail that only a few doctors make claims for the vitamin:

> The sales of vitamin E, helped by the claims of health food faddists and **a few** doctors, have doubled in the past five years.

But even if more than a few doctors support vitamin E, there are other ways to play down their support:

> The sales of vitamin E, helped by the claims of health food faddists and **some** doctors, have doubled in the past five years.

There is a big difference in tone between **some doctors** and just **doctors.** The phrase **some doctors** implies, as **doctors** alone does not, that there is another group of doctors who have made no claims for vitamin E and who may perhaps reject such claims. But the support of doctors for vitamin E can be weakened still further without making your statement seem exaggerated or biased:

> The sales of vitamin E, helped by the claims of health food faddists and **even** some doctors, have doubled in the past five years.

The word **even** suggests your surprise that doctors, who should know better, have made such foolish claims.

You can control tone not only by your choice of words and details but also by your sentence structure. To make your implied criticism more forceful, reorder your sentence so that the criticism occurs not in the relatively weak middle of your sentence but at its emphatic beginning or end position:

> The claims of health food faddists and even some doctors have helped double the sales of vitamin E in the past five years.

> OR

> In the past five years sales of vitamin E have doubled, thanks to the claims of health food faddists and even some doctors.

Now let's suppose that you wanted to create a sentence not critical but favorable in tone toward the increased sales of vitamin E. You can do so by choosing words and details with more positive associations:

> The sales of vitamin E, helped by statements from health food **experts** and doctors, have doubled in the past five years.

> OR

> The sales of vitamin E, helped by **reports** from health food experts and doctors, have doubled in the past five years.

> OR

> The sales of vitamin E, helped by the **testimony** of health food experts and doctors, have doubled in the past five years.

Because **experts** seem more trustworthy than simple **enthusiasts** and because both **reports** and **testimony** carry more weight than mere **statements,** the three sentences above are more favorable in tone than the original toneless version. But you can go even further in creating a positive tone by making the doctors who support vitamin E more prestigious:

> The sales of vitamin E, helped by the testimony of health food experts and **a number of** doctors, have doubled in the past five years.

> OR

The sales of vitamin E, helped by the testimony of health food
experts and a number of **leading** doctors, have doubled in
the past five years.

OR

The sales of vitamin E, helped by the testimony of health food
experts and a number of leading **medical authorities,**
have doubled in the past five years.

The phrase **a number of doctors,** even if it actually refers to but
three or four doctors, sounds more impressive than **a few doctors, some doctors,** or **doctors** alone. And **leading** doctors
are supposed to be more reliable than doctors who are not leaders,
although certainly not as reliable as leading **medical authorities.**

The previous sentences about vitamin E range from negative
to positive in tone, but they are alike in that each is formal, serious,
and relatively impersonal. If you want to make your sentence less
formal and more personal, you have a number of options. The
simplest way to personalize its tone is to introduce yourself into the
sentence as "I":

I find it hard to believe, but the sales of vitamin E, spurred on
by the claims of health food faddists and doctors, have
doubled in the past five years.

OR

The other day **I** read that the claims of health food faddists
and doctors have helped double the sales of vitamin E in
the past five years.

OR

I never thought that any vitamin would become glamorous,
but vitamin E certainly has. Thanks to the claims of health
food faddists and doctors, its sales have actually doubled in
the past five years.

The sentence can also be made more informal if you establish a
relationship between yourself and the reader. One way of relating
to your reader is by asking a question:

Why have the sales of vitamin E doubled in the past five years? Largely because of the claims of health food faddists and a few doctors.

OR

Who is responsible for the skyrocketing sales of vitamin E over the past five years? Mainly health food faddists and a few doctors.

An even more direct way of relating to readers is by addressing them as "you":

You may be surprised to learn that over the past five years the sales of vitamin E have doubled, in large part because of the claims of health food faddists and doctors.

OR

Did **you** know that, thanks to the claims of health food faddists and doctors, the sales of vitamin E have doubled in the past five years?

The informality of your writing will usually be increased by contractions, slang, and short, simple words instead of longer, more complex ones. Informal writing often includes exclamations, deliberate sentence fragments, and short as opposed to long sentences:

It's hard to believe but **it's** true. In just five short years the sales of vitamin E have doubled! **Why?** Because doctors and health food **buffs** have been telling people that **it's** good for their health.

OR

This may surprise you but twice as much vitamin E is sold today as five years ago. **Twice as much!** And **I'll** tell you why. It's because people have **swallowed** what some doctors and natural food **fans** have told them.

The more informal your writing becomes, the more it will sound like spoken rather than written language. Whether you want to give your writing the informal qualities of spoken language or the formal qualities of written language depends on what strategies you decide are most effective for achieving your overall purpose.

The paragraph provides even more options for controlling tone than the sentence. Here is a paragraph on student loans that seems impartial in tone:

> Many college graduates claim bankruptcy in order to avoid repaying money borrowed from the federal government to finance their education. In fact, over $500 million is now owed the government by more than 300,000 student borrowers. Statistics show that students are not good risks. Whereas the student default rate now stands at 12.2 percent, banks report that nonstudent loan delinquency seldom exceeds 3 percent. Apparently, the lack of money is not the only reason for nonpayment. Through its computers, the Department of Health, Education and Welfare recently discovered that 300 of its employees, some currently earning up to $33,000, had defaulted on student loans.

This is the kind of paragraph a newspaper reporter striving to be objective might write. It does not indicate through its word choice, sentence structure, or selection of details either anger or amusement, either approval or disapproval of the students who default on their loans or of the government which apparently tolerates it. But the paragraph does indicate, especially through its formal wording and complete absence of humor, that the student loan situation is important enough to be taken seriously by the reader.

The same paragraph can be rewritten to make it less serious and more playful, to create a tone of mild amusement with the students who take advantage of the government:

> One of the more popular pastimes of college graduates is claiming bankruptcy to avoid repaying money borrowed from the government to pay their college costs. Right now Uncle Sam is out some $500 million owed by more than 300,000 student borrowers. Unfortunately for the federal treasury, students are not the best loan risks. Whereas the student default rate has hit 12.2 percent, banks say that nonstudent loan repayments seldom go above 3 percent. Among the most interesting facts recently turned up by computers of the Department of Health, Education and

> Welfare is that 300 of its own employees, some making as much as $33,000, had managed to avoid repaying their student loans.

The paragraph is no longer wholly serious because the failure to repay student loans has become merely a **popular pastime,** presumably little more important than such other pastimes as golfing or watching TV. And that well-paid HEW employees have defaulted on student loans is nothing to take seriously, just an **interesting fact.** Much of the original wording of the paragraph has been made less formal in keeping with the paragraph's changed tone. The **government** has been reduced to **Uncle Sam,** always a slightly comic figure. The formal **to finance their college education** has become **to pay their college costs.** In the same way, words like **exceeds, discovered,** and **earning** have been replaced by their informal equivalents—**go above, turned up,** and **making.** Through its tone the paragraph communicates the writer's attitude that there's nothing to get excited about. Just sit back and smile.

Of course, there may be good reason for concern. In that case the writer will eliminate whatever seems casual or informal in the paragraph and, most importantly, add details that make clear the serious consequences of allowing students to continue defaulting on their loans:

> At a time when funds are sorely needed for federal programs to protect the environment and to quicken the economy, college students are refusing to repay money borrowed from the government to finance their education. The situation is serious. Either by claiming bankruptcy or by simply ignoring requests for repayment, over 300,000 student borrowers have deprived the American treasury of half a billion dollars. Whereas banks report only a 3 percent delinquency rate on nonstudent loans, the student default rate has climbed to an astounding 12.2 percent. Withholding money owed the government has become so widespread that the Department of Health, Education and Welfare recently discovered defaults on student loans by 300 of its own employees, some earning up to $33,000. If defaults continue, the student loan program which has helped so many re-

sponsible men and women may be dismantled because of an irresponsible few.

There is nothing amusing in this paragraph. From the first sentence to the last, it is serious, even urgent in tone. Its urgency is created in part through the opening assertion that the money collected from student loans could be used for programs that most Americans believe to be vital—programs affecting the environment and the economy. The sense of urgency is maintained up to the paragraph's most striking point, deliberately placed in the emphatic concluding sentence: the entire student loan program is jeopardized by defaults. No longer is nonpayment a popular pastime bothersome only to Uncle Sam, but a grave threat to the education of millions of Americans.

The paragraph's urgency of tone is controlled not only through the choice of words and the selection of details but through sentence structure as well. The first and last sentences both make use of strategies of repetition, which are especially appropriate in formal and serious prose. The first sentence uses the balanced phrases **to protect the environment** and **to quicken the economy,** and the last sentence contrasts **responsible** with **irresponsible.** The pattern of paired coordinators, another mark of a serious and deliberate prose style, is found in the construction of the third sentence. The short second sentence, "The situation is serious," is constructed to gain emphasis and impact from its position between two longer, more complex sentences. Through its tone the whole paragraph communicates the writer's feeling that there is cause for deep concern.

The next paragraph also expresses concern but without the positive suggestion that we can act to improve the situation. Instead, the tone of the paragraph is bitter and cynical:

Whatever else they got out of their four years at State U., college graduates have surely learned how to rip off Uncle Sam. In fact, claiming bankruptcy to escape repaying their student loans must now rank with pot smoking and wife swapping as the favorite pastimes of college grads. Some 300,000 of them have already bilked the federal treasury of $500 million, and you can bet that's not the end of it—not with one out of every eight student borrowers refusing to pay. The Department of Health, Education and Welfare recently took the time to find out that 300 of its own employees, some making salaries three times fatter than the national average, had squirmed out of debts they promised to repay. The only question is who deserves more of our scorn—the swindlers from college or the fools from Washington?

The tone of the opening sentence indicates what the rest of the paragraph makes clear—the writer hates colleges and college students. The first sentence suggests that students are likely to learn little from college except how to scheme and cheat, and the second sentence extends student immorality into the areas of drugs and sex. But the writer's contempt for college students is matched by a loathing of government officials, the ones who finally "take the time" to discover what any ordinary American would have recognized long before. Assuming the role of that ordinary American, the writer refuses to use fancy, intellectual terms like **default, delinquency,** and **dismantled;** instead, the words are coarser, tougher—**rip off, bilked, stupid, fatter, squirmed, swindlers,** and **fools.** Despite the tough, earthy language and the writer's attempt to relate to the readers—"**you** can bet that's not the end of it" and "who deserves more of **our** scorn"—the paragraph communicates a sense of futility and bitterness. Its tone suggests the writer's attitude that there's nothing to do about the entire rotten mess but to get angry.

The above paragraphs on student loans are all relatively clear in tone and straightforward in attitude, but the paragraph below seems somewhat more subtle, perhaps because it is serious and playful at the same time:

Despite soaring tuition fees and room-and-board charges, some college graduates have hit upon a practical plan for reducing the costs of higher education. They simply claim bankruptcy to avoid repaying money they had borrowed from the government to attend college in the first place. Word of the plan must be spreading, for over 300,000 grads have freed themselves of $500 million in federal debts. So long as Washington remains untroubled by the bulging 12.2 percent student default rate—the rate of nonstudent loan delinquencies is a modest 3 percent—students should seriously consider allowing the government to finance their schooling. And after they graduate, they may be able to count on further help. Computers of the Department of Health, Education and Welfare recently discovered that 300 college graduates who defaulted on their student loans are now employed by HEW, some earning as much as $33,000.

It is the paragraph's wording that makes its tone seem playful, especially phrases like "college graduates have **hit upon,**" "They **simply** claim bankruptcy," "grads have **freed themselves,**" "So long as Washington remains **untroubled,**" and "**allowing** the government to finance their schooling." Yet beneath the playfulness, the paragraph is serious in implying that the government is foolish to permit abuse of its student loan program and even more foolish to reward with high-paying jobs those who have abused it. At the same time the writer of the paragraph suggests—with a touch of cynicism—that so long as governmental action seems to invite students to default, they would be fools to pay.

The five paragraphs on student loans illustrate some of the options for defining and controlling the tone of your writing. Try experimenting with word choice, detail selection, and sentence structure until you have created the tone best suited for communicating your attitudes and feelings.

Controlling Tone

Each of the following three paragraphs has a definite tone. Let's assume you've decided that this tone is inappropriate for the purpose of your essay. By using different words, reconstructing sentences, adding and omitting details, or making any other changes, rewrite each paragraph to give it the tone suggested by the directions.

Example

After four days of college life, I've had enough and I'm ready to leave. My clothes have been disappearing one by one into my laundry bag, but they are not clean, folded, and ready to wear the next morning as they were at home. After almost a week without my favorite television programs, I still haven't adjusted to the loss. The supply of snacks ran out yesterday, leaving me totally dependent on the trash that the dining hall calls food. Worst of all, I haven't been able to figure a way to bring my old jalopy to campus, so I have nothing to do with my spare time. Oh, how I wish I were home. (Rewrite the paragraph to make it more playful, less serious.)

↓

After four days of college life, **I've convinced myself** that I've had enough, and I'm ready to leave. My clothes have been disappearing one by one into my laundry bag, but **for some reason** they are not clean, folded, and ready to wear the next morning as they were at home. After almost a week without **Cookie Monster and the rest of the Sesame Street gang, the first pangs of going cold turkey are beginning to set in.** The supply of **Taco Doritos** ran out yesterday, leaving my room totally void of **munchy snacks.** Worst of all, I haven't **yet** been able to figure a way to fit a **grand piano** into my room, leaving me with nothing to do with my spare time but **chase after girls.** Oh, how I **long for the finer things in life!**

A. Not only did Stephen Foster's heart not yearn for the "Swanee" River before he made it famous in his song "The Old Folks at Home," the overrated songwriter never even saw the muddy stream. His first version of the song used the *Pee Dee River*, but Foster decided a softer sounding name would have more commercial appeal, so he found the Suwannee River on a map and then falsified its name. He never even bothered to find out that the Suwannee runs through the swamps of northern Florida and Georgia without so much as touching a plantation. (Rewrite the paragraph to make its tone less nasty.)

B. Of course, it's possible that some of the sightings of flying saucers are actually close encounters of the third kind—encounters with extraterrestrial life. Scientists do believe that 80 of the 300,000 planets in our galaxy have intelligent life. It is even likely that 40 of them have civilizations more advanced than our own. But each of those 40 planets is at least 11,500 light years from earth. So, besides the time—a lot—it would take the energy equivalent of 139,000,000,000,000,000,000 kilowatt hours of electricity to move a space ship to this planet in order to fly around a swamp and excite earthlings. And that's just for a one-way trip. In other words, it's more probable that flying saucer sightings are close encounters of the fourth kind. Close encounters with swamp gas. (Rewrite the paragraph to make its tone more serious and less skeptical.)

C. It was a simpler, happier, and more satisfying world that Archie and Edith Bunker sing about every week on "All in the Family," a world where "girls were girls and men were men." It was a world of strong, silent Hemingway heroes—hunters, soldiers, and athletes who went out into the jungle and brought home the spoils. Waiting to meet them with open arms were sweet, available women who willingly accepted their subordinate position and were happy to be conquered. Truly, those were the days. (Rewrite the paragraph to give it a hostile, disapproving tone.)

Sentence Combining Exercise

Combine the sentences below into a humorous paragraph. Choose from the options in parentheses the one that most effectively helps create a humorous tone. Feel free to add or delete details, to change sentence structure, and to select words and phrases different from those within the parentheses.

THE DASTARDLY DUCKS

1. There are (busybodies, dedicated souls, people).
2. They (are opposed to, fight, wage war on) pornography and vice in the media.
3. They should (examine more carefully, scrutinize, take a closer look at) the Donald Duck comic books.

4. The comic books present a picture of the family and of American capitalism.
5. The picture is (dirty, sordid, unwholesome).

6. The Duck family is (fragmented, imperfect, incomplete).
7. The Duck family is (motherless, without a mother, without a woman in the house).
8. Donald Duck raises three (kids he tries to pass off as nephews, supposed "nephews," young boys who are obviously illegitimate).

9. You can't turn a page in the comic book without (observing, seeing, spotting) a duck.
10. The duck is (naked, nude, unclothed).
11. Even the ducks that (are attired, dress, wear clothes) cover only their tops.
12. They never cover their more (essential, private, significant) (bodily areas, parts, places).

13. The only example of a successful businessduck is Scrooge McDuck.
14. Scrooge McDuck is (frugal, miserly, money-grubbing).
15. Scrooge McDuck is a (millionaire, tycoon, plutocrat).

16. (All in all, If everything is taken into account, Thus), Donald Duck comics (have, offer, purvey) vice and corruption.
17. It is as much vice and corruption as a (copy, issue, volume) of (*Hustler, Playboy, Reader's Digest*).
18. The (copy, issue, volume) is (average, representative, typical).

Creating Tone

Each of the following three paragraphs is relatively impartial in tone. By using different words, reconstructing sentences, adding and omitting details, or making any other appropriate changes, rewrite the paragraph to give it a more definite tone. You may create the tone called for in the directions, or you may create any other tone you want.

Example

A football widow is not a woman whose husband perished on the stadium parking lot. No, it's just that her husband watches football on television every Saturday and Sunday and every Monday night during the football season. She has her weekends all to herself because, when she tries to talk to her husband, she is usually told to start crocheting a sweater for the neighbor's poodle. Instead, she'll probably join a bridge club, go bowling with her friends, or bake batches of chocolate chip cookies. (Rewrite the paragraph to make it either more serious, more angry, or both.)

A football widow is not a woman whose husband died on the stadium parking lot, although she often wishes he had. She is a woman whose husband is addicted to watching football on television every Saturday, every Sunday, and every Monday night from late August to early January. She is a woman afraid to talk to her husband—except to offer him a brew—for fear she will be ignored, shut up, or told where to go. And sometimes she does go—to the bridge club, to the bowling alleys, or to have an affair with her daughter's math teacher.

A. Each year, fraternities and sororities replenish their ranks through a process known as "rush." Ostensibly a group of open houses and parties for the purpose of making friends and learning about the Greek system, rush is also a screening process for choosing acceptable pledges. It is a procedure whose structure is bound by tradition, allowing the participants to be closely scrutinized in a variety of social situations. The brothers and sisters compare the newcomers, from the first beer bash through the final dinner party, seeking people with a strong affinity for their group. These people are tendered an invitation to join the fraternal organization at the close of rush activities. (Rewrite the paragraph to make it either more hostile or more favorable in tone to fraternities and sororities.)

B. Some people can't understand why the Equal Rights Amendment has run into difficulties in the ratification process. As an outgrowth of the democratic tradition, the measure seems to many a natural step in political evolution. However, there is a tightly knit and vocal group of people, predominantly women, who are opposed to the ERA on basic philosophical principles. Their campaign to halt the amendment has been so successful that ratification now appears doubtful. The failure of the ERA would signal a defeat for the women's liberation movement and a triumph for traditional values. (Rewrite the paragraph so that its tone clearly indicates that you either support or oppose the ratification of the ERA.)

C. We've all used mnemonic devices, memory aids, to help us recall information. Probably the most famous is the tune by which everyone learns the ABCs. A recently published book entitled *A Dictionary of Mnemonics* lists hundreds of memory devices used by schoolchildren and scholars from the middle ages to the present. It includes a rhyming poem for those who wish to list the rulers of England from the eleventh century, another that gives the value of pi to the twentieth decimal point, and a sentence whose initial letters indicate the order of the planets: "**M**en **v**ery **e**asily **m**ade **j**ugs **s**erve **u**seful **n**octurnal **p**urposes." (Rewrite the paragraph with a tone of doubt and skepticism about the value of mnemonic devices.)

Sentence Combining Exercise

Read over the following sentences in order to decide on the tone you want to create. Then combine the sentences into an essay with a clearly defined tone. You may change words or phrases and add or eliminate details.

AREN'T YOU GLAD YOU USE DIAL?

1. Americans have always lived by aphorisms.

2. Ben Franklin's Poor Richard became famous for teaching us this.

3. "A penny saved is a penny earned."
4. "Hard work never hurt anyone."

5. We believed the aphorisms.
6. And we became a great nation.
7. We saved our money.
8. And we worked hard.

9. But there is one aphorism.
10. We took to it more than the others.
11. It is "cleanliness is next to godliness."

12. So we made a fetish out of keeping clean.

13. Suppose ads are a reflection of our life-style.
14. Then we spend half our lives ridding our homes of offending odors.
15. We spend half our lives ridding our bodies of offending odors.
16. Offending odors would betray a lack of cleanliness.

17. And we spend a lot of money on odor-reducing products.
18. We spend more than $300 million a year on mouthwashes.
19. We spend over $500 million a year for deodorants.

20. The competition among companies is so keen.
21. Two of the largest ones have staffs of trained judges.
22. The companies sell us these products.
23. The judges' only job is this.
24. They sniff armpits.
25. This is to ascertain the effectiveness of the deodorants.

26. No one would fault Americans for wanting to smell good.
27. No one has taken a crowded bus in Rome, Italy on a warm day.

28. But it may be this.
29. We carry the effort too far.

30. In fact, odors do occur.

31. People do not keep clean.

32. But bacteria cause odors.
33. And deodorants do little to prevent bacteria.
34. Mouthwashes do little to prevent bacteria.

35. For instance, mouth odor is caused by the bacteria from tooth decay.
36. Mouth odor is caused by the bacteria from throat infections.
37. Or mouth odor is caused by the bacteria from postnasal drip.
38. Mouthwashes will relieve none of these.

39. And deodorants do little more than this.
40. They mask the odor of decomposing sweat.

41. In effect, we could be as clean and sweet-smelling by proper oral hygiene.
42. We could be as clean and sweet-smelling by daily bathing.
43. And we could save a great deal of money.

44. Poor Richard may have been right.
45. But Listerine is a put on.

46. You may be glad you use sprays.
47. You may be glad you use roll-ons.
48. You may be glad you use mouthwashes.
49. But hardly anyone else notices.

Revising for Consistency of Tone

Each of the paragraphs below is confusing because of inconsistency of tone. Following the specific directions, revise each paragraph to create a consistent tone that makes your feelings and attitudes clear.

Example

Many states are instituting proficiency examinations for graduating high school seniors. They test, for example, the students' ability to read newspapers and magazines, to write checks, and to find names in phone books. Educators hope that proficiency testing is a first step in assuring that, when you've finally gotten the old diploma, you can really do some of the things you're supposed to be able to do in the twelfth grade. (Rewrite the last sentence to make it consistent in tone with the rest of the paragraph.)

↓

Educators hope that proficiency testing is a first step toward assuring that graduation from high school means a student has achieved twelfth-grade skills.

A. The government obviously resorts to secrecy whenever its agencies conduct research which the public has good reason to suspect is either cruel or unethical. The army has secretly subjected dogs to torture endurance tests and, in the 1950s, hid from the public its testing of LSD and other dangerous drugs on unsuspecting American soldiers. Of course, the army is not the only governmental agency guilty of concealing its inhumane and immoral experiments from the public. Even the Department of Transportation admitted that for years it has used human bodies in auto crash tests to study the effectiveness of air bags. I tend to believe, and so do many of the people I've talked with, that the interest of the public would best be served if the government occasionally made available the nature and purposes of any experiment that might conceivably prove to be questionable. (Rewrite the last sentence to make it consistent in tone with the rest of the paragraph.)

B. Although successful people and failures both agree that luck and connections are the main ingredients of success, they view these factors differently. The guys 'n' gals who've never made it to the top say that forces they can't control prevented them from doing more. They view luck as a turn of the roulette wheel or a throw of the dice, as an almost magical force. They believe that connections are an accident of birth. But that's not the case for those who've made it. Oh, no! Those who have succeeded attribute their accomplishments to their own talent and effort. They see luck in terms of timing, of taking advantage of opportunities as they arise. And according to these Joes and Janes, connections are not really a birthright. No way! They're the result of keeping your nose to the grindstone. One essential difference, then, between those who succeed and those who fail seems to be the extent to which they accept responsibility for controlling their own lives. (Rewrite the middle of the paragraph to make it consistent in tone with the first and last sentences.)

C. The national parks, which were set aside by an act of Congress to keep the American wilderness going, have become tame and polluted, little more than drive-in Holiday Inns complete with newfangled, computerized reservation setups. Trails that were once loads of fun to explore have been paved over for the convenience of tenderfeet. Park rangers now spend more time picking up litter and putting out fires than caring for Yogi Bear, Boo Boo, and all their friends and relatives. Walking among the candy wrappers, beer cans, and spray-painted boulders—some of them are decorated with really interesting designs!—campers smell gas fumes more often than the scent of pine. Even the whispering wind is likely to be drowned out by the roar of trail bikes or by the chatter of portable radios. When will Americans shape up? (Rewrite the paragraph to make it consistent in tone. Decide whether to make its tone serious or playful and formal or informal.)

Sentence Combining Exercise

Combine the following sentences into an essay which describes and explains the simplicity and symmetry of an authentic Chinese table setting. Create the style and tone appropriate to an essay on simplicity and symmetry. Since style and tone are in part controlled by sentence length, there are no white spaces to indicate where one of your sentences may begin and another end. Instead, the white spaces suggest where you may begin and end your paragraphs.

CHINESE TABLE SETTINGS

1. Dragons adorn most Chinese restaurants in America.
2. Exotic lights adorn most Chinese restaurants in America.

3. Hanging wind chimes adorn most Chinese restaurants in America.
4. Restaurants in China are actually quite different.
5. Restaurants in China stress economy.
6. Restaurants in China do not stress effect.
7. The table setting is an example of this economy.
8. The table setting is the most characteristic example.
9. An authentic Chinese table is an embodiment of symmetry.
10. An authentic Chinese table is an embodiment of simplicity.
11. It is a perfect embodiment.
12. The embodiment is from the decorations to the place settings.

13. The dinner table is in a well-lighted room.
14. The dinner table is round.
15. The dinner table is covered with a cloth.
16. The cloth is white.
17. The cloth is simple.
18. There are six to eight chairs.
19. One chair is directly across from another.
20. The chairs are wooden.
21. The chairs surround the table.
22. There is a set of serving dishes.
23. The dishes rest in the middle of the table.
24. A soup bowl is in the middle.
25. The soup bowl is large.
26. There are smaller dishes.
27. These dishes are for the main courses.
28. These dishes are situated around the soup bowl.
29. These dishes are like the chairs.
30. These dishes are arranged symmetrically.

31. The individual place settings are equally simple.
32. A plate sits in the center.
33. The plate is used for foods.
34. The plate is used for scraps as well.
35. On the plate is a soup bowl.
36. The soup bowl is small.
37. A china spoon rests inside the soup bowl.

38. A pair of chopsticks lie immediately to the right.
39. The chopsticks may be made of plastic.
40. The chopsticks may be made of wood.
41. The chopsticks may be made of ivory.
42. At more expensive restaurants the chopsticks are of ivory.
43. The chopsticks are usually without design.
44. A tea cup is located directly behind the chopsticks.
45. The tea cup is small.
46. The tea cup is porcelain.
47. The tea cup has no handles.
48. A wine cup sits to the right of the tea cup on most occasions.
49. The rice bowl is the most important piece.
50. The rice bowl is placed in the upper left-hand corner of the setting.
51. The rice bowl is placed directly across from the tea cup.
52. A dip dish is placed between the tea cup and the rice bowl.
53. The dip dish is tiny.
54. The dip dish concludes the setting.

55. The setting is simple.
56. Chinese table settings are not all alike.
57. The dishes have shapes.
58. The dishes have designs.
59. The dishes have colors.
60. They are limited only by one's imagination.
61. Landscape scenes often decorate the cups and plates.
62. The scenes are brightly colored.
63. Animals often decorate the cups and plates.
64. The Chinese rely even more on something else for excitement.
65. The Chinese rely on the food.
66. The meal is served.
67. Then, shrimp, beef, peas, pineapples, and rice fill the bowls.
68. Shrimp, beef, peas, pineapples, and rice punctuate the simplicity of the table.
69. The simplicity is punctuated with shapes.
70. The simplicity is punctuated with colors.

71. The simplicity is punctuated with aromas.
72. The simplicity of the table is not merely for the sake of simplicity.
73. The simplicity of the table is not merely for the sake of symmetry.
74. The simplicity of the table is designed to accentuate the natural beauty of the food.

17. Summing Up

Revising Paragraphs I

Revise the following paragraphs using the strategy indicated in parentheses. Make any other changes you feel are necessary.

A. The image of the movie hero has changed in recent years. No longer does he have to be tall, strong, and firm like Clark Gable. Now he can be short, fragile, and sensitive like Woody Allen. He doesn't have to be like Cary Grant any more—cool, detached, and well groomed. Like Dustin Hoffman, he can be neurotic, involved, and unkempt now. (Repetition/Balance)

B. College students often wonder whether their four years in school might not be better spent at a job. Recent research on the benefits of higher education indicates that a college degree will return an average of 9 to 14 percent interest in increased earning power over a lifetime. It is shown that college graduates will enjoy their jobs more than those without a degree, have stronger family bonds and smaller, healthier families. (Coherence)

C. A great pitcher doesn't need a lot of "stuff," just two good pitches. Sandy Koufax, for instance, pitched mainly fastballs and curves. His powerful fastball set up batters, kept them on their toes, alert, and quick to swing the bat. His curve put the batters away. He baited them with a fastball and struck them out with a curve. (Rearrangement for emphasis)

D. Moviemakers constantly try to add realism to their product. Some of the gimmicks they've employed, such as sound, wide screen, and technicolor, have caught on and become part of the industry. Other gimmicks, like 3-D and Sensurround, proved an annoyance and quickly died. Now odors have been added for a new dimension of realism by some owners of porno movie houses. The day may not be distant when some enterprising porno flick owner combines the odors with 3-D and Sensurround, and the prospect boggles the mind. (Emphasis)

E. Did you know that it is commonly thought that left-handedness is an inherited trait, like blue eyes or blond hair? Well, it is. But doctors—when they're not playing golf—are now beginning to investigate the possibility that left-handedness may be caused by stressful births which reduce the supply of good old oxygen to the left side of the noggin, the side that controls language functions and right-handedness. The incidence of stressful births is twice as high among southpaws than righties, and dullards with language disorders have a higher incidence of left-handedness than the normal population. It may be that left-handedness is the most common and harmless effect of birth stress. But then again, what do doctors know, anyway? (Tone)

Sentence Combining Exercise

Combine the following sentences into an effective essay.

SPARE THE ROD

1. Genie was found by the authorities in Los Angeles.
2. Genie was 14 years old.
3. Genie looked like an emaciated six year old.

4. She could not talk.
5. She could not chew food.
6. She could not use a toilet.

7. Genie had been locked in a small room.
8. Genie was often strapped in an infant's potty chair.
9. Or Genie was caged in a crib.
10. The crib was covered with wire mesh.
11. She was fed nothing but baby food.
12. She was never spoken to by her parents.
13. These happened from the age of 20 months.

14. She cried.
15. Or she made a sound.
16. If so, then her father beat her.
17. Her father claimed this.
18. Noise upset him.

19. Genie's is a case of child abuse.
20. The case is extreme.
21. The case is unusual only in its severity.

22. The National Center on Child Abuse documented this.
23. There were a half million cases in the United States in 1976.
24. The cases were of child abuse.
25. And experts at the center estimate this.
26. The number is only half of the actual cases.

27. The problem is so severe.
28. One out of every 33 children is probably abused.
29. Or one out of every 33 children is probably neglected.

30. Child abuse now ranks fifth among the major causes of childhood deaths.
31. It ranks behind accidents.
32. It ranks behind cancer.
33. It ranks behind congenital abnormalities.
34. And it ranks behind pneumonia.

35. The statistics seem to indicate this.
36. Americans are growing more violent toward their children.
37. Or the statistics seem to indicate this.
38. We are developing a social layer.
39. The social layer is of evil people.
40. The evil people abuse their own flesh and blood.
41. They do this with ropes.
42. They do this with sticks.
43. They do this with boots.
44. And they do this with hot irons.

45. But probably neither of these is the case.

46. The statistical increase probably indicates nothing more than this.
47. Doctors report child abuse cases.
48. They report more often now than they did in the past.

49. And surprisingly few parents are truly evil.
50. Parents abuse their children.
51. This is according to the authorities.

52. In fact, child abusers are not evil.
53. In fact, child abusers are not even readily identifiable.

54. They come from every race.
55. They come from every religion.
56. They come from all levels of society.

57. But they do have some characteristics in common.

58. They are isolated people.
59. They have few friends.

60. They are distrustful of others.

61. Most of them have a low tolerance for frustration.
62. They strike out when their children cry.
63. Or they strike out when their children upset their plans.
64. Most of them are like Genie's father.

65. Usually they have been abused themselves as children.

66. In fact, the children of child abusers will probably emulate their parents.
67. They will strike out at their own offspring.
68. Or they will strike out at society.

69. One recent study reveals this.
70. Half the delinquents in South Carolina detention centers have been abused by their parents.
71. Sirhan Sirhan had also been abused by his parents.
72. James Earl Ray had also been abused by his parents.
73. Lee Harvey Oswald had also been abused by his parents.
74. John Wilkes Booth had also been abused by his parents.

75. Child abuse is now recognized as a national problem.
76. But the law can do little to help the children.
77. Child abuse is so difficult to prove except in extreme cases.

78. Experts agree.
79. Parents must be educated.
80. Parents abuse their children.
81. This may enable them to cope with frustration.
82. This may alleviate the problem.

83. So, many cities now sponsor programs.
84. The programs relieve family tension.
85. The programs teach parents to enjoy their children.

86. And a nationwide program has been established.
87. It is for parents who wish to help themselves.
88. It is called Parents Anonymous.

89. Suppose such programs had existed 20 years ago.
90. Then Genie might have had a normal life.
91. Then half the delinquents might be learning to be useful citizens.

Taking It Apart

Make each of the long, unwieldy sentences below into a more effective short paragraph of two or more sentences. Correct problems of coherence, emphasize the controlling idea, and make the tone consistent and appropriate.

Example

Tourists to Douglas, Wyoming, are surprised to see the 8-foot-tall jackalope statue in the center of town, although residents, discounting rumors that a local taxidermist created the "horny rabbit," insist that the jackalope, an animal with the body of a rabbit and the antlers of a deer, does exist, the Douglas Chamber of Commerce being so sure of the animal's existence that each year it sells thousands of jackalope hunting licenses to be used—would you believe?—between the hours of midnight and 2 A.M. every June 31.

Tourists to Douglas, Wyoming, are surprised to see the 8-foot-tall jackalope statue in the center of town. But residents insist that the jackalope, an animal with the body of a rabbit and the antlers of a deer, does exist. They discount rumors that a local taxidermist created the "horny rabbit." In fact, the Douglas Chamber of Commerce is so sure of the animal's existence that each year it sells thousands of jackalope hunting licenses to be used—would you believe?—between the hours of midnight and 2 A.M. every June 31.

OR

It is only between the hours of midnight and 2 A.M. every June 31 that licenses are valid to hunt jackalope—an animal with the body of a rabbit and the antlers of a deer. Yet thousands of the licenses are sold by the Douglas, Wyoming, Chamber of Commerce. The residents of Douglas have erected an 8-foot-tall statue to the jackalope in the center of town—in direct defiance of those who would spread the rumor that a local taxidermist created the animal. Still, tourists are surprised to see the statue and often doubt the veracity of the story of the "horny rabbit."

A. Authorities usually claim that criminals are produced either by bad environments or by mental illness, but a new study indicates that criminals are not products of bad environments and are not mentally ill, but, simply, bad and antisocial people who enjoy lying, stealing, embezzling, and killing, and think about crime constantly, the way an alcoholic may think about liquor, being cured with the same kind of therapy that helps alcoholics, in other words, with a kind of "Criminals Anonymous."

B. Theology and psychology often explain the same phenomena in different ways, the Bible, for instance, relating the story of Nebuchadnezzar, a Babylonian king who was turned into a beast, made to lie in the fields and eat grass with the animals, which was a humbling experience for the man who had built the Hanging Gardens, but psychologists would say that he had been afflicted with lycanthropy, a mental illness that makes people think they are animals, which is the same thing that affects Lon Chaney in the movies, when he supposedly turns into a werewolf at the appearance of the full moon.

C. The British Broadcasting Company may have proven Joseph Conrad, who speculated that the behavior of civilized people is but a thin veneer covering a truly primitive nature, correct when, in order to film a documentary on life in the Iron Age, the company hired a group of ten men and women to live in an ancient villlage just outside of Stonehenge, where they had to weave cloth, make tools, farm in ancient ways, and practice the Celtic religion; for, after a year, their behavior changed and they walked more slowly and talked more slowly and slept longer and were less inhibited about nudity and more self-sufficient but also more primitive, for instance, at the planting ceremony, where they forced one of the group to be lashed as a sacrifice to ensure a good harvest.

D. If you want to play caterpillar, ringalevio, elbow tag, or vampire, but are afraid that you are too old and would be embarrassed, go to Kansas City, where the group of people in all age groups—6 to 60—meets every Sunday in a park to play their favorite childhood games, bumping into each other, running around shrieking like vampires, or hiding from whoever is "It," and the participants saying, "It's good clean fun and good exercise as well," and besides, what else is there to do on a Sunday in Kansas City?

E. People who ordinarily would not cheat or steal will often lie about their educational backgrounds in order to impress people, gain political power, borrow money, or boost their own egos, and so graduates of nonprestige schools like Lydia Pinkham College will claim to have graduated from Harvard or Yale, one man even figuring a way to get his picture in the Harvard yearbook, though he had never taken a class at that university—the problem becoming so severe that Ivy League schools are now threatening to sue imposters, who, according to one psychiatrist, believe that they have gone to the prestige institutions because "they wished so badly that they had."

Sentence Combining Exercise

Combine these sentences into an essay of no more than 200 words. Choose only those details that most directly support the thesis and omit the rest.

"THE JEFFERSONS"

1. TV networks have been accused of exploiting blacks.
2. TV networks have been accused of picturing blacks only as buffoons or servants.
3. Blacks have been pictured in a world filled with admirable white characters.
4. This has been in the past.

5. The networks have overcompensated.
6. The networks have tilted the balance the other way.
7. They give us shows with black characters and white characters.
8. The black characters are admirable.

9. The white characters are buffoons and servants.
10. This is in an attempt to rectify past discrimination.
11. This is now.

12. "The Jeffersons" is a case in point.

13. Every black character on "The Jeffersons" is praiseworthy.
14. Even those with obvious flaws are praiseworthy.

15. George Jefferson is prejudiced toward whites.
16. George Jefferson is overbearing toward economic inferiors.
17. George Jefferson is the central character.

18. Yet he comes off as lovable.
19. This is because he is funny.
20. This is because he is smart.
21. This is because he is quick-witted.

22. The other characters laugh off his flaws.
23. Thus they minimize his offensiveness.
24. They endorse his reprehensible attitudes.
25. This is clear.

26. Louise Jefferson is a sensible and intelligent woman.
27. She successfully mediates all conflicts.

28. She has a quick wit.
29. She has a clear head.
30. She has a maternal attractiveness.

31. Their son and his wife are a model couple.
32. Their son is Lionel.
33. His wife is Jennie.
34. They are attractive.
35. They are considerate.
36. They are insightful.

37. Even George's mother wins our sympathy.
38. She does this though she is close-minded.

39. She does this because her stubbornness is amusing.
40. She does this because her biting criticism is amusing.

41. The maid delights us with her intelligence.
42. The maid delights us with her "jive."

43. Jennie's mother rounds out the black cast.
44. Jennie's mother is beautiful.

45. All these black characters are essentially positive.
46. Their negative qualities are minimized.

47. The few whites appear regularly.
48. They are more or less buffoons.
49. They contrast with the black characters.

50. Their primary function is this.
51. They provide the blacks with objects for ridicule.

52. An Englishman plays the perfect fool.

53. He is tall.
54. He is gawky.
55. He is eagle-beaked.
56. He appears ridiculous because of his lack of common sense.
57. He appears ridiculous because of his clumsiness.

58. Jennie's white father is a favorite target.

59. He is nervous.
60. He is fat.
61. And he is a silly worrywart.
62. This is in comparison to his wife.

63. The final white character serves one purpose.
64. He is a doorman.
65. His purpose is to exemplify the money-grubbing employee.
66. His purpose is to exemplify the anything-for-a-buck employee.

67. The white characters form a sorry group.
68. They are floundering nincompoops.

69. "The Jeffersons" reveals the failure of the TV networks.
70. The networks have not come to grips with discrimination.

71. They reverse white and black roles.
72. This succeeds only in perpetuating existing racial prejudice.

73. "The Jeffersons" is hardly a realistic portrayal of black life-styles.
74. It is no more realistic than "All in the Family" in portraying white life-styles.

75. Surely TV can do better than Archie Bunker.
76. Surely TV can do better than George Jefferson.

77. What would be wrong with a show that had realistic black and white characters?
78. What would be wrong with a show that did not have stereotypes?

Revising Paragraphs II

Revise the following paragraphs using the strategy indicated in parentheses. Make any other changes you feel are necessary.

A. There are two elementary symbols in Western literature, light and dark. Light signifies purity and life. Corruption and even death are signified by dark. Our literature is filled with this contrast. When St. Paul is struck by a blinding light, he is transformed from a sinner to a follower of Christ. Lucifer rebels against God in *Paradise Lost* and then he is plunged into "darkness visible." (Repetition/Ellipsis)

B. Most people think of archeological expeditions as fascinating treasure hunts to uncover the glories of the past. The occasional discovery of strange and magnificent artifacts, like those from King Tut's tomb, or of important religious documents, like the Dead Sea Scrolls, support an image in the public mind. Most expeditions are tedious to anyone but a dedicated scholar interested in the mundane, everyday existence of ancient peoples. On the site the archeologist's patience is tried by insects, poor food, bad weather, primitive accommodations, and meddling by local officials. Difficult months of excavation are more often rewarded by pottery shards from ancient trash heaps than by glittering monuments of civilizations. (Coherence)

C. While most energy research is directed at deriving power from the sun or harnessing the wind and waves, some researchers think they've found a short-term answer to the energy crisis in CRAP, the Calorific Recovery Anaerobic Process, Inc. CRAP, an Oklahoma-based company that converts cattle manure into methane, sells 1.6 million cubic feet of gas to utility companies. That's the output of its "harvest" of the waste of 100,000 cattle. By recycling the estimated 380 tons of U.S. manure, CRAP could supply nearly 5 percent of the nation's natural gas demands. Then the only thing worse than an Arab oil embargo would be an epidemic of bovine constipation. (Tone)

D. Though many of America's actresses, including Susan Blakely, Farrah Fawcett, and Jaclyn Smith, began as models, few models have become accomplished actresses. Maybe modeling and acting are too different. Modeling demands the passive skill of being photogenic and of functioning simply as a beautiful doll on which to display a product. Acting demands the active skill of projecting a personality and creating a character out of the playwright's lines, on the other hand. (Emphasis)

E. Politicians and entrepreneurs can get into trouble with the federal government for "laundering" money through Caribbean bank accounts. But in the early 1900s the U.S. Treasury Department actually did launder money. It had a machine that washed, rinsed, and dried old bills. Workers then ironed the bills, which were put back into circulation. The Treasury Department, though, began to destroy old money rather than launder it, after 1921. It seems that laundered money feels different and is easier to counterfeit. (Rearrangement)

Sentence Combining Exercise

Combine the following sentences into an effective argument for or against abortion by (1) omitting any details that do not support your position and (2) completing the essay with details that do.

ABORTION

1. Surgical abortion remains the only certain way.
2. It terminates unwanted pregnancies.
3. It is an ancient method of birth control.
4. It is a widespread method of birth control.

5. Abortion has become more popular all over the world.
6. At the same time new surgical techniques have made abortions safe.
7. They are more safe than full-term pregnancy and childbirth.

8. Abortion was generally used when pregnancy resulted from rape or incest.
9. It was used when the mother's life was endangered.
10. Or it was used when this was likely.
11. The child would be born defective.
12. This was in the past.

13. Abortion is increasingly considered as an option.
14. It is an option when the regular method of birth control fails.
15. This is now.

16. The debate over surgical "abortion upon request" has divided this country.
17. Few other issues have divided the country like this since Vietnam.
18. The debate is intense.
19. The debate is often bitter.

20. The Supreme Court paved the way for legalized abortion.

21. The legalized abortion would be throughout the United States.
22. It did this in 1973.
23. It did this when it handed down two important decisions.

24. These rulings forbid any attempt.
25. The attempts would deny a woman an abortion in the first three months of pregnancy.
26. The rulings were based largely on the grounds of privacy.

27. The government may place restrictions on the abortion procedure.
28. This can happen only after the fetus reaches a state of viability.

29. Several groups decried the decisions.
30. The groups were opposed to abortion.
31. They said the decisions violated the rights of the fetus.
32. Their decrying almost immediately followed the Court's actions.

33. The groups argued this.
34. The fetus is a human being.
35. And abortion is murder.
36. Quite simply, it is murder.

37. The Court avoided the theological problem.
38. The theological problem is in determining when a fetus becomes human.
39. The Court based its judgment on the concept of viability.
40. The concept of viability is medical.

41. That is, the fetus is not yet an individual.
42. And the fetus is therefore not subject to constitutional protection.
43. This is true if the fetus cannot sustain its own life outside the womb.

44. The mother is the one entitled.
45. She is entitled to legal support of her right.
46. Her right is to decide this.
47. What is in her own best interest?

PART THREE

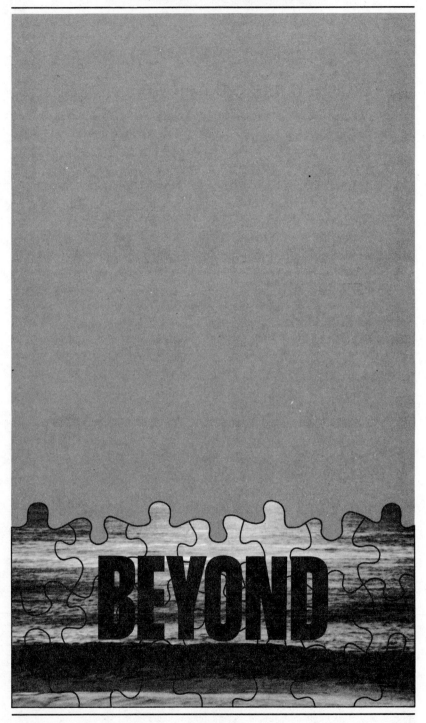

18. Toward Selecting and Organizing Ideas

You usually start writing only after you've collected some information. You do enough reading, remembering, and thinking until you've accumulated a set of related ideas and supporting details, often in the form of notes. Then the process of selection and organization begins. Suppose that, beginning only with the vague purpose of writing about Charles Lindbergh's historic transatlantic flight in 1927, you collect the following notes:

> Lindbergh was 25 years old when he flew from New York to Paris.
> The solo flight was from Long Island to Orly Airport.
> It took 33 hours.
> Onlookers thought he was doomed to failure.
> He had flown and navigated mail planes for years.
> He had been a stunt pilot on the barnstorming circuit.
> He had set out to win the $25,000 prize offered for the first nonstop flight across the Atlantic.

He had studied all the planes available and chose the Ryan monoplane.

He had it modified and supervised all the modifications.

The wingspan was extended 10 feet for more lift.

He added stronger landing gear.

The fuel capacity was increased from 50 to 450 gallons.

He had enough fuel for a 300-mile navigational error.

He replaced the original seat by a cane chair to save weight.

He installed a 200 h.p. radial air-cooled Wright Whirlwind engine.

The plane had a 130 mph top speed.

He had no radio.

He navigated with a magnetic compass and mariner's sextant.

He flew 10 feet above the waves to keep track of wind direction and wind speed.

He had a bottle of water and five sandwiches—two ham, two beef, one egg with mayonnaise.

His first landsight was Ireland, just as he had planned.

After the flight, he was made a hero, and songs were written about him.

One song was "Lucky Lindy."

Which of these ideas and details you select and how you arrange them depends on your purpose. If you had been a newspaper reporter in 1927, your story would probably begin with a paragraph whose purpose is to communicate the basic facts of Lindbergh's flight. The basic facts will emerge from your notes if you ask yourself a set of six questions known in journalism classes as the "Five W's plus H": Who? What? Where? When? Why? and How?

Who?   Charles Lindbergh, a 25-year-old former mail pilot.

What?   Flew nonstop across the Atlantic.

Where?   From Long Island to Paris.

When?   Landed this morning after a 33-hour flight.

Why?   A $25,000 prize.

How?   In a Ryan monoplane, solo, navigating with a compass and sextant.

With the answers to these six questions, you can construct an appropriate opening paragraph for a longer article on Lindbergh's flight:

> Charles Lindbergh, a 25-year-old former mail pilot, landed in
> Paris this morning after a 33-hour solo flight from Long
> Island. Lindbergh flew a modified Ryan monoplane and
> navigated with a compass and sextant. He is expected to
> claim the $25,000 prize for being the first person ever to fly
> nonstop across the Atlantic.

This paragraph primarily communicates facts. But most of the
paragraphs you write in college will go beyond stating facts in order
to explain, analyze, or interpret them. Such paragraphs are usually
most effective when unified by a controlling idea.

A controlling idea, sometimes called a topic sentence, helps
you to separate what is relevant from what is irrelevant. If your
controlling idea is that Lindbergh succeeded because of his knowledge, experience, thoroughness, and luck, you will probably see at
once that some of your collected notes are irrelevant and should be
discarded. For example, the facts that Lindbergh had no radio and
that he took along five sandwiches are not clearly connected to the
reasons for his success. In the same way, the facts that the flight
took 33 hours, that it began in Long Island and ended at Orly
Airport, or that it won Lindbergh $25,000 are not directly related to
knowledge, experience, thoroughness, and luck. By omitting such
irrelevant material and by including only details that develop the
controlling idea, you can construct a unified and effective paragraph:

> **Lindbergh was successful in flying nonstop across
> the Atlantic because of his knowledge, his ex-
> perience, his thoroughness, and his luck.** He knew
> airplanes both as a pilot and navigator. He had gained
> extensive flying experience from mail runs and the
> barnstorming circuit. He carefully selected his own plane
> and thoroughly modified it for the arduous flight by extend-
> ing its wingspan, installing stronger landing gear, and in-
> creasing its fuel capacity. And, as popular songs like
> "Lucky Lindy" made clear, he had plenty of luck.

Aside from providing a principle for selecting ideas and details, the
controlling idea often suggests a principle of organization as well.
Here the controlling idea has four parts—knowledge, experience,
thoroughness, and luck—and each of the subsequent sentences in
turn illustrates one of those four parts.

From the same controlling idea, many different paragraphs can be constructed, depending again on your selection and organization of ideas and supporting details. One useful option is to begin your paragraph with a question that the remainder of the paragraph answers. In such a paragraph your controlling idea may be positioned not at the beginning but at the end:

> Why was Charles Lindbergh able to succeed in flying nonstop across the Atlantic when others before him had failed? For one thing, he knew airplanes both as a pilot and navigator. For another, he had gained extensive flying experience from mail runs and the barnstorming circuit. Perhaps most importantly, he carefully selected his own plane and thoroughly modified it for the arduous flight by extending its wingspan, installing stronger landing gear, and increasing its fuel capacity. Finally, as popular songs like "Lucky Lindy" make clear, he had plenty of luck. **Lindbergh succeeded because of his knowledge, experience, thoroughness, and luck.**

Whenever you have difficulty finding a controlling idea, it's helpful to start asking questions about the information you've gathered. For example, one of your notes says that Lindbergh was "made a hero" after his flight. A question you might ask yourself and then try to answer is whether Lindbergh really deserved to be made into a hero. The question itself indicates the topic of a potential paragraph or essay, and your answer to it helps define a controlling idea. If you answer that "Lindbergh deserved his status as a hero" and choose that statement as your controlling idea, the next step is to select from your notes those details that are relevant and to discard those that are not. The most relevant details for establishing Lindbergh's heroism relate to the length and difficulty of his journey, to his primitive flight instruments, and to the uniqueness of his achievement. Those details might be organized into a paragraph like this:

> Charles Lindbergh was hailed as a hero when he landed safely in Paris because, by flying nonstop across the Atlantic, he had done what had never been done before. And he did it under almost impossible conditions. He piloted a single-engine Ryan monoplane capable of no more than

130 miles per hour. He flew alone for 33 hours, without a radio and with only a sextant and magnetic compass for navigational help. He often cruised but ten feet above the ocean waves in order to estimate wind speed and wind direction. Because his was truly a heroic feat, **Lindbergh deserved to be a hero.**

Details in the earlier paragraph explaining why Lindbergh succeeded were deliberately omitted from this paragraph because they were no longer relevant. The details about Lindbergh's knowledge, experience, thoroughness, and luck did not directly support the controlling idea that "Lindbergh deserved to be a hero." As always, it is your controlling idea that determines which details are relevant and which are not.

If you had asked how Lindbergh modified his plane instead of why he succeeded or whether he deserved to be a hero, still another paragraph with a different controlling idea could have grown out of your notes. From the details that Lindbergh changed the plane's original wingspan, landing gear, engine, fuel capacity, and seat, you might have written a paragraph developing the idea that after Lindbergh modified his plane, even its manufacturers couldn't recognize it:

The plane Charles Lindbergh flew nonstop across the Atlantic only began as a Ryan monoplane. That was before Lindbergh started modifying it. First, he extended the wingspan by ten feet and added stronger landing gear. Then he increased its fuel capacity from 50 to 450 gallons and installed a 200 horsepower Wright Whirlwind engine. Before he was through, he even replaced the original seat with a lightweight cane chair. When he was done, **the original builders probably wouldn't have recognized their own creation.**

Once again, the controlling idea governed your selection and exclusion of details. Because the details of Lindbergh's difficult flight and primitive instruments did not help develop a controlling idea about plane modifications, you carefully excluded such details from your paragraph.

Sometimes your controlling idea and even the purpose of your paragraph become clear to you only after you have begun writing. Just as often, what you have written may give you new ideas for developing the paragraph. Here is a paragraph you might have written to support the controlling idea that Lindbergh was a skillful planner, pilot, and navigator:

> When 25-year-old Charles Lindbergh took off from Long Island to claim the $25,000 prize for flying nonstop to Paris, most of the onlookers thought he was just another exbarnstormer doomed to failure. They didn't know that **"Lucky Lindy" was a skillful planner, pilot, and navigator.** He had carefully chosen the Ryan monoplane and supervised its modifications. He had installed a 200-horsepower radial air-cooled engine that gave him a top speed of 130 miles per hour. He had the wingspan extended by ten feet for more lift. And he had the normal 50-gallon fuel tank increased to 450 gallons. He was an excellent navigator and pilot who kept track of wind direction and wind speed by flying ten feet above the ocean. When he sighted land, it was precisely where he expected—in Ireland.

But after completing such a paragraph, you might begin to see a new idea emerging—the contrast between the nickname "Lucky Lindy" and the facts indicating that Lindbergh had prepared for his flight with great care and skill. To develop this contrast as the controlling idea of a revised version of your paragraph, you would first want to return to your notes for additional supporting information. There you would find two further details to illustrate Lindbergh's careful preparation—his experience as a pilot of barnstormers and mail planes and his carrying enough fuel for a 300-mile navigational error. By incorporating these details and excluding others, by revising and rearranging sentences, but especially by emphasizing in both your first and last sentences the contrast between luck on the one hand, care and skill on the other, you are now able to construct a new and highly effective paragraph:

> **Though the world called him "Lucky Lindy"** after he became the first person to fly nonstop across the Atlantic, the 25-year-old **Charles Lindbergh had actually depended on skill and careful preparation** for the

flight. He was an expert pilot and navigator with years of experience flying barnstormers and mail planes. He carefully selected the Ryan monoplane from among the available aircraft as the best suited for his difficult task. And he personally supervised its modification, which included extending its wingspan by ten feet and increasing its fuel capacity by 400 gallons so as to allow for a 300-mile navigational error. When "Lucky Lindy" touched down in Paris 33 hours after leaving Long Island, it was because he had left little to luck.

Your major options in constructing paragraphs and essays include defining your controlling idea, carefully selecting your supporting details, and then arranging both idea and supporting details into an effective whole.

Sentence Combining Exercise

Combine the following sentences so as to develop either (1) the argument that the government should not enact rent control laws because they would inhibit free enterprise or (2) the argument that the government should enact rent control laws because they would benefit low and fixed income renters without cost to taxpayers. Exclude from your essay the facts or details which do not help develop the thesis you choose. Develop your essay with some paragraphs unified by a controlling idea.

RENT CONTROL

1. The federal government invested millions of dollars.
2. The money was invested in a low income housing project.
3. The housing project was in Atlanta.
4. A study found the buildings unfit and unsafe four years later.

5. This sort of thing happens all too often.
6. It happens in a time when housing is needed.
7. It is needed for low income families.
8. The need is bad.
9. It is an example of the foolishness of many government ideas.
10. The government ideas relate to housing.

11. Another of the government's ideas is rent control.
12. It was designed to protect the rights of renters.
13. Instead it serves to deny landlords the rights of ownership.

14. But one of the government's ideas may protect low and fixed income renters.
15. One of the government's ideas is rent control.
16. It may do this effectively.
17. It may do this during inflationary times.

18. Rent control is simply a form of price control.

19. Rent control laws have been enacted.

20. Governments of cities have enacted them.
21. The cities had housing vacancy rates below 5 percent.
22. This has been in the past.

23. Rent control fixes a ceiling.
24. The ceiling is on the amount of rent.
25. The landlords may charge their tenants the amount of rent.

26. The rates of future increases are also fixed.
27. They are fixed according to this.
28. What do lawmakers consider reasonable?
29. They are fixed so that landlords may get a fair return.
30. The return is on their investment.

31. This means this.
32. A family cannot legally be asked by its landlord to pay $350.
33. The family pays $175 a month for rent.
34. This is when its current lease is renewed.

35. In fact, suppose the rent is to be increased at all.
36. Then the family must be told in advance.
37. It must be told the amount of increase.

38. The idea is noble.
39. But there are problems in rent control planning.

40. "Reasonable rates" is a vague term.
41. "Fair returns on investments" is a vague term.
42. The government must define these terms.

43. The terms would be defined by government officials.
44. Therefore this is likely.
45. These rates will be set below this.
46. What would landlords consider reasonable?

47. Old people need this kind of protection against inflation.
48. Old people are on fixed retirement incomes.
49. And low income renters need this kind of protection against inflation.

50. Rents take as much as two-thirds of older peoples' income.
51. This happens even at present rent costs.

52. Many low income families set aside 34 percent of their salaries.
53. This is so they can pay rent.

54. And prices are rising faster than pensions are increasing.
55. Prices are rising faster than wages are increasing.

56. Furthermore, landlords claim this.
57. Rents do not rise fast enough.
58. The rises do not make the construction of new buildings worthwhile.
59. This happens even without rent controls.

60. One developer asserts this.
61. He needs to raise rents from 10 to 12 percent annually.
62. This is just to stay even.
63. He is in California.

64. An issue of *Business Week* reports this.
65. An 87-year-old pensioner and his wife watched their rent increase from $295 a month to $445 a month.
66. This increase happened in just four years.
67. They were in a high-rise building for older people.
68. The building was in Santa Monica, California.

69. Therefore controls are needed.
70. This is clear.

71. Older people can barely afford to pay their rent.
72. Low income families can barely afford to pay their rent.

73. There is rent control.
74. New construction is inhibited.

75. Even the existing low income housing deteriorates.
76. This is because less money is available.
77. The landlords can't provide adequate maintenance.

78. Rent controls are unprofitable.
79. Rent controls are unmanageable.
80. They are also detrimental to the quality of low income housing.

81. The government has moved with noble intentions.
82. It has done this too often.
83. Then it creates more problems than it solves.
84. It did this in the Atlanta housing project.

85. It should let rent controls alone.
86. It may create another boondoggle.

87. Controls would help.
88. They would assure these people this.
89. They will have to pay no more than a rate.
90. The rate would be fixed by the government.
91. It would be legally binding on the landlord.

92. The government is wasting its revenue.
93. The waste is on low income housing projects.
94. The projects are poorly conceived.
95. Instead, the government should do something constructive for the needy.
96. Imposing a national system of rent control would do something constructive.

97. And a national system of rent control wouldn't cost the taxpayer a cent.

Sentence Combining Exercise

Construct a unified and ordered paragraph by picking one of the three statements below to serve as a controlling idea and then choosing appropriate supporting details from the notes.

1. Game show prizes aren't always as good a deal as they seem to be.
2. Game shows use gaudy sets, sex, and gimmicks to create excitement.
3. Game shows thrive on placing contestants in humiliating situations.

GAME SHOWS

Notes

1. Game show hosts are usually young and attractive.
2. They dress in the latest fashions.
3. Game show sets are alive with flashing lights and gaudy colors.
4. Women assistants on shows like "The Price Is Right," "Let's Make a Deal," and "Treasure Hunt" are dressed in sexy outfits.
5. On "The Price Is Right" contestants called down from the audience are told to run from their seats to the stage.
6. They often exhibit no regard for others sitting in their area.
7. Contestants on all the shows are encouraged to use cutthroat tactics to eliminate their competition.
8. Prizes like cars, boats, and furs are displayed in the flashiest way possible to make them appear more exciting.
9. Contestants display their greed when they consider the value of their prizes or decide which door to choose.
10. Most shows don't allow winners to substitute cash value for the prizes.
11. When prizes do arrive, they are often defective, the wrong model, or the wrong color.
12. People from certain areas of the country have no use for sailboats, scuba gear, or snowmobiles—common game show prizes.
13. Since taxes on prizes are high, many winners are forced to sell their prizes for money to pay the taxes.
14. Winners frequently report having to wait for months before getting their prizes.
15. Some people have strong moral objections to fur coats—common prizes.
16. Certain prizes require expensive upkeep.
17. Many of the game shows are gimmicky.
18. They are geared to creating a false sense of suspense.
19. Contestants often act like children in order to amuse the host or audience.
20. When contestants win prizes, they often become hysterical and cry.

21. Hosts take advantage of contestants' peculiarities to make them look ridiculous.
22. The "Newlywed Game" exposes intimate personal information about couples and encourages family arguments on stage.
23. "Let's Make a Deal" forces people to dress up in ridiculous costumes.
24. All the shows encourage contestants to go for the most expensive items displayed.

Sentence Combining Exercise

Select and organize any four or more notes below into an effective paragraph that is unified by a controlling idea. Then select and organize another set of four or more notes into a second paragraph that is unified by a different controlling idea. For both paragraphs, feel free to add details or ideas of your own.

PHYSICAL FITNESS

Notes

1. More than $200 million worth of tennis clothes are sold annually.
2. Fitness enthusiasts gain a renewed sense of vitality, of a goal conquered, and of confidence in coping with life.
3. Up to two-thirds of the joggers suffer injuries serious enough to put them out of action for two weeks or more.
4. Sex and age are no barrier to physical training.
5. Tennis players and racquetball enthusiasts suffer tennis elbow, the inflammation of the tendon that joins the forearm muscles to the elbow.
6. There are more than 1300 books on fitness in print now.
7. The upsurge is beginning to pay off in a decrease in the mortality rate from heart attacks—30 percent lower since 1950.
8. *Runner's World* magazine increased from 35,000 circulation in 1975 to over 200,000 circulation by 1978.

9. Middle-aged joggers in poor condition may be setting off heart attacks if they begin without proper advice.
10. A recent Gallup poll indicates that 47 percent of Americans take part in some form of physical fitness daily.
11. Most joggers suffer shin splints or damage to the cartilage behind the kneecap.
12. Jogging is one of the best cures for depression, report many psychologists.
13. Exercise can become an addiction, and those who exercise become evangelists, recruiting others.
14. More than 100 of 3000 runners in a recent marathon in Honolulu, Hawaii, had previously suffered heart attacks.
15. The United States now has over 500 racquetball clubs.
16. Some joggers report a feeling of euphoria—not unlike a drug-induced high—from runs of more than three miles.
17. Fitness buffs are rejecting sports like golf and bowling for jogging, bicycling, tennis, swimming, and racquetball.
18. Some people jog in $100 jogging suits—with stripes down the sides—and $50 shoes.
19. More active sports—like jogging and tennis—are good for the heart, lungs, and circulatory system, according to many doctors.
20. Jogging helps protect against two causes of heart attacks—inactivity and tension.
21. There are over 8 million joggers in the country, over 29 million tennis players.
22. There are now over 3000 health clubs and spas around the nation with millions of total members.
23. Catering to fitness has become a huge industry.
24. YMCA membership has increased by 16 percent in the past decade.
25. Some doctors don't agree that exercise helps our health. They claim that any healthful benefits of exercise come from the more temperate life associated with exercising.
26. Addidas alone sells over 200 styles of athletic shoes.
27. Over $2 billion worth of sports equipment is sold every year.

INDEX

Page numbers in italics indicate the principal discussion of the term.

78 79 80 7 6 5 4 3 2 1